R3.00

# THE AFRIKANER'S INTERPRETATION
## OF
## SOUTH AFRICAN HISTORY

# The Afrikaner's Interpretation

## of

## South African History

F. A. VAN JAARSVELD

*Professor of History in the*
*University of South Africa*

1964

SIMONDIUM PUBLISHERS (PTY.) LTD.

P. O. BOX 3737 · CAPE TOWN

DEDICATED TO
MY ESTEEMED TEACHER AND PROMOTOR
PROF JHR DR P. J. VAN WINTER

# CONTENTS

Preface                                                                            vii

The Ideas of the Afrikaner on his Calling and Mission                                1

The Awakening of the Afrikaner to an Awareness of his History                       33

The Afrikaner's Image of his Past                                                    46

Biographies of Voortrekker Leaders                                                   71

The Anglo-Boer War and the Historical Writings of
  Dr. W. J. Leyds                                                                    94

History and Politics                                                                105

Interpretations and Trends in South African Historical Writing                      116

On Objectivity, Subjectivity and Relativity in the Writing of
  History                                                                           166

The Purpose and Significance of the Teaching of History                             173

Dangers Latent in the Teaching of History                                           182

On the Teaching of "General" History in South African
  Schools                                                                           189

On the Teaching of "National" History in South African
  Schools                                                                           196

# PREFACE

The lectures and studies selected for inclusion in this volume were published originally in Afrikaans in various magazines, books and brochures. It is hoped that their translation into English may now render them accessible to a wider circle of readers.

I have chosen those themes that bear on the interpretation of history, historical writing and the teaching of history in South Africa. Although my main concern is with the Afrikaner's interpretation of and attitudes towards South African history, notice has also been taken of the standpoints of the English-speaking and non-white communities. (See *Interpretations and Trends in South African Historical Writing*.)

The first essay, *The Ideas of the Afrikaner on his Calling and Mission*, attempts to shed light on the traditional approach and frame of mind of the Afrikaner and its application to the changed world of today, especially in the field of race relations.

The five studies that follow are intended to show the role of history in formulating the philosophy of life and outlook of a people – how it influenced a people's thoughts and thus became a determinant in political and human relationships.

The origin and development of the Afrikaner's conception of his history is traced and the growth of his image of history delineated, also the parallelism between the historical experiences of a people, its vision of the past, and the form taken in its historical writings. The material presented may lead to a clearer comprehension of the Afrikaner people and explain why they have pursued a course that has made them the cynosure of world-wide attention.

Historical teaching in South Africa is dealt with in the remaining essays; this is a subject that has been widely discussed, often heatedly, in the press during the past decade and still gives rise to lively debate.

Quotations from Dutch or Afrikaans newspapers, periodicals and books have been translated into English; I did not refer to any contemporary translations and it is possible that the present translations may not follow the identical language of earlier versions. I referred to the original Dutch or Afrikaans texts throughout.

Before the present translation was undertaken I revised the

essays and introduced minor changes into the text without altering any of my main conclusions. The studies were originally prepared for various occasions and an element of overlapping in some of the sub-divisions cannot be ruled out. Except for some compression, I have not effected any substantial alteration lest the unity of an essay be impaired.

In conclusion, I wish to express my gratitude to the editors and publishers who granted me permission to republish the articles in translated form.

Last but not least, my thanks are due to my colleague and friend, Mr A. M. Davey, who undertook the translation.

University of South Africa,                    F. A. VAN JAARSVELD
Pretoria
June, 1963

# THE IDEAS OF THE AFRIKANER ON HIS CALLING AND MISSION *

I

At the present time one is frequently confronted with the assertion that the Afrikaner people has been assigned a place in the southern corner of Africa for "a purpose" and to fulfil "a mission". Such sentiments find expression in sermons, in letters published in the press and particularly in the speeches of those who are in the fore-front of political and cultural affairs. The validity of the claim is usually taken for granted. To the audience for which it is intended, it sounds a pleasing note: To those of differing standpoints e.g. the non-whites or the English-speaking group, it has less appeal – they are apt to see in it all manner of sinister intentions. The subject often gives rise to comment in the press, in speeches or in books. In a South Africa in which the Afrikaner holds the political reins and in a changed world in which reference has been made to "the century of the black man" it might be profitable to investi-gate these assertions of "calling" and "mission" and their con-comitant, the idea of a select destiny as a chosen people.

These claims are far from being creations of yesterday; they lie deep-rooted in South African history; they have links with the spiritual, social, political and economic circumstances that contri-buted to the evolution of the Afrikaner people and they are pointers to past, present and future. Furthermore, the idea of divine election, purpose or calling has ties with the process of self-assertion of the Afrikaner and with his nationalism.

This study has as its objective an historical investigation of such assertions made during the 19th and 20th centuries and will en-deavour to show the relationship of their content to the crises sur-mounted by the Afrikaner people. How did beliefs alter with the passage of time and in changed circumstances? How does the Afri-kaner's account of himself before the world of to-day, compare with that put forward in previous times? What does he regard as

*Lecture delivered at a meeting of the Afrikaans Cultural Council of Pretoria on the 25th October, 1961.

his present purpose and calling? Has he succeeded in fulfilling the purpose, charge or calling that he assumed unto himself in earlier times?

Our first step in this study will be to outline the general background to show that the idea of a calling is not peculiar to the Afrikaner people and that *inter alia* the British and Americans were (and still are) inspired by it. The investigation then proceeds to the roots of the idea among the Afrikaners, as reflected in their traditional attitudes towards the Bantu, the English-speaking and one another and then to the concept of divine election which has a close affinity with its treatment in the Old Testament.

This is a study in the history of *ideas*. It makes no claims to completeness since a whole volume could be devoted to the subject. If it should stimulate any history or theological student to a more detailed study or to a *theological* interpretation, I should consider myself amply rewarded.

2

From the very earliest times civilised peoples were possessed of the idea that they were superior to others and had a purpose or calling to dominate and assume the leadership of neighbouring peoples. It was for this reason that the Greeks and Chinese spoke of the uncivilised peoples as "barbarians".

In the old dispensation, the most striking example of a calling is to be found among the Hebrews, *vide Deuteronomy* 14 : 2: "For thou art an holy people unto the Lord thy God, and the Lord hath chosen thee to be a peculiar people unto himself, above all the nations that are upon the earth". The hallowed mission of a chosen people is the leit-motif of the history of the Jews as recounted in the *Old Testament*. They were the bearers of a covenant with Jehovah; they were summoned out of Egypt, freed from the bonds of Pharaoh and led through the desert to the promised land in which they were settled in the midst of other nations. They were inspired with a belief in their special charge and purpose and with a Messianic expectation.

In the *New Testament* (Romans 8 : 30) we read: "Moreover whom he did predestinate, them he also called". In the new dispensation the idea of calling is prominent but it is a calling of the Word and is always a summons to emulate Christ and enrol in His service. This calling was to be the determinant of the course set by Christendom.

Anyone who makes a study of modern nationalism will be struck by the fact that each European people that developed a sense of identity and national consciousness considered itself "chosen" and felt aware of its special "calling", "purpose" or "mission" within the circle of its neighbours. The Old Testament conception of the select destiny of the Israelites lay at the roots of these notions. One can also see in them a secularisation of the New Testament's idea of the calling of the Christian i.e. a translation from the religious to the national sphere. The idea of a national calling or purpose therefore carries a religious impress.

One of the first of the modern nations to experience a national awakening dating from the 17th century, was England. The idea that the English, like Israel of old, were a chosen people with a mission, was established firmly under Cromwell's leadership and Puritan domination; its origins lay in Calvinist influences and the Old Testament. With the growth of England's political power from the time of Queen Elizabeth, the religious motive from which the concept arose, receded into the background. In the period that followed the Puritanical and Glorious Revolutions the English acceptance as axiomatic of the belief that they were a chosen people acquired an increasing political significance.

England conceived herself to be *the* nation that was summoned to mastery of the oceans and then to supremacy over the greater part of the globe,[1] but at the same time her people were to be the bearers of the idea of *freedom* for mankind and for the smaller nations.[2] The supra-national element, which was of Hebrew derivation, gave rise to the idea that it was to be England's mission to lead and protect all the Protestant nations.[3] In the 19th century a British-Israelite society even went so far as to declare that the English race was sprung from the ten lost tribes of Israel![4] With the advent of the New Imperialism of the 19th century, the belief in a special calling as a chosen people loomed large; it was linked to a powerful resurgence of British nationalism that began to display an overweening self-confidence and self-glorification. The verses of Swinburne and Kipling proclaimed the predestined leadership of the British over other peoples.[5]

Joseph Chamberlain declared that the Anglo-Saxon race "is infallibly destined to be the predominant force in the history and civilization of the world."[6] Books, such as those of Seeley, *The Expansion of England* and Charles Dilke, *Problems of Greater Britain*, fostered the belief in an imperial mission. In South Africa Cecil Rhodes expressed his credo: "Only one race approached God's ideal type, his own Anglo-Saxon race; God's purpose then was to make the Anglo-Saxon race predominant, and the best way to help on God's work and fulfil His purpose in the world was to contribute to the predominance of the Anglo-Saxon race and so bring nearer the reign of justice, liberty and peace."[7] Through the agency of Sir Alfred Milner the idea of "British supremacy" in South Africa was to lead directly to the Anglo-Boer war of 1899–1902.[8] In the last quarter of the 19th century British expansion in South Africa, although achieved at the expense of Boer and Bantu, was based on the idea of a mission i.e. that the Anglo-Saxon race had to expand in the interests of *progress, civilisation* and *humanity*. In certain British circles the belief still persists that the present emancipation of the British colonial peoples marks the conclusion or fulfilment of their mission.

The Puritan Pilgrim Fathers transplanted the idea of a calling to America: They identified themselves with Israel of old that had moved into the Promised Land. God had reserved it for His chosen people and led them to it when the time was ripe. It was their mission to draw the oppressed from the old world and offer them a new fatherland, a new life and liberty.[9] Gradually ideas of "Manifest Destiny" and a "Call to Greatness" took form: It was to be their mission to liberate and rejuvenate mankind. In the process of the emancipation of the colonial peoples and resistance to Communism the old idea of mission donned a new garb. "For them (the Americans) the Mission of America is synonymous with a will to dominate, to play the part of a New Rome, to make the next hundred years the American Century with all the pursuit of self-aggrandisement that that name implies."[10] Herman Melville expressed the idea of a calling as follows: "We Americans are a peculiar, chosen people, the Israel of our times; we bear the ark of the liberties of the world."

By 1848 we perceive the ideas of mission, calling and special election in practically all the nationally conscious European nations. After the French Revolution, which created the modern French nation, the French cherished a belief in their civilising mission,[11] the German idea of a mission based on the superiority of their culture dates from their wars of liberation;[12] after 1830 the Poles believed that their mission was martyrdom in the cause of liberty.[13] The Russians conceived the belief that they were the Third Rome that would bring the true faith to Europe. At present their idea of mission is embodied in a sort of messianic belief that they should extend Communism throughout the world and liberate colonial and other peoples.[14] There are many others cases in point.

Modern nationalism originated with the French Revolution and Napoleonic Wars. European scholars who have studied the nationalism of modern nations agree that the national awakening of a people, by and large, was the result of pressure, danger or attacks

4

from without on its identity. The nation justifies its existence and aspirations and tries to prove its worth by raising the appeal of a special assignment, purpose, calling or destiny which, in the case of a disaster such as befell Germany, can be transmuted into *Schicksal* (fate): And so the whole idea encompasses the future, present and past of the nation. The conception of a special destiny leads to the growth of a historical legend and of a national ideology; the conception of a calling gives form to the nation and with it a feeling of uniqueness, assurance and self-esteem. Each nation acquires an ideology of special destiny that is inseparable from its national historical legend;[15] the Afrikaner people is no exception.

3

Before we investigate the specific content of the idea of the Afrikaners' calling, it is necessary to explain *the background* that produced it and to see what the Afrikaners thought of the *non-whites* and the *English-speaking colonists,* and of *themselves* and their own *history* i.e. what their particular place was in the pattern of the constituent groups of our country's population. We have noted how the Calvinists who settled in North America believed that they were God's chosen people whose footsteps had been directed to the land of Canaan. This belief was decisive in so far as it led to the near-extinction of the redskin and the preservation of the whites; by way of contrast, the Catholic colonists mingled and inter-married with the dark-skinned races.[16]

It is difficult to establish whether sentiments similar to those of the Calvinists in America animated the Dutch colonists who settled at the Cape in 1652 and later, but it was apparently not the case. There was little place for evangelical or missionary zeal in the commercially-minded and practical Netherlanders.[17] Of all the Protestant peoples who settled in overseas countries, they displayed the greatest racial tolerance.[18] Investigators conclude that race and skin pigmentation played no part in the 17th century Cape Colony and that there was no prejudice towards coloured peoples until the 18th century was well-advanced.[19] There are examples of inter-marriage and social intercourse to support these conclusions.

Where then did the current conceptions of white *superiority* and resistance to equalisation and blood admixture arise? Research workers consider that they developed during the 18th century. We know that the Afrikaner people became a separate people in that century, with their own identity and beliefs. In addition to physical detachment from their mother country, isolation in the interior,

5

social and economic factors, influences such as the Calvinist heritage and the Old Testament went into the moulding of the Afrikaner. We know that from the beginning of the settlement "Christian" and "heathen" were distinguished from one another. During the second half of the 18th century there was an increasing tendency for the use of these terms synonymously with "white" and "coloured".[20] And so the whites came to feel that they were "masters", distinct from the coloureds who performed the more elementary types of work; the latter were referred to later as "schepsels" (creatures).[21] In 1830 we read of "Christen en beschaafde Natien" (Christian and civilised peoples – white) as opposed to "Heidensche Volken zoo als de Hottentotten, de Kaffirs, enz." (Heathen peoples such as Hottentots, Kaffirs, etc.)[22] "Civilised" and "uncivilised" thus became terms associated with whites and coloureds, respectively.

Here we detect the influence of the Old Testament. The coloureds were held to be an inferior race, designed by the will of God to be hewers of wood and drawers of water. In 1703 the Church Council of Drakenstein wrote to the Convocation of Amsterdam on the subject of Hottentots whom it wished to convert "so that the children of Ham would no longer be the servants of bondsmen". In its reply the Convocation expressed approval and the hope that "one day God would lift the curse from the generation of Ham."[23] Approximately a century later a Cape colonist recorded his belief that the Hottentots were the descendants of Ham and therefore condemned by the Almighty to subservience and abuse.[24]

This notion still persists among the Afrikaner farming community. Our records are dotted with pronouncements that support this contention – to give a few examples: In 1892 an Afrikaner from the Transvaal spoke of the non-whites as "the generation of Ham – the menials"[25] and in 1895 we encounter the assertion that "the sons of Ham alone are accursed" coupled with the rhetorical query "Here on earth the Lord has made this difference and who will change it?"[26] In 1909: "Providence had provided that he (the non-white) should remain a drawer of water and a hewer of wood."[27] In our time (1958) a complaint was voiced that the non-white was still regarded "as a God-given and permanent drawer of water to minister to our comfort." "It is shocking", the writer continues, "to see how many of our people [the Afrikaners] cherish this belief."[28] In 1960 Dr. G. D. Scholtz felt it necessary to sound a note of warning against "the so-called superiority complex of the white race in relation to the non-white races and the belief that the Bantu were the descendants of Ham and therefore condemned to exist as servants of the whites." He added that a commission of

6

learned theologians of the *Gereformeerde* Church reported in 1958 that there were no biblical grounds for the assumption that the Bantu were the descendants of Ham or that any sort of curse attached to them.[29]

Research workers into the problem of race in recent times have also shown that there is no such thing as an inferior or superior race. There are indeed great differences in physical appearance, social relationships, patterns of conduct, cultural achievements and spiritual development, but none of these gives rise to a superior or an inferior race.

Another assumption that still persists also has partial links with the Old Testament; it is the Afrikaners' rejection of *admixture of blood* and *equalisation*. As the isolation of the Dutch colonists in the remote interior increased, so did their literal application to themselves of the contents of the Old Testament. It was as a chosen race that the Israelites had received a divine injunction not to inter-marry with the Canaanites. The non-whites of South Africa were identified therefore not only with the children of Ham but also with the Canaanites of the Promised Land; they were referred to by the Boers as "Naatsies" (The nations without the law)[30] whilst the term Philistines was also used.[31] This approach was particularly apparent after the Great Trek. When Commandant P. E. Scholtz had subdued the chief Sechele during the 1850's, he declared that he had acted in the matter in accordance with the divine law that had been entrusted to Joshua.[32] Contemporary writers e.g. Livingstone, Holden, Proctor, McKinnon, Bryce and others, noted that the Boers of the Republics conceived themselves to be Lord's chosen ones to whom the non-whites had been delivered as under-lings and servants.[33] The Christian convictions of the Boers and their sense of mission towards the non-whites apparently restrained them from following the precedents of extermination that are to be found in the Old Testament – and such policies of decimation as were put into practice in America. Defensive references to this aspect have been made on many occasions – even during the present period.

Anna Steenkamp listed one of the causes of the Great Trek as "the equalisation (of the non-whites) with "the Christians"; this, she considered, "was in conflict with the laws of God and with natural distinctions of origin and belief."[34] It is hardly surprising to find that the Trekkers in their republics would admit of no equality between white and coloured in church and state. When Union was eventually brought about the former republicans opposed the extension of a non-white franchise to the North. General De Wet's adjudgement was typical: "Providence had drawn the line

7

between black and white and we must make that clear to the Natives and not instil into their minds false ideas of equality".[35] Since that time racial legislation, with which we are all familiar, has been enacted.

The traditional attitude of the Afrikaners towards *the English-speaking* has been determined by two factors – firstly, by *British policy towards the non-whites*, and, secondly, by *the Afrikaner's own struggle for independence and separate identity*. One discerns the influence of the Old Testament in this context too. The first clash of significance was due to the British 19th century philanthropic policy of effecting the "equalisation" of the non-whites. The farmers of the Eastern frontier came to the conclusion that the British were backing the coloureds against them. The reaction was the Great Trek (1836–'38) which was seen as a necessary step to secure their safe existence for the future beyond the borders of the colony and for the retention of their philosophy and way of life. After that phase the Afrikaners saw the English-speaking as traducers who continually presented them to the outside world as suppressors, ill-treaters, enslavers and exterminators of the natives; during the 19th century they were continually on the defensive to counter such charges.[36] Moreover they accused the British of siding with the natives in the case of armed clashes and of inciting the latter, or of furnishing them with weapons, so as to secure political advantages or territorial expansion.

In the British "liberal" policy of "equality and fraternity", leading to the franchise, the Afrikaners saw dangers ahead for the whites.[37] They held the view that "only a Boer knows how to deal with a Kaffir and keep him in his place". Nowadays many Afrikaners still believe that the future of the country cannot be entrusted to the English-speaking section; this is coupled with a distrust of the English-speaking, for, if the latter came to hold power, they might well concede the franchise to the non-whites and so jeopardize the future of the whites. The belief still persists that only the Afrikaner has "a solution" to the problem of the non-whites. To-day, as in the 19th century, the "English" newspapers and publications are charged with responsibility for the discreditable image of the Afrikaners in the outside world and of presenting the Afrikaner's case "incorrectly". In fact, a feeling has grown among the Afrikaners that the English-language press in South Africa has contracted some form of alliance with the non-whites against the Afrikaners.

In the second place, the Afrikaners have seen in the British the "suppressors" "persecutors" and "enemies" of their *freedom*. This resulted in a continual feeling of distrust and sense of injustice[38] particularly after the inroads into Natal (1842), the Free State (1871) and Transvaal (1877). The awakening of an Afrikaans nationalism between 1877 and 1881 was largely a reaction to the British annexationist policy. Out of the crucible of 1899–1902 the Afrikaners emerged with a stronger and more comprehensive nationalism. They saw the war as a war of annihilation that was intended to eliminate them as a people. Milner's policy of anglicisation drove home the conviction that the English-speaking would not concede the Afrikaner his own separate language, culture or philosophy of life and that at all times the Afrikaner would have to fight to obtain his rights and to maintain his identity. The Afrikaners cherished the belief that they alone were "true patriots" since the English-speaking community was invariably opposed to the acquisition of South Africa's own symbols of nationhood and to a greater degree of independence.

The Old Testament is again of importance in this context. In 1848 when Sir Harry Smith prepared to use armed force against the Voortrekkers on the banks of the Orange River, General Andries Pretorius notified him that they (the Trekkers) were as Israel standing before Pharaoh.[39] In 1871 we read of "the yoke of Pharaoh"[40] and in 1882 the Rev. S. J. du Toit declared that the English were their "chastisers" and that through the former's acts of oppression the Afrikaners had become a nation. He asked: "who has taught us a sense of unity as a people?", and supplied the answer: "None but England by her oppressions. Who has aroused a spirit of fraternity and patriotism throughout South Africa? None but England through the blows of her lash".[41] In 1898 we encounter the contention that "the war of Liberation (1881) and nothing less was necessary to create and animate a national feeling in South Africa."[42]


4


The British policy of opposition to the Great Trek and the Boer republics was the linchpin in the final casting of the *pattern of thought* of the 19th century Afrikaner. Mention has been made of the natives whom the Boers saw as children of *Ham* and *Canaanites* in their efforts to sustain themselves as a group apart. The *British administration* had stood in the shoes of *Pharaoh* and oppressed them in Egypt – a country that they had had to forsake to seek freedom: And so the exodus to the *Promised Land* was undertaken. The Voortrekkers and their descendants in their new home (*Israel*) felt that they were waging a struggle for survival

9

against "Pharaoh" and "the black Canaanites". They literally applied to themselves the history of Israel as set forth in the pages of the Old Testament.

When one pauses to wonder why the parallel with Israel was carried to such lengths, one recollects that, quite apart from the political circumstances, the way of life of the Boers was similar to that of Israel of old. The stories of the Old Testament could never have made such a deep impression on urban communities. One has to appreciate the loneliness, the vast expanses of the veld, the trek into the unknown with all their possessions and livestock, the patriarchal nature of family relationships and of forms of government, the starry firmament by night and the scorching sun by day and the dangers of wild beasts and barbarians that threatened their existence from day to day. For the Afrikaners the parallel with the chosen of the Lord grew into a form of mystecism; by their suferings in fulfilling God's calling they would be purified. English historians of the 19th century were impressed by the consciousness of the Republicans of the background of the Old Testament.[43] It bound the community together, fostered its unity, secured it against miscegenation and degeneration and inspired it with courage to combat the British and barbarians alike: above all, it was a civilising influence that bestowed positive values, law and order on the community.

The documents of the 19th century are replete with pronouncements that support such contentions. One may quote a few of them to illustrate the Boer image of himself. Voortrekker terminology shows the direct influence of the Old Testament. Maritz spoke in 1837 of the new land "overflowing with milk and honey;"[44] they appointed "Judges" to rule over them;[45] some of them wished to call Natal "New Eden";[46] Sunday was "the day of the Sabbath";[47] their trek was a wandering in "the desert";[48] before Blood River they entered into "a compact" with God[49] while references to "promised land", "the God of our fathers" and the place name "The River Nile" too show how literally they applied the words of the Old Testament. It is recorded that many of Potgieter's group of Trekkers believed that they were a chosen people of God journeying to the land of Canaan with their leader as a second Moses.[50] The Rev. W. Robertson who was in touch with the Voortrekkers in 1836 stated that many of them believed in the prophecy of Joel "that they are to flee to another country and that their emigration is therefore necessary for the fulfilment of these parts of scripture". Robertson added: "From their reading more in the Bible than other books, the arguments to be used with them are better, when taken from thence than elsewhere."[51]

It is not surprising that the Rev. Mr Smit, the Voortrekker pastor, drew on the Old Testament for almost all of his texts.[52] This is also true of the Transvaal ministers of religion who made frequent use – particularly at public gatherings – of "the Trek" from Egypt and the trials of Israel in Canaan as the topics of their sermons. The role of the minister of religion in the history of the Afrikaners still awaits treatment. Let us refer to a few examples. On the 16th December, 1895, a clergyman delivering the main address at a commemorative occasion, basing his words on *Numbers* 14 : 24. Inter alia, he remarked: "When we think of the former emigrants, the Voortrekkers of yore it is then revealed unto us how God, in His divine providence, dealt with them, even as He dealt with the Israelite nation of old; that he summoned them to the same task; Canaan was inhabited by heathen alienated from God . . . Israel was bidden make it the Lord's dwelling-place."[53] At a Dingaan's Day commemorative gathering at Petrusburg in the following year a clergyman quoted *Ruth* 1 : 16 and 17 and recalled the tribulations of the Israelites in Egypt; whilst they groaned under the yoke of mighty Pharaohs one never heard of gatherings of the people and yet such convocations of the people were necessary "to give instruction on the national existence."[54] Such commemorative gatherings of the Afrikaner owed their origin to the Old Testament; they were instituted in 1880 to reaffirm the vow taken at Blood River.

There are many interesting examples of the way in which the history of the Transvaal Boers was *likened* to that of Israel; it will suffice to refer to two of them. There are the typical words of President M. W. Pretorius in 1871 on the occasion of an address to three hundred Boers at Rustenburg; he had the older members of the community seated in the front rows. "His Excellency then addressed himself to the original Voortrekkers, calling them Fathers of Israel, and depicting and likening them to the chosen of the Lord, who even as the Israelites had trekked from Egypt to escape Pharaoh's yoke, had themselves withdrawn from the yoke of the detestable English Government to found their own Government and administration."[55]

When the Transvaal War broke out in 1880, an Afrikaner clergyman of the Transvaal saw it in the following terms: "Behold the armies of salvation of the Lord; we were as Israel of old – before us lay the Red Sea, behind us was the Egyptian host and on either side of us were lofty mountains. We could but look up and cry to God and He heard our voice."[56]

Comparisons with Israel are still made; only recently *Die Trans-valer* declared that "the Afrikaner who has accepted the Bible as his guiding rule in life still sees a considerable measure of resemblance between the history of his own people and that of Israel . . . The people of Israel invoked the Old Testament as a reason for not mingling with other races; so does the Afrikaner".[57] In various quarters it has been remarked that South Africa in present times has become the "Israel of Africa".[58] There has also been a revival of similar comparisons from the pulpit.[59]

Is there any ground for the identification of the trials of the Afrikaner people with those of Israel or for the acceptance of analogies in the histories of the two peoples? Furthermore, is it permissible, whether in sermon or public speech, to assert, without further qualification, that the Afrikaner people is a chosen people? The history of ancient Israel was *religious history*: Church and people were terms that were practically synonymous – a situation that no longer obtained with the advent of the new dispensation. The Rev. I. F. Retief has recently pointed out that there is no reason for conceding that any modern people is a peculiar or chosen people in the sense of Israel of old. To speculate whether there really is an analogy between us and Israel of old, the Rev. Retief concludes, merely leaves us in the realms of *speculation*. He also considers that there is no scriptural exposition or evangelical exegesis of it. Practically every nation can adduce examples from its history which within certain limits, have a similarity to biblical history.[60]

Just as the Israelites of old looked back on their trials and recalled them during national gatherings, so too did the Afrikaners of the 19th and 20th centuries. They usually referred to God's guidance and Providential direction during their tribulations. In 1841 Andries Pretorius said that during the years of the Trek they had enjoyed the visible guidance and protection of God.[61] In 1885 someone else spoke of "a twofold delivery by which God saved our people in 1838 and again in 1880-'81 and delivered them from peril and misery so great that our people could see no salvation other than through Almighty God."[62] After the battle of Blood River *De Zuid-Afrikaan* was convinced that "if we consider the commencement of the emigration and its present outcome, then we can only adhere to the belief that the hand of the Lord is with the Boers and that woe will be upon any man who opposes them".[63] Time and again President Kruger reminded his people that they should not pride themselves on their own achievements but that the God of their Fathers[64] and "General Jesus" had supported them and that their leaders had merely been tools in the Divine hand.[65] Before and during the Anglo-Boer War we know how the President pointed to history to show what "miracles"

God had wrought for the Afrikaners and that it was within His province to do so again and confer victory on them. They were to fight in His name[66] – for the God of Israel was still the same God. On all sides there was the conviction that their history, character and God's purpose with them, had been revealed.[67] Nowadays one still reads that: "The child should see from the pages of history how God led the people" and that a nation fulfils "a purpose"[68] and that "the Lord's guidance has been transparently visible in the history of our people from 1652 to the present."[69] Gradually history has been invoked to show how God was on the Afrikaners' side and that therefore He will come to their aid in the future. At the outbreak of the Anglo-Boer War biblical texts were used to encourage the people.[70]

It is a matter of common knowledge that the revelation of God's aid at Blood River, Majuba and Doornkop gave rise to an overconfidence in the Afrikaners when they declared war in 1899. Shortly before the war, Milner, who was aware of these convictions of the Afrikaners, observed: "The Higher Powers seemed twice [Majuba and Doornkop] in the past to have directly intervened and wrought a miracle for the Afrikaners: why not a third time? It is small wonder that the pious parsons of the Dutch Reformed Church really believe that the Lord of Hosts is always on the look-out and will get them out of any tight place. But I have my private heresy and doubt whether He will always do it."[71]

In this context there is another aspect to be considered. Afrikaner leaders have a predeliction for seeing themselves as men with a calling. Among such leaders this was true of Retief[72] and President Kruger. During the Rebellion of 1914 Generals Beyers and De Wet felt themselves "called" by God to act since "the matter had finally been shown to be the Lord's will."[73] In 1961, when dealing with the republican ideal, Dr. Verwoerd said: "It is the privilege of the leaders to be used by the Ruler of Nations and by their people as the vanguard in the fulfilment of this ideal."[74] After the unsuccessful attempt on his life, he was convinced that God's hand had been outstretched over him for a purpose – a purpose that also related to South Africa. "May it be granted to me to fulfil that purpose faithfully".[75] Other Afrikaners also saw in this deliverance "the Hand of God"; the Prime Minister had to be saved "so as to lead our people to victory".[76] When one of our cabinet ministers stated publicly in 1958 that it was his conviction that the Afrikaner leaders had been summoned by God, each to fulfil a special purpose, there was a considerable rumpus in the English-language press.[77] The triumphs of the Afrikaners at the ballot-box were ascribed repeatedly to "the Hand of God"[78] and the coming of the

Republic as "the will of God".[79] The leader of the Nationalist Party in Natal recently declared on various occasions that God was on the side of the Afrikaners and for that reason all would go well with the country.[80] In the meantime the Bantu also began to believe that God was on their side and that he would eventually lead them to victory.[81]

Pronouncements such as these evoke reaction from the other population groups in South Africa. *Adamastor* wrote in 1950: "The God of the Afrikaners is a very powerful, very exclusive and very fierce God . . . He turns His face away from skins that are not white . . . He has a traditional dislike for English-speaking folk . . . His benignity is preserved for the Afrikaans-speaking people; did He not bring them through the valley of shadow on to the Highveld of the Transvaal so that they could get away from the British?" He saw the people (*die volk*) through critical eyes – "the people chosen by God to rule South Africa in perpetuity and impose the tortuous intolerance of their eighteenth century outlook upon a nation calling itself Christian and a democracy."[82] There are also repeated references to the "tribal God" of the Afrikaners.

## 5

And so we return to the point at which our survey began: the Afrikaner's idea of his calling or his conception of a national purpose or destiny. At first the term "the Afrikaner" applied to the republican Afrikaners of the Trek period. It was only during the years 1877–'81, when Afrikaner nationalism originated, that the term acquired an extended meaning to include those of Afrikaner stock still living in the Cape and Natal colonies.

In what special circumstances do we encounter pronouncements on "calling" or "mission"? As in the case of other nations, usually during times of *crisis* i.e. when a group or people finds itself in a situation in which it feels that its existence, ideas, values and future are threatened and seeks to justify or defend them. Three major crises of this nature marked the history of the Afrikaners during the 19th and 20th centuries. The first occasion was the Great Trek period. (The "Balkanisation" of South Africa"); the second was the period in which British pressure endeavoured to force political unity (the "wars of liberation" (Vryheidsoorloë) resulting eventually in Union); the third crisis arose with resistance to foreign pressure and internal upheaval during the era of Anti-colonialism.

The first great crisis of which the Afrikaners had a *conscious* awareness was the withdrawal (Great Trek) of a part of "the people" from the British-controlled Cape Colony and the establishment of independent republics in the teeth of British and Bantu opposition. It reached its climax in such military engagements as Vegkop, Kapain and Blood River against the Bantu and Congella and Boomplaats against the British. In the broader sense it was a withdrawal to the interior in protest at the philanthropic movement from overseas that threatened established Boer notions concerning their relationship to the non-whites and it was a movement to create new states in which they could put into practice their views on the state, government and the place of the non-white. During the Great Trek the British (Government, philanthropists and missionaries) asserted that the emigrants would subject, exterminate and enslave the non-whites so as to possess themselves of land. The Voortrekkers were very sensitive to such accusations in view of the fact that the Trek followed shortly after the emancipation of slaves and because there were many armed clashes. The emigrants continually tried to defend themselves and explain their intentions to the outside world. Retief felt that he was "summoned" by God to the leadership so as to ensure their establishment in the interior and believed that "ere long, God in his compassion, will bring us in safety to our appointed destination."[83] Maritz, Potgieter and Pretorius all expressed the hope that somewhere in the interior the emigrants would become "a nation" and that there an abode would be prepared for the whole Afrikaner race. To quote the words of Andries Pretorius which reflect a sincere faith and a great reverence: "Since such things flow from the Almighty, if it be His wise will and pleasure, we shall there become a nation and live to His honour."[84]

These references also touch on the Trekker's idea of *a mission;* they are directed towards the future. A nation has still to be moulded, and a *free* nation at that, detached from British authority and safeguarded from the non-whites. This brings us to two lines of thought. Besides that which we have outlined, there was that of some of the Cape Afrikaners who had not accompanied the Great Trek and who visualised *fraternisation* of and eventual *fusion* or *unification* of the colonists of Dutch and English descent. It was only during the 1870's that the prospect of independence, a republican South Africa and an *Afrikaans* language took root in the Cape Colony; to this we shall return later. The Afrikaners' ideas on their mission and the image of the future, with all that is involved, is a theme in itself to which a whole book could be devoted.

As to the idea of a calling, it is common knowledge that the Cape

Synod disapproved of the Great Trek and did not follow in the footsteps of the migrants since it was unconvinced that the Trek was an imperative step brought about by Divine Providence.[85] *De Zuid-Afrikaan*, however, hoped that, under God's guidance, the Trekkers would be the instruments to sow the seeds of Christianity among the barbarians.[86]

The *Voortrekker-volksraad* (Council of the people or parliament) met the waves of criticism and speculation in 1841, and explained the advantages arising from the exodus from the Cape Colony: "that we hope to convince the world that far from destroying or ruining the Heathen races in these parts, we are an instrument in God's hands that will put an end to plunder, murder and violence among them and so provide greater security for the Cape Colony and will promote the extension of Christian civilisation among many thousands whose existence hitherto has been rooted in darkness. This fact will readily be acknowledged if regard be had to the Heathen already under our protection and those others with whom we have established peacable relations."[87]

From the Trekker's conception of their special calling (an instrument in God's hand) one infers the following: The sense of responsibility of Christians towards heathen, of a higher towards a lower form of civilisation; the protection of the heathen people from internecine murder, plunder and violence; the shielding of the Cape Colony from inroads by natives; the promotion of "Christian civilisation" and the encouragement of the spread of "Evangelical doctrine and the education of the Heathen races."[88] The Trekkers thus saw themselves as the instruments in God's hand who would *civilise* the non-whites and assist in their conversion to Christianity or, in other words, as the bearers and distributors of the torch of civilisation in Stygian darkness. If these had been their only intentions they would certainly never have left the Colony, but interwoven with these ambitions were national ideals such as the urge to achieve security, self-preservation, the creation of a home in which they could continue to follow the traditional way of life that was threatened in the Colony, etc. There was furthermore a confusion of the role of the church with that of the people although one might add that people and church (a congregation on trek) were indistinguishable from one another as separate entities at that time.

It is a fact that Trekkers put an end to tribal wars; but it is true too that they took no trouble to organise mission work from their ranks among the natives. Prior to 1899 none of the three Afrikaner churches in the Transvaal had missionaries in the field. When a certain Afrikaner, C. F. Weyers, acting on his own initiative, held services for non-whites at Potchefstroom in 1861 without obtaining the Government's permission, he was fined 250 rix-dollars.[89] Many of the Trekkers in the Transvaal had an animus towards mission activity as is evidenced by the opposition encountered by the first missionaries of the Cape Dutch Reformed Church in the Zoutpansberg during the 1860's.[90] In principle the Transvaal state was not opposed to mission work but the missionaries of the London Missionary Society were suspect in view of the Boers' experiences of Read, Van der Kemp and Dr. Philip in the Cape Colony. In 1852 the missionaries Edwards and Inglis were ejected from the Transvaal[91] and Livingstone was accused of supplying fire-arms to the natives. On the other hand German missionaries were admitted since it was believed that they taught the natives to work and to respect the white man. Whether the Voortrekkers put into practice their feeling of a calling or not, they "felt it was their duty not only to pioneer the way to the Heathen but also to open the hearts [of the natives] and make them receptive to the Gospel."[92]

We then arrive at the second great crisis in the history of the Afrikaner people – the efforts to undo the South Africa that had come into being during the period 1836–1854 and to substitute for it a politically united country under the British flag. This struggle against British Imperialism had three points of climax – the Transvaal War 1880–'81, the Jameson Raid, 1896 and the Anglo-Boer War 1899–1902. Its underlying purpose was the retention of the fruits of the Great Trek and the sequal of that movement – the independence of the Republics. The first two collisions brought success to Republican arms: the last resulted in their downfall. From this issue a new South Africa arose – a Union in which Boer and Briton were to wage a struggle for hegemony during the en-suing sixty years and one in which the Afrikaners strove to retain their identity as a people.

In 1877, there were accusations on the part of the British and complaints akin to those made at the time of the Great Trek i.e. that the Transvaal Republic had not done what was expected of it i.e. to establish the rule of law and order in the interior – coupled with the charge that the non-whites had been enslaved and op-pressed. It was for these reasons (among others) that Shepstone and Carnarvon intended to annex the Transvaal. There were objections to the annexation and an increasingly robust resistance that cul-minated in an outbreak of hostilities in 1881. This period of crisis compelled the Afrikaners to reconsider their "select destiny", "calling", and "mission". Their review had two angles to it; firstly it was *retrospective;* their calling was not projected into the future to show what their future actions would be, but, was viewed at it were, in reverse, in an interpretative way so that *history* could show what "the purpose" or "calling" was. In the second place it was directed towards the future. The first-mentioned aspect had particular reference to the non-whites while the second was concerned with independence.

As to the first: President Kruger and Piet Joubert wrote to Sir Michael Hicks Beach in 1878 to the effect that the Transvaal "was a flourishing and self-supporting state, a source of strength and security to neighbouring European settlements and a centre from which Christianity and civilisation were spreading rapidly into Central Africa. It formed a barrier between Natal and the natives of the interior and was also a source of strength and assurance to the [Cape] Colony".[93] In another letter to the Aborigine's Protection Society (1884), President Kruger and the Rev. S. J. du Toit refuted charges of ill-treatment of the non-whites and adduced statistics to show what the Transvaal had meant to its non-white inhabitants. According to the President, the natives who were placed under the protection of the Trekkers when the latter arrived in the Transvaal, some 30,000 had grown to approximately 700,000 by 1884 – proof enough that they had not been exterminated but, on the contrary, protected. "The [original] small groups of natives", Kruger stated, "were poverty-stricken individuals who sought shelter in holes and caves and lived in constant fear of attacks by neighbouring tribes who murdered their wives and children and destroyed their cattle". He also pointed out that despite the whites and natives having lived side by side in the Transvaal for more than a generation "one nowhere encounters children of mixed colour – proof that the female native has not become the victim of sensual urges, as so often happens in the other colonies".[94]

In comparing the pronouncements of 1878 with those of the Voortrekker *Volksraad* of 1841, one sees an evident resemblance: "Christianity and civilisation" and protection of the white colonies and the natives from internal strife are in the forefront as a kind of proof of fulfilment of a calling. When we think of the current situation President Kruger's views hardly sound an unfamiliar note.

But there was more to it than that. Many convictions such as the following were expressed: "The Afrikaners have received a Providential summons to trek through South Africa as the pioneers of civilisation so that Africa may be civilised and the heathen natives won over to Christianity and civilisation",[95] or: "Our Afrikaner Boers are summoned to be the pioneers of Christianity and civilisation".[96] In retrospect the Great Trek was seen *as a mission;* it had been bound to happen;[97] the Trekkers had not turned aside; they were "sent by God, the Achiever of all things, in His eternal wisdom" – Who had also charged the Afrikaner Boer "with the mighty task of winning Africa for Jesus the King".[98] It was particularly the clergymen who emphasised this. The Rev. Mr. Cachet pointed out that where the Boers paved the way, the English trader or missionary followed in their wake. He had forgotten that before the Great Trek there was already a considerable number of English-speaking missionaries in the interior.

We now come to the second aspect, a special destiny and mission, which contemporaries used indiscriminately along with "calling". The image of Israel's trek out of Egypt into Canaan which dated from the Great Trek was extended to include the whole colonial period. So that a writer who was discussing the origin of the Afrikaner nation wrote that "our generation (like Israel of old that was taken as vinestock from Egypt and planted and nurtured in Canaan) was taken, by God's Providence from Holland, France and Germany, and planted and nurtured as a people in Africa".[99] There were repeated references to the "noble" origins of the Afrikaner people such as to their having been "religious refugees led to this place to find liberty".[100] The Rev. S. J. du Toit said that God had placed the Afrikaners in Africa and given them the Afrikaans language.

It was in these years too that the Afrikaner Bond in the Cape Colony propagated the idea of a free and independent South Africa. The slogan was "Africa for the Afrikaners".[101] In the Transvaal this sentiment was echoed in the much-quoted words of Pres. Kruger (in reality coined by Dr. Jorissen): "Whether we conquer or whether we perish, Freedom will emerge in Africa, as it did in the United States of North America, as surely as the sun rises out of the morning clouds. And then from the Zambezi to Simon's Bay it will be a case of Africa for the Afrikaner". This utterance was typical of the mood that prevailed at the outbreak of the First Transvaal War of Independence. During that war many Afrikaners turned their thoughts to their mission. A Free Stater, for example, exclaimed: "I consider and believe that this land is the land ordained by God since time began in which we should wage our final fight for freedom".[102] A group of Transvalers proclaimed that "God rules and is with us. It is His will that we should unite as one nation and create a unified South Africa that is free of British authority. The future lies with us."[103] The war did not realise these expectations. However, such hopes were typical of the image of the future implanted in the minds of many Afrikaners although all did not cherish such sentiments. This image was the antithesis of that envisaged by English-speaking South Africa – a united South Africa under the British flag. Notwithstanding the assertion in *De Express* of the 6th November, 1884 that "we believe in a future South African Republic", this goal was not to be achieved until 1961.

It has often been alleged that President Kruger cherished an ambition of this kind; that is not the case. After the Transvaal War of 1880–1881 he and many others, thought only in terms of an independent Transvaal and the maintenance of *the identity* of the Transvalers. Kruger believed that freedom was "a gift from the Lord" that was to be preserved inviolate. Other Transvalers thought that "our God wills that we be a free people, free from oppression"; one of them pleaded for the adoption as their motto of "For the Lord and for the Fatherland, with our God for our Liberty".[104] In the words of an observer, Lord de Villiers, "the preservation of their independence is a sacred mission".[105]

Coupled with this idea was another – that in the attainment of their mission the Afrikaner people should retain its identity. In 1883 a minister of religion delivered the following exhortation: "You are Afrikaners! This you are by Divine ordinance and you will never become Englishmen!"[106] This mood was particularly predominant after the influx of the Uitlanders to the Rand. The Afrikaners were continually warned not to abjure their "origin", to honour their language and to keep their religious faith. "The Afrikaner people must not be cast into the melting-pot to emerge in such way that its identity and character is submerged or lost".[107] In 1892, Dr. Mansvelt expressed his faith in the future of the Afrikaner people: "After so much strife and suffering to win and develop this lovely and richly-endowed land, and after their having opened the way for the spread of the Gospel and civilisation, I do not believe that Providence has destined [the Afrikaners] to disappear from history without trace and to give way to others".[108]

During the Anglo-Boer War Kruger remarked that Lord Salisbury had said that the Afrikaner people should not exist; Kruger's rejoinder to this was that God had said "such a people shall exist" and that having once set His hand to such a task God would not abandon it.

After the war there were those who thought that the destiny of the Afrikaners lay in fraternisation with the English-speaking people so that this combination could give rise to a united South Africa under the British flag. Others thought the goal was retention of a separate Afrikaner people with its own language and culture – a parallel development with the English language group. The slogans "preserve and build", "bring together those who belong together from inner convictions", and the like, were based on the belief that it was God's will that the Afrikaners should survive as a separate people. Many thought that the mission was the conversion of South Africa into an independent Republic – the statements of some of the leaders of the Rebellion may be cited to support this. In 1906 President Steyn asked the Afrikaners to bear their burdens "until the Almighty achieves His purpose with this people".[109] Dr. Malan's words too strike a typical note: "The history of the Afrikaner reveals a determination and definiteness of purpose which make one feel that Afrikanerdom is not the work of man, but a creation of God. We have a Divine right to be Afrikaners. Our history is the highest work of art of the Architect of the centuries".[109a]

## 6

We then arrive at the third great crisis that has affected the Afrikaners as a people. It is seated in the *Anti-Colonialism* that is sweeping away the European colonial empires of the past four centuries. We are living in the era of the *black man's emancipation* throughout the world – Africa in particular. The remote Boer of the 19th century never dreamed that a day would dawn when the descendants of his "inferior" labourers would demand equal political rights and recognition of their human dignity and that they would receive support from beyond the country's borders. However, a few warning notes had been sounded that passed unnoticed in their day.

In 1884 *De Express* recognised the particularly great difficulty of the native question. All was quiet at that time but for how brief a period would it last? "In very truth", went on this article, "anyone conjuring up visions of the future would be inclined to despair of the continent's future".[110] With the British policy of "equality and fraternity" in mind the same newspaper prophesied in 1897: "The day will come when every European will realise that it is impossible for the whites, (a minority in relation to the natives) to make Africa a white man's land unless they combine their forces"[111] – a conclusion that equally well might apply to 1963. The paper was convinced that the policy of equalisation in the Cape Colony would inevitably result in the long run in the black man becoming the master of the white. "Under such circumstances", it queried significantly, "would the white man defer to the black?" In the same year Dr. J. W. G. van Oordt posed the question of whether the whites "clearly called to be the aristocracy and the salt of the country" might not one day be doomed to dependence on the masses, and black masses at that.[112]

The relatively weak philanthropic stream of the 19th century that contributed to the mass migration of a small group of Afrikaners into the interior, has swelled into a universal torrent since the Second World War; this time it threatens not a section of the Afrikaners only, but the whole of the white community, including the English-speaking. At the very time when the Afrikaners secured political domination over the English-speaking and resurrected the two small Republics of the 19th century in the form of a Republic spanning the whole of South Africa, they found themselves facing a threat of world-wide dimensions from the East, Africa – and the West – from a position as isolated as that of any nation has been.

The change in the world that crumbled the foundations of security beneath the feet of the Afrikaners, impressed itself on some of their leaders soon after the Second World War. It gained increasing emphasis during election campaigns and on public platforms on special occasions. It was realised that the non-whites had weight of numbers and that a concession of "one man, one vote" which the outside world had begun to claim, could lead to a "black" South Africa. With an eye to the *future* an ideology known as *apartheid* (or later as "parallel development", "autochthonous development" or "separate development") was evolved, drawn from traditional views on colour, equalisation, levels of civilisation, segregation, etc. It envisages a South Africa in which a "white" state will exist alongside "non-white" states or "Bantu homelands" in which latter the non-whites will have the same rights, political, social and economic, in their *own* territories as only the white man presently enjoys. It is a policy that reflects a similarity with recent trends in the rest of Africa that have brought independent ,,black" states into being.

After three hundred years of a process of economic integration of whites and non-whites this ideology offers the Afrikaners "a mission", that of dissolving, dividing and separating the main constituents of the population – each into separate areas in which each can develop according to its own character. The process will demand "sacrifice". The whites have to be "re-educated" to do their own manual work. And so we find rebuttals of the contention that the non-whites were destined to be the domestic servants and to minister to the comfort of the whites. If this separation is not carried out, the alternative prospect held out is "perish".

Underlying this ideology too are the traditional ideas of select destiny, calling and mission. They are all *interwoven* in the ideology as will be shown presently by referring to various pronouncements on the subject. Some theologians have harnessed biblical texts to bolster the ideology but others have stated that it is incorrect to invoke biblical grounds in support of our ideologies. Some learned men assert that God has drawn a line of distinction between peoples, and more emphatically between races, and that in distinguishing races and nations, He fulfils part of the divine scheme of things. Israel, for example, had to refrain from close association with other peoples: An admixture of races would make the goal of separate peoples unattainable and integration would lead to the downfall of "Western civilisation" in South Africa. There exists a belief that the Afrikaners have a "calling" from God to effect the *separation* of white and black to the end that the whites may "permanently" be able to fulfil their "calling". The racial problem therefore has a religious core.

I shall refer to a few recent verdicts to illustrate the mood in our day. In 1946 we read in *Die Volksblad:* "World affairs, moving at a furious pace, have brought our people to a second moment of crisis in which everything is at stake. We stand before a second Blood River . . . for even from Europe, our ancestral home . . . come ominous voices. Western civilisation has destroyed itself in a titanic struggle . . . and with it the Divinely ordained divisions between East and West and between the white men and the colour-ed races have vanished from the face of the earth . . . Before that tribunal of confused nations . . . the Boer people has been dragged, found guilty and given a sentence of doom . . . the judgment be-ing that the descendant of the Voortrekker will no longer have a right to draw a dividing line between the black man and himself! . . . The hour of crisis is at hand; the hour of decision as to the continued existence of the Boer people in South Africa, won at so great a cost, is *now*. Here is the setting of the final trial of strength between Christiandom and heathendom. If this outpost of Western civilisation crumbles, then 'finis' may be written to our nation and country . . . then the Communists will rule, the forces of darkness, the heathendom of the East".[113] In the same year the Rev. J. F. Mentz declared: "If we Afrikaners do not unite and snatch our country from the hands of the black masses who are pressing on our heels, we – those who wish to remain white – may have to flee".[114]

In 1959 Professor S. du Toit warned that the extension of the franchise to the non-whites would practically amount to suicide for the whites and that with it would go the possibility of a reversion to barbarism. "If we believe that we still have a calling and a task", he added, "then we may not destroy ourselves . . . We are determined to remain here. We have no other fatherland and, if our good intentions are disregarded, we shall defend ourselves to the uttermost".[115] Approximately one year later, his colleague, Professor H. G. Stoker felt that "our arguments should be sustained rather by faith in God's guidance, by our God-given calling, and by the rightness of our cause . . . the present situation is grave, critical and dangerous. Against us we have the antipathy of the states ruled by coloured races (including the black states in Africa) and the criticism of the West, with the possibility of more positive action on the part of the latter (and even of UNO) in an attempt to force us to give the franchise to natives in the white areas" . . . He warned against any concession in this respect . . . : "We should live with a truer and intenser confidence that God presides over the fortunes of our country and that here we have a God-given calling. This was the spirit that animated our forefathers at the battle of Blood River . . . Our refusal to make a concession [of the franchise to non-whites] is also religious in its essence and relates to our firm belief in the calling to which God has summoned us here in South Africa".[116]

You will have noticed in the meanwhile that we have again arrived at the idea of calling and mission. What does that encompass and how is it expressed? It would be possible to compile a whole volume of select readings of recent pronouncements on the subject as it affects the Afrikaner people. I shall quote a few examples before proceeding to analyse their content. The Rev. W. A. Landman wrote: "We believe that as a people we have had a calling from God and we believe that we have a god-given task in relation to the non-whites in this African continent. God brought us here for a purpose".[117] A more detailed description of the purpose, calling or assignment is lacking. In 1957 one of the *Transvaler's* readers wrote "that God has summoned the white man and set him apart to build a separate nation in South Africa and to spread the gospel of Jesus Christ among the Heathen . . . To achieve this calling the white man has been bidden to act as the guardian, master and spiritual leader of the black man. To do that the white man has to have at his command the authority needed to uplift, Christianize and evangelise the black man; the purpose of this is that the black man who is still a child from the point of view of civilisation, shall grow and develop in due course in his own area, with his own language, according to the nature of his kind and in accordance with his own traditions . . . We are in the process of setting the world an example since we know and believe that God wills it thus".[118]

On the 28th April, 1959, *Die Transvaler* replied to an attack by *The Star* on the Afrikaner's philosophy of life: "The Afrikaner believes that his struggle for the continued existence of the whites in this country will be crowned with success . . . He also believes that the Supreme Being brought him to this country by divine

24

purpose and that the fulfilment of that purpose is his primary task and a matter of principle on which there should be no speculation for the sake of material well-being or for temporary advantage. When a God-given calling has to be fulfilled, self-interest and opportunism do not count".[119] The implication of this – *apartheid* is not only a purpose but also a calling.

In September, 1959 the Rev. F. O'B. Geldenhuys spoke of the Afrikaner's "God-given mission – to be the bearer of light in Africa".[120] A month later a correspondent wrote: "We are a people with a calling who have to carry the light of the Gospel to the heathen in South Africa".[121] In January, 1961 an Afrikaner said that it was our divine purpose "to spread the Gospel of Light, and salvation, to heathendom that lived in darkness and, in doing this, to prevent their exterminating one another".[122] The history of the past 300 years, declared Professor J. H. Coetzee, has led us to believe "that we have a calling that is of God's counsel".[123] The Rev. J. J. Swart concluded "that as a people we had received a calling to spread the evangelical message of light from the southern end of Africa to the darkness of the North".[124]

A speaker at a meeting in April, 1961 told his audience that it was our calling "to spread the light of the Gospel in Dark Africa" and that to ensure the abiding nature of this calling we had to sustain ourselves as a *white* people".[125] *Die Transvaler* considered that our calling was seated in "the assurance of the continued existence of white civilisation"[126] and in upholding "western culture and civilisation" in this "outpost".[127] The emphasis is increasingly shifted from "Evangelical and Christian" civilisation to the preservation of the white man. Dr. Verwoerd declared on the 30th September, 1961: "South Africa has a greater task than that of establishing Christian civilisation in Africa. It must become the firm base for the *white man* when he has his back to the wall from which he can again advance . . . Our strength lies not in our numbers but in our *faith*".[128] On various occasions Dr. Verwoerd has heartened the people in terms such as: "Let us enter the future with full courage and faith, with our eyes raised Above to Him who planted us here for a purpose";[129] or: "The people of South Africa were not planted here to vanish".[130] In conclusion, the utterances of two cabinet ministers: Mr. P. M. K. le Roux felt assured that "a people that believes in its calling can have no doubts about its future"[131] and Mr. M. C. de Wet Nel said: "Let this Republic be a model of good race relations to the whole world. We are a people with a calling and cannot fail."[132] According to these expositions the whites are destined to set the world an example in arranging racial and communal affairs on peacable lines.

Let us take a closer look at these assertions (culled from thousands of examples) on the theme of purpose and calling. If we compare them with the expressed convictions of the Voortrekkers in 1841 we find that the ideas on dissemination of the Gospel, Christian civilisation and defence against non-whites as well as against rival white neighbours, have remained substantially the same. There has only been a shift of emphasis; this accords with changed circumstances although the situations of 1841 and today are rather alike. In both situations the Afrikaners felt called on to defend and justify their convictions and actions *against an outside world* – the only difference today being that the dimensions are wider. Nowadays the Afrikaners see South Africa as an advanced post and a bastion of the white man or of white civilisation in a black continent whereas in the 19th century similar views were held in respect of a portion of the interior only.

The shift in emphasis is interesting. In the 19th century it fell on the *promotion* of "Christian civilisation" among "the heathen" and on the enforcement of order through the eradication of "plunder, murder and violence"; today it rests on the *maintenance* of white civilisation with the stress falling on *white*. The whites and the whites alone (according to these views on "calling") can be considered worthy bearers of western civilisation; the viewpoint does not take cognisance of the Christianisation or westernisation of non-whites (for the old "purpose" or "calling" of bringing the Gospel to them still holds good). A glance at statistics shows that only some 3% of the non-whites of South Africa are members of the three Afrikaans churches – that figure having been attained after more than a century since we recognised the call "to spread the Gospel of Light". The fact that the stress has moved to *maintenance* of *white* civilisation so that the call to Christianise can be answered "permanently", leads one to wonder sometimes whether the "calling" is an existentialist manifestation. When the Afrikaners need encouragement or comfort in difficult situations are they not likely to deceive themselves by falling back on convenient slogans?

The idea is used thoughtlessly on occasion or without amplification of the content. What is meant e.g. by "The Afrikaner, summoned by Providence, remains on the path of destiny"?[133] It seems curious that the words "calling" or "purpose" should so frequently tend to have a soothing and flattering effect on speaker and audience. How very comforting! But – to quote *Die Burger* on this subject, "it is an extremely uncomfortable business to have a calling since that involves responsibility and sacrifice".[134]

When the idea of calling emanates from a political platform one is apt to wonder whether it is being used to sustain an ideology during a time of crisis. Is not the "calling" of "separation" to secure "the continued existence of the white" perhaps a device "to secure the continued existence of a particular regime"? If some are "called" who are the others? People who are *not* called? Yet from this latter quarter rises a slogan similar to that used by the Afrikaners in 1881: "Africa for the Africans". And may not investigation show that the non-white too says: God planted us here with a purpose and gave us a calling – perhaps that of becoming masters of the white men?

It is noticeable that many Afrikaners have a *fatalistic* attitude towards the racial question and the future of the whites: They seem to believe that all will be well and that there can be no misfortunes as long as they believe in a "calling". Their assurance is based on the following assumptions: "Do not feel uneasy about the future – just believe in God; He has led us whites in South Africa safely until now. He will never allow us to yield to the threats that loom up at many points on "the trek-path of South Africa". As a counter to such notions Dr. J. A. Schutte sounded a note of warning in 1959: *actions* must go hand in hand with faith. A theory or an ideology cannot rescue us.[135]

Opposed to "belief" in a "calling" or "special destiny" which permits of no doubts as to a "future", is the idea of *fate*. There are many who entertain doubts as to the future of the white man in a continent that is "bound" to become "black". Their arguments rest on historical precedents: Since the early Christian civilisation totally vanished from North Africa why should not the same fate befall ours? or: Where a higher civilisation hinges on non-white labour, the black proletariat will inevitably come to power at some future date. Even if such arguments are meant to focus attention on the seriousness of the situation, they do have a touch of *defeatism* about them. There are those who speak of leaving the country because they have doubts as to its future; and there we see the idea of inevitable ruin at work – anticipating a time when the threats will have turned into *fate*.

A few more observations remain; they concern the content of the pronouncements on the "calling" to bring the Gospel to the non-whites. In the first place one may query the correctness of the assumption that it is the privilege of the whites to act as the sole trustees of Christiandom in South Africa. Professor E. S. Mulder feels that the white man cannot lay a claim to a monopoly in this field but that he has a right to uphold his existence in the country.[136] In the second place may we assert that the maintenance of the position of the "white man" here is a "superior task" to that of establishing "Christian civilisation"? Or what is meant by such terms? In the third place there is a confusion of the functions of *people* and *church*. The people is assigned a task that in its essence belongs elsewhere. A people, a natural human community, cannot act *per se* as the expounder of the Gospel. It is the church whose calling it is to bring the message of deliverance. But on this subject *Die Kerkbode*[137] recently said that although some members of the people might not be active propagators of the Gospel, it did not follow that the whole people forfeited its right to existence. The "Gospel" should not be a people's defensive umbrella – nor a factor that aids in the peoples' dissolution. In other words, one should not say that it is our "calling" to spread the Gospel when one envisages it as one of the ways that will help to preserve our white skins intact. Neither is it permissible to say: We have already brought Christianity to most of the coloured races: Perhaps it is the Lord's will that the brown and the black man should succeed to the task of the white and that the white man should now disappear from the scene!

Every nation has its ideal. This ideal acts as a binding force. The ideal, as it were planted in the future, is the goal towards which the people strive as they move on into that future. We recall the ideal of independence which the Afrikaners sustained during and after the Great Trek, through the lifetime of the two republics and until our day when it was fully realised in the establishment of the Republic of South Africa. When the ideal is attained, the binding force which it evoked, may weaken and relaxation and diffusion may set in.

At present it seems as if the old ideal has given way to a new one – an endeavour to arrive at a "solution" of the racial problem since that is necessary to secure the "abiding" independence and continued existence of a "white" Republic. It is furthermore recognised as an attainable objective. One wonders at times whether temporary political goals are projected on to our image of what we imagine God's "calling" and "mission" to be. From the various views I have mentioned, it would seem that there is much confusion.

Is there not a danger that a people may become too wrapped up in itself – to the point of self-deification? Against such possibilities there should be constant vigilance.

1. *Cf.* Wilhelm Wundt: *Die Nationen und ihre Philosophie* (Leipzig, 1916), pp. 39–40.
2. *Cf.* Hans Kohn: *Nationalism – Its Meaning and History* (New York, 1955), pp. 16–17.
3. *Cf.* Frederick Hertz: *Nationality in History and Politics* (London, 1957, 4th ed.) pp. 305–6.
4. Boyd C. Shafer: *Nationalism Myth and Reality* (London 1955), p. 20.
5. *Cf.* Friedrich Hertz: *Nationalgeist und Politik* (Zürich, 1938), pp. 242–3; Lemberg, p. 293.
6. *Cf.* J. A. Hobson: *Imperialism* (London, 1938) p. 160.
7. Basil Williams: *Cecil Rhodes* (London, 1938, 4th ed.) p. 50.
8. J. S. Marais: *The Fall of Kruger's Republic* (London, 1961), Chap. XI and pp. 326–7.
9. *Cf.* Hans Kohn: Nationalism, pp. 12–30.
10. Edward M. Burns: *The American Idea of Mission.* (New Brunswick, 1957), p. 32.
11. Eugen Lemberg: *Geschichte des Nationalismus in Europa,* (Stuttgart, 1950), p. 165.
12. *Ibid.,* p. 169.
13. *Ibid.,* p. 182.
14. *Cf.* Hanno Kesting: *Geschichtsphilosophie und Weltbürgerkrieg* (Heidelberg, 1959), pp. 201–2;
Shafer: *Nationalism,* p. 179; *vide* also
Hans Kohn: *Pan-Slavism – Its History and Ideology* (1953) pp. 104–5.
15. *Vide* also Hertz: *Nationality,* pp. 19, 43, 45; and Lemberg: *Nationalismus,* pp. 19, 154, 163, 168, 176, 182 and 213.
16. Arnold Toynbee: *A Study of History,* Vol. I (4th ed. 1948), pp. 211–212.
17. Eduard Sieber: *Kolonialgeschichte der Neuzeit* (Berne 1949), p. 61.
18. *Cf.* Hertz: *Nationality,* pp. 60–61.
19. I. D. MacCrone: *Race Attitudes in South Africa* (1937), p. 41.
20. P. J. van der Merwe: *Die Trekboer in die Geskiedenis van die Kaapkolonie* (1938), pp. 256–257.
21. *Vide* e.g. *De Zuid-Afrikaan,* 22.2.1833, "Een Opmerker" (An Observer") to editor; *ibid.,* 26.8.1831, "Een Aanschouwer" ("An Onlooker") to editor.
22. *Zuid-Afrikaan,* 10.9.1830, leading article.
23. C. Spoelstra: *Bouwstoffen voor de Geschiedenis der Nederduitsch-Gereformeerde Kerken in Zuid-Afrika* (Amsterdam, 1906), Vol. I, p. 34 and Vol. II, p. 15, letter d.d. 4.4.1703.
24. Cited by G. D. Scholtz in "Die Ontstaan en Wese van die S.A. Rassepatroon" in *Tydskrif vir Rasse-aangeleenthede,* July, 1958, p. 147.
25. *De Volksstem,* 23.2.1892, I. J. Breytenbach to editor, 15.2.1892.
26. *De Volksstem,* 5.1.1895, J. J. Ferreira to editor.
27. L. M. Thompson: *The Unification of South Africa* (London, 1960) p. 333, J. P. G. Steyl in the Parliament of the Orange River Colony.
28. *Die Tranvaler,* 7.3.1958, B. A. P. Naudé to editor (Readers' views).
29. *Ibid.,* 16.3.1960, report of a speech delivered in Cape Town. The older generation among the Afrikaners still believe, as did their forefathers, that the descendants of Ham are black and that they migrated to Africa. They believe that it stands recorded in the old Dutch "State" Bible. However no-one has been able to trace this authority!
30. *Cf. inter alia Voortrekkerargiefstukke,* pp. 29–30 (Letter – 1838).

31. *Vide inter alia Die Patriot,* 18.4.1879, letter from "K" in the Orange Free State; McKinnon: *South African Traits,* p. 223.
32. See W. Kistner: *The Anti-Slavery Agitation against the Transvaal Republic 1852–1868 (Archives Year Book,* 1952, Vol. II), p. 211. The author gives a good analysis of the attitude of the Boers towards the non-whites.
33. *Cf.* Livingstone: *Missionary Travels* (1857); W. Holden: *History of the Colony of Natal* (1855), p. 390; J. Proctor: *Boers and Little Englanders* (1897), p. 3; Bryce: *Impressions of South Africa,* p. 118.
34. G. S. Preller: *Voortrekkermense II,* pp. 30–31.
35. L. M. Thompson: *op. cit.,* p. 219.
36. There is a pressing need for a series of studies on themes such as the Boers' assessment of the British and vice versa and also of British and Boer attitudes to one another – not political relationships but human relations. Similarly in the case of the whites and non-whites: What did the Boers think of the non-whites and vice versa? Such investigations would do a great deal to put race relations on a rational footing.
37. *De Express,* 7.3.1899, leading article.
38. *Cf.* F. A. van Jaarsveld: *The Awakening of Afrikaner Nationalism* (1961).
39. F. A. van Jaarsveld: *Die Eenheidstrewe van die Republikeinse Afrikaners* (1951), p. 68.
40. *De Tijd,* 9.2.1871, report by J.F.
41. *De Volksstem,* 29.3.1882.
42. *De Express,* 15.4.1898, leading article.
43. *Cf.* e.g. Colquhoun: *The Africander Land,* p. 212; A. Wilmot: *The Story of the Expansion of South Africa* (1899), p. 163; John Noble: *South Africa, Past and Present* (1877), p. 169; G. M. Theal: *History of South Africa,* IV, p. 445.
44. *De Zuid-Afrikaan,* 5.5.1837, letter written from Blesberg, 17.3.1837.
45. G. S. Preller: *Voortrekkermense,* I. p. 297.
46. G. S. Preller: *Voortrekkermense,* II, p. 102.
47. *Voortrekkerargiefstukke,* p. 233.
48. *Ibid.,* p. 150, speech of A. W. J. Pretorius at Vet Rivier, 1841.
49. *Cf.* e.g. *Gen.* 31:44–48; 33:20; 35:1, 7; *Psalms* 50: 14 and 15.
50. F. Lion Cachet: *De Worstelstrijd der Transvalers* (1882), p. iii *n.*
51. A. Dreyer, *Die Kaapse Kerk en die Groot Trek,* p. 7, letter Robertson to John Fairbairn, 13.3.1836.
52. *Vide* G. S. Preller: *Voortrekkermense,* II, pp. 108, 114, 269 etc.
53. *De Express,* 27.12.1895.
54. *De Express,* 18.12.1896.
55. *De Tijd,* 9.2.1871, report by J.F.
56. *De Express,* 9.2.1882, report by two clergymen (Van Wijk and Fraser).
57. *Die Transvaler,* 13.7.1961, leading article.
58. *Ibid.,* 9.7.1960, leading article.
59. E.g., *vide* the Rev. G. J. J. Boshoff: *U Volk is my Volk* (1959).
60. *Die Kerkbode,* 29.6.1960, pp. 919–920.
61. *Voortrekkerargiefstukke,* p. 149.
62. *De Volksstem,* 8.8.1885, D.D.D. to editor; see also the report by A. W. J. Pretorius on the battle of Blood River in *De Zuid-Afrikaan,* 16.2.1839.
63. *De Zuid-Afrikaan,* 26.4.1839.

64. *Staats Courant* Z.A.R. 1881, p. 38, letter of Kruger's, 7.3.1881.
65. *De Express*, 5.1.1882, report of President Kruger's address at Paardekraal.
66. *Gedenkschriften* (1902), pp. 249, 255, 264.
67. C. N. J. du Plessis: *Uit de Geschiedenis van de Z.A. Republiek en van de Afrikaanders* (2nd ed. 1900), p. 256; *De Express*, 30.6.1899, letter to editor from D. J. Pretorius.
68. *Onderwysblad*, 1.5.1955.
69. *Die Transvaler*, 29.5.1959, letter from W. F. Botha.
70. *De Express*, 22.8.1899, leading article referring, *inter alia*, to *Psalms* 20:8; 33:16, 17; 147:10–19; *Hosea* 14:4; *1 Sam.* 17:45, 47 etc.
71. Cecil Headlam: *The Milner Papers* II, p. 286.
72. *Zuid-Afrikaan*, 10.11.1837, letter.
73. M. C. E. van Schoor: *Die Vrystaatse Helpmekaar* (1960), pp. 21–22.
74. *Die Transvaler*, 17.8.1961.
75. *Ibid.*, 21.5.1960, radio talk by the Prime Minister on 20.5.1960.
76. *Ibid.*, 20.10.1960, letter from A. J. B. Vosloo; 21.10.'60, letter from Mrs. J. du Toit.
77. See *The Star*, 13.11.1958.
78. See, for example, Jannie Kruger: *President C. R. Swart* (1961), p. 130.
79. *The Star*, 9.2.1959, p. 8.
80. See reports in *The Star*, 24.8.1961 and 6.10.1961.
81. *Vide Bantu World*, 3.1.1953.
82. Adamastor: *White Man Boss* (London), 1950, pp. 16, 20; *The Star*, 17.10.1961, p. 6.
83. *De Zuid-Afrikaan*, 10.11.1837, letter from Retief.
84. Dreyer, *op. cit.*, p. 13, letter from Pretorius to the Rev. Van der Lingen, 23.7.1838; see too *De Zuid-Afrikaan*, 10.8.1838, letter from Gert Maritz to G. Joubert, 8.6.1838.
85. Dreyer, *op. cit.*, p. 3.
86. *De Zuid-Afrikaan*, 29.12.1837, leading article.
87. *Voortrekkerargiefstukke*, p. 120, Volksraad in a letter to Governor Napier, 14.1.1841.
88. *Ibid.*, p. 119.
89. Transvaal Archives, *Landdrost Potchefstroom* 196, criminal cases, Vol. 2, session of landdrost and councillors, 13.3.1861.
90. G. D. Scholtz: *Die Geskiedenis van die Nederduitse Hervormde of Gereformeerde Kerk van Suid-Afrika*, Vol. I (1956), p. 225.
91. See J. A. I. Agar-Hamilton: *The Native Policy of the Voortrekkers* (Cape Town 1928), pp. 127–129.
92. A. Dreyer, *op. cit.*, p. vii.
93. J. F. van Oordt: *Paul Kruger* (1898), p. 216, letter d.d. 10.7.1878.
94. *De Express*, 16.1.1884.
95. *De Express*, 17.4.1884, referring to a booklet by C. P. Bezuidenhout.
96. F. L. Cachet: *Vijftien Jaar in Zuid-Afrika* (1875), p. 234.
97. *Cf.* F. L. Cachet: *De Worstelstrijd der Transvalers* (1882), pp. 40–41; G. B. A. Gerdener: *Sarel Cilliers* (1925), p. 23.
98. The Rev. C. Spoelstra: *Het Kerkelijke en Godsdienstig Leven der Boeren na de Groot Trek* (1915), introduction p. 8.
99. *De Express*, 17.4.1884, dealing with C. P. Bezuidenhout's publication.
100. See, as a typical example, *De Express*, 18.3.1886, letter from W. Coetzer.
101. *Cf. De Express*, 2.2.1882 and 15.4.1898.

102. J. D. Weilbach and C. N. J. du Plessis: *Geschiedenis van de Emigranten-Boeren en van den Vrijheidsoorlog* (1882), pp. 253–254.
103. *De Volksstem*, 13.1.1877.
104. Concerning Kruger's views see *De Volksstem*, 5.1.1888; the other quotations are those of views expressed by C. J. Bodenstein and S. J. M. Swanepoel in *De Volksstem* of 4.1.1882 and 25.10.1892, respectively.
105. J. S. Marais: *The Fall of Kruger's Republic* (1961), pp. 331–332.
106. *De Express*, 5.4.1883; see also ibid. 12.4.1883.
107. *De Express*, 15.2.1887, article by "Oom Willem"; *De Volksstem*, 25.8.1890, letter from "Protest"; 28.9.1895, letter from A. Boshoff.
108. *De Volksstem*, 7.1.1892.
109. J. J. Oberholster: *President Steyn aan die Woord*, p. 147.
109a. E. Robbins: *This Man Malan* (Cape Town 1953), p. 7.
110. *De Express*, 11.12.1884, leading article.
111. *Ibid.*, 17.9.1897.
112. See his book *Slachtersnek* (1887), p. 140.
113. 16.12.1946, leading article.
114. Day of the Covenant celebration, Bloemfontein, 16.12.1946.
115. *Die Transvaler*, 8.9.1959, address to the Afrikanerkring, Melville.
116. *Woord en Daad*, 17.8.1960, p. 2.
117. *Ons Rassevraagstuk, die Wêreldmening en Ons Toekoms* (Stellenbosch, 1955), p. 23.
118. *Die Transvaler*, 25.7.1957, letter from "Quo Vadis".
119. *Die Transvaler*, 28.4.1959.
120. *Die Transvaler*, 17.9.1959.
121. *Die Transvaler*, 14.10.1959, reader's views.
122. *Die Transvaler*, 5.1.1961, p. 10, letter from L. J. Buitendach.
123. *Die Transvaler*, 10.9.1958.
124. *Die Transvaler*, 18.1.1961, p. 1, (Chairman of the Afrikaners Christian Movement).
125. *Woord en Daad*, 21.4.1961. My italics.
126. *Die Transvaler*, 27.5.1961, leading article. My italics.
127. *Ibid.*, 25.8.1961, leading article.
128. *Die Transvaler*, 2.10.1961, report of a meeting at Standerton. My italics.
129. *Die Transvaler*, 1.6.1960, p. 11, col. 6, address at a commemorative occasion, Bloemfontein.
130. *Die Transvaler*, 21.5.1960, radio talk to the nation on 20.5.1960.
131. *Woord en Daad*, 6.1.1961.
132. *Pretoria News*, 4.9.1961, report of a speech delivered in the town hall of Pretoria North.
133. Prof. Abel Coetzee: *Die Afrikaanse Volkskultuur* (1960), p. 147.
134. *Die Burger*, 1.1.1947.
135. *Die Transvaler*, 13.6.1959.
136. *The Star*, 8.9.1961, report of a lecture.
137. *Die Kerkbode*, 14.12.1960, pp. 836–837.

# THE AWAKENING OF THE AFRIKANER TO AN AWARENESS OF HIS HISTORY*

I

It is well known that the Afrikaners of a previous generation were acutely interested in their history. As far back as the 19th century there was plenty of evidence of this interest. Several Afrikaners in the Cape contributed articles or delivered lectures on such topics as the Huguenots, the Dutch East India Company's period of rule at the Cape and the Great Trek. It was only during the second half of the 19th century, however, that a fairly widespread awareness of their history as a whole became apparent among them. This awareness was not always manifested in historical writing; it was often given expression to in speeches, pamphlets or published letters – usually on political subjects. However, a few books were published to which we shall refer. It is interesting to note the striking relationship that there was between the dawning of the Afrikaner's awareness of his history and his realisation of himself in national terms during the period 1868–1881. I shall try to explain this relationship and reveal something of the nature of the process that resulted in the Afrikaner becoming a historically conscious individual.

We can best begin by describing the condition of the Afrikaans-speaking population shortly before the seventies and eighties of the last century. At that time terms such as "South Africa" or "Afrikaans people" had no spiritual or political meaning for them; since they lacked unity and national consciousness, such terms could not denote a "fatherland" or "nation". In short, they had not yet become "nationally" minded. Over a distance of nearly 1,500 miles, stretching from the Cape to the Zoutpansberg there were isolated groups and there was only a limited intellectual exchange. The Republican North and the Colonial South were

---

* This essay was first published in *Standpunte* X, No. 4, Cape Town, 1956, pp. 42–53. It has been revised. Quotations from Dutch and Afrikaans sources have been translated into English in this text. For more particulars see my *Die Afrikaner en sy Geskiedenis* (Nasionale Boekhandel, 1959).

sundered and had few sentiments in common, (although there were unconscious ties of blood, language, and religion). The Great Trek lay at the roots of this division. Only some of the Colonial Afrikaans-speaking people had joined the Trek and they had done this not because of theoretical ideals of freedom not because they were "nationally awakened" nor yet because they were exceptionally "good Afrikaners"; long years of pressure on the eastern frontier – losses of property, the uncertain existence and doubts concerning their future – had developed some sense of group consciousness among them and, more specifically, a racial and political aware-ness. Those who remained behind in the Cape did not have this continual stimulus; moreover they were relatively isolated in the country districts and lived at a distance from the British authorities. In these circumstances they lacked a sense of identity and it was possible that they might gradually become anglicised; they were unaware of the need of a language and history of their own. They had few of the stimuli necessary to promote a community of in-terests, political realisation, solidarity and the concept of a common cause.

On the other hand the Great Trek itself, their establishment in new countries, clashes with the Bantu and the British, loss of life and land – all these factors gave rise to a feeling of solidarity among the emigrant farmers, a sense of their own worth, of being involved in a common destiny and of a group-awareness to which attached an "own" history – even if this history was but a phase through which they had lived and still recollected. The substance of this history was based on little more than "grievances" and its "starting-point" went back hardly further than the time of the departure from "the motherland" (Cape Colony). As long as the British authorities continued to bring pressure to bear on the emigrants there was a possibility that a genuine sense of national awareness might develop among them, but before that stage was reached, the pressure was relaxed with the signing of the two Con-ventions, 1852–1854; after that the bonds tended to slacken and dissolve and there were internal dissensions so that in the eighteen-sixties individualism, local disputes and civil strife were the pre-vailing symptoms in the Transvaal. The pioneers lacked the will to establish a positive commonwealth and there were insufficient bind-ing factors to promote unity and a true national consciousness. A "Republican" was not necessarily a nationally-minded person.

2

The renewed attack of the British Government on the independ-ence of the Republics was to alter this state of affairs. Due to its geographical position the change first came about in the Orange Free State. It occurred in 1868, due to resistance encountered in their war with the Basutos and the leadership of President J. H. Brand who became the symbol of their unity; binding forces drew the Free Staters together as a conscious group and with a newly-discovered perception of their national "personality". The pressure that was brought to bear by the British over annexations after that wounded their feelings of self-esteem, led to a strong group-consciousness and a feeling of solidarity and of a common destiny; it was a spur to national awareness and in the Free State that was revealed as their fatherland; the "people" became the "nation".

In their indignation at the threat from outside they gave thought to themselves and their history. The Great Trek, its causes, their treatment by the British, the struggle to sustain an existence – these were all recalled and served to emphasise the importance in the pages of history of the Afrikaans-speaking Free Staters. Questions were posed as to their origin, place and future in South Africa and the answers became facts in a collective sense of identity that united the community in sentiment from within. It was in this spirit that the first Free State and Afrikaans historical writing (although it appeared in the Dutch language) saw the light of day with its essence the relation between "Boer and Briton" and with the Great Trek as its starting-point.

It was not merely fortuitous that financial support of the Free State Government made possible the publication of H. J. Hofstede's *Geschiedenis van den Oranje-Vrijstaat* (1876). The title reflects a limited vision that was not yet extended to the confines of South Africa as a whole. It was intended to be "a work devoted to the fatherland . . . for our Burghers" and for "posterity" who had to remember "what their fathers had done and had suffered". He wished to stir and "uplift their national feelings" and to express "the love that tingles our hearts with warmth for the country in which we now live in peace and to raise our thankful voices for all the love and support that Providence gave our forefathers during their trials and tribulations". An appeal was made to the youth to hold the "freedom" of their country to be "precious", the land "that had been purchased at so high a price and for whose liberty rivers of blood had been shed". "Heroes" like Wepener and Dreyer were mentioned. Notwithstanding its factual errors and lack of cohesion, the Volksraad welcomed the book's appearance "since it made known to the world the numerous grievances of the Afrikaners, and of this people, in particular".[1] At a time of crisis it created a point of departure in their history which gave the Free Staters a background and a frame on which they could weave their

35

dreams of the future. It was the product of an awakening of a national feeling.

The First Transvaal War of Independence, 1880–1881 broadened *Free State* patriotism into a *South African* patriotism.[2] A feeling of affiliation and of a common home, origin and destiny merged the "volk" into a greater people drawn towards a common future and one in which the political ideal expressed was that of a united South Africa. In contrast to Hofstede's book, the small publication of C. P. Bezuidenhout, *De Geschiedenis van het Afrikaansche Ge-slacht van 1688 tot 1882*,[3] provided common basis for the origins, formative background, establishment and meaning of the existence of the Afrikaans-speaking as a people. They had opened up the interior for Christianity and civilisation. They were therefore presented as forming a unity, alive to their course in the present and the future and aware of past origins. The idea of freedom, of a common future and calling and of a God-given task to be undertaken – all these beliefs pointed to a quickened sense of self-awareness and of consciousness of the past.

There followed an interest in the collection of source material dealing with their forebears and a great veneration of their predecessors. There was a collection for "a national monument to commemorate the valient Voortrekkers and Piet Retief" and all the heroes".[4] The stronger the national awareness became in the eighties, the greater was the need felt for "clear and correct" facts of the previous generation in school books and that these facts should be presented from an Afrikaans viewpoint.[5] According to the Free Staters, English text-books (e.g. Wilmot's) depicted their history in "the blackest and dirtiest colours" and conveyed "a wrong impression" of their "beloved state" to the children. The "unjust and scandalous" deeds of the British should be exposed "to the world" and school books should serve to arouse a national feeling among those who lacked it or whose feelings were insufficiently strong; "a genuine nationhood" should be cultivated.[6] The past was also used to stimulate enthusiasm for burning political issues of the day e.g. "Brothers, think of the precious blood shed by our forefathers" or "The Afrikaners have a history. It teaches us of their struggles and self-sacrificing love of freedom" or "Bear the Voortrekkers in remembrance. They have taught us".[7]


3


The Afrikaans-speaking of the Cape Colony who lacked stimuli and sufficient welding forces, were not yet "nationally" minded and did not at first seem conscious of the great historic role that they were destined to fulfil. Although it was in the role of spectators that they witnessed the drama of British annexations unfolding beyond the Orange and Vaal Rivers between 1868 and 1877, they gradually came to enter into and share the feelings of their distant kinsmen. Reflection and growing indignation led to "discovery" and appreciation of the Republican North and of themselves as an entity. The Republicans were rediscovered as "a stem of our own tree"[8] and "offshoots of the Colony"[9] who "had originally been one with us and would have remained one with us".[10] If it had not been for the Trek "the bonds that held us together as one people would never have been sundered."[11] The annexation of the Transvaal and its "War of Liberation" sent a "national impulse of sympathy" through them too for the war was also "a war waged against us".[12] "Setting aside the ties of blood, your interests are our interests, your well-being is our well-being, your suffering, our suffering"[13] for "from the Cape to the Soutpansberg we are one family".[14] And so there was a "discovery" of the Great Trek and their "kinsmen" of the interior were lauded as the "pioneers" of civilisation and Christianity; the Cape Afrikaners were filled with "pride" too at the achievements of the uneducated Boers. It was then only that the concepts of "one people, one country, one language", "the Afrikaans people" and "South African fatherland" originated. Common ties of blood, a common habitat and a common destiny again overrode geographical barriers and brought about a feeling of unity. In these circumstances there emerged in small circles as yet the new ideal of a united South Africa that was to be created from within and which was to find expression in the Afrikaner Bond. With an eye to the future, they analysed the situation in which they found themselves, giving particular thought to the place of the Afrikaans-speaking at political level and the possibility of Anglicisation. This in its turn led to their discovery of their own potential political power coupled with the fact that they occupied a subordinate position in the Colony that might conceivably result in their absorption into the English community. *Language* and *history* were the means by which their continued existence could be achieved for *Afrikaans* as a language could win a whole future for them and history could nourish the idea of nationality. In this situation the *Genootskap van Regte Afrikaners* (The Society of Right-minded Afrikaners) came into being with *Die Patriot,* its newspaper charged with carrying out the work of convincing the Afrikaners. In this great crisis – continued existence versus submergence – dividing lines were drawn and the people were continually faced with the choice of being "loyal" or "dis-

loyal'' or ''genuine'' and ''true'' as opposed to ''wrong-minded''
and ''faithless'' – a situation which, in its turn, induced a defensive and conservative frame of mind.

The problem of the future and the analysis of their own time
would also lead the ''Patriots'' back into the past although it was
felt that they ''had practically no past but did have a future''.[15]
National self-discovery resulted in questions being put as to who
they were, what their place in the past had been, how they had
been treated by the British Government, and what direction they
were to take in future. They therefore accounted for their origin
and their right to exist as a separate group with its own identity.
It was at this stage that the Huguenots were ''discovered'', that the
language ordinances were revealed to be ''unjust'' and acts of
''suppression'' and that attempts were made to show that Afrikaans was a separate language. An appeal was also directed at the
youth to preserve ''the heritage of our devout forefathers''[16] and to
cleave to that which was ''their own'' – descent, language, morals
and tradition. Here one discerns the common binding forces. Their
history had as its content, the struggle between Boer and Briton and
the treatment of the Republics was seen as ''unjust'' and ''oppression''.[17] The past was presented as being one laden with grievances
and British policies were depicted as ''crimes''.[18] This historical
awareness of themselves resulted too in the collection of historical
source material ''so that the remembrance of our forefathers does
not die out''.[19] *Die Patriot* had a special column for ''Afrikaans
history'' and pleaded for a monument to the Huguenots. Readers
were encouraged to write ''an original Afrikaans history in which
our domestic way of life, morals, customs, character and nationality, past and future, language and rights in the face of alien intrusion would be done full justice''.[20] The paper also called for an
''epic poem'' on Piet Retief. The underlying intention was to foster
self-esteem and pride.

''British History'' and ''Cape History'', so it was discovered,
were calculated to extinguish any ideas of ''nationality''. ''It is
high time that our children should be made acquainted at school in
their own language with the *true* history of the land of their birth.
For too long we have received stones in lieu of bread, snakes instead of fish and scorpions rather than eggs''.[21] According to ''Cape
History'' England was ''all-important'' and ''the Afrikaner always
in the wrong''. History could foster patriotism. ''Is the time not
more than ripe'', wrote one Afrikaner, ''for some capable persons
to write a concise history of our country for us ordinary people, so
that there may come an end to the dissemination of such one-sided
histories as those of Hall, Wilmot and Chase that libel the Afri-

38

kaner?"[22] "Criticus" considered it a "scandal" that there was no history in "the language of the country" and the Rev. S. J. du Toit pointed out that the "poor Boer" was always shown in a bad light and complained that the British works contained "twisted" and "partisan" presentations and reflected "narrow-minded prejudices".[23] C. P. Hoogenhout seethed with indignation at W. Holden's *History of the Colony of Natal* (1855) in which "the Afrikaner Boer was jeered at and insulted". "Who is there who does not shudder at such infamous and shameless untruths? . . . the book is full of hatred, envy and lies."[24] Self-discovery directed attention to history and the indignation that this aroused led to a demand for an "accurate" presentation of the facts.

It is not to be wondered at that the first history written in *Afrikaans, Die Geskiedenis van ons Land in die Taal van Ons Volk* (1877) (*The History of Our Country in the Language of Our People*) testifies to a wounded self-esteem and that it sets out to put the facts "right" from an Afrikaans point of view. As opposed to the existing works that viewed everything through "English spectacles" and in which "the unfortunate Afrikaner was always put in the wrong", it would "tell things as they really were".[25] It is not for nothing that one reads in the foreword: "Tell the truth, correct the lie and again bring to notice the deeds and fortunes of our forefathers". By way of introduction the book commences with Diaz and concludes with a "United States of Africa" that becomes the starting point of their "present". Although the book lacks cohesion, is too much of a chronicle and inaccurate – due to lack of sources and ignorance of European philological-critical methods – it does furnish for the first time, the common background of the Afrikaners of the Republics and of the Colony. The Great Trek was depicted as an occurrence in which branches from the mother-tree took root. According to the book the Afrikaans-speaking people through-out South Africa had an inner unity in their "national" history. The essence of the book's content is the grapple of the Boer and Englishman; it is built up as the defence of a case, as a refutation of charges, as an exoneration and as a corrective of wrong presentations. Furthermore it unmasks British actions and combines both prosecution and condemnation in doing that. Indications of motives are lacking and the presentation is invariably charged with an emotional overtone. The book's spirit and mood is nationalistic and the purpose is "to acquaint our children from their childhood of the trials and sufferings of their fathers in this land where foreigners now seek to tread us under foot"; they are required to learn to "keep faith" with their "devout forefathers" and to steer clear of "novelties" and alienation; in brief, the book is designed to serve as a cohesive force. Its mood is well reflected when it deals with the Slagtersnek episode: "Weep Afrikanders! – Here lie your flesh and blood! – Martyred in the cruelest fashion!" Or in the case of the Great Trek. "What Afrikander is there whose heart does not miss a beat when he reflects on the reason for the exodus? Anyone who remains cool after reading of the oppression, injustice and disasters suffered by the poor Boers is unworthy of the name of Afrikander". The book testifies to the racial gulf created by the British annexations; it was intended to bolster awakening national feelings of which it was a product itself.

The reception the book had also testifies to this. In *Die Patriot's* view "it was the light of South Africa that had opened our eyes" and had made them appreciate something that they should have realised long before, the need "to awaken a sense of nationhood".[26] A correspondent put it as follows: "The need for a history of this kind was great. What is the best way to develop a sense of nationhood and to strengthen the harmonious bonds of affection among the people? Surely it lies in a thorough knowledge of an interest in the history of the people of one's own country. Everyone who holds the memory of his devout parents to be sacred, rejoices when he reads their history in his own language and his heart warms to his fatherland when he learns of the trials, the courage, the patriotism, but especially of the simple, genuine piety of his ancestors . . . Our Afrikaans spirit and feelings are presented in inimitable fashion in this history of ours".[27] The impact of the book on a Free Stater was typical: "If I had to tell you here everything that I felt when I read it (the book), then the columns of your *Patriot* would be absolutely too small to contain it . . . Please see that thousands of copies of your little history book are printed so that every true Afrikander can have one in his possession and so that all may know what South Africa cost their forefathers".[28]

4

Owing to its remoteness the Transvaal did not experience the full pressure of British policy before 1877. But with the loss of their independence and "the foe" in their midst the Transvalers saw things with other eyes and compared conditions before the annexation with those that succeeded it; this gave rise to indignation, reflection and joint consultation at large gatherings of the people and thus to a unifying aim. In this way their home that had previously lacked a proper appreciation was seen as "the fatherland" and a feeling of nationhood was born. Horizontal antipathies were spanned and a quickened awareness of their status as a group developed that bore witness to feelings of solidarity and self-respect. It was only in the crisis when the country had been "lost" that self-respect was "discovered" anew and that a feeling of unity and common destiny developed that was to be fortified in the blood-shed of the "War of Freedom" of 1881. The fact that the Free Staters and the Cape Afrikaners showed so much sympathy for the Transvalers and strove to help achieve the latter's independence had the effect of drawing them into the historical image of the Northerners, and in the North too the concept of one "South Africa" and one "Afrikaner nation" took root. In 1880 the following remarks were addressed to the colonial Afrikaners from the Transvaal: "After all we are one nation, of one blood and of one bone and one flesh"[29] and "The whole of South Africa, from the shores of Table Bay to the borders of the Limpopo will be united ere long in a Bond of unity with the accomplishment of a community of one South African people as its aim".[30] And so from the North too the schism of the Great Trek was bridged and the groups of people welded into one large community with a common habitat and ties of blood. To many South Africa had become a "fatherland" for the "Afrikaans people".

As in the case of the Cape Colony, the crisis evoked reflection on future, present and past. Contemplation of their past gave them historical dimensions in their new condition of self-awareness and gave the "volk" historical stature – but oneness with the "other" Afrikaners elsewhere in South Africa. Unity entered into the common totality of recollections even if this "history" was a tabulation of grievances and a story of clashes between Boer and Briton and its spirit that of "wrongs", "injustice" and "oppression". The Great Trek was interpreted as "a sacred passion for freedom" and Slagtersnek received considerable notice. In the opening of the interior for "Christiandom and Civilisation" was seen the purport of their history. In this case too history took the form of defence of a case, of justification of their existence and independence, of an exposure of the imputations made by the British, of refutals of the latter's accusations and of a denouncement of British policy. *Het goed Recht der Transvaalsche Boeren* (1883) ("The Just Cause of the Transvaal Boers") of J. A. Roorda-Smit and F. Lion Cachet's *De Worstelstrijd der Transvalers* (1882) ("The Intense Struggle of the Transvalers") are sufficient examples to illustrate the content and method of presentation of this history.

In *Wie zijn Wij?* (1881) ("Who are We?"), a manifesto signed by President Kruger, (but actually written by Dr. E. J. P. Jorissen), that testifies to a time of questioning, the author pro-

41

ceeded beyond the limited bounds of historical presentation that had always begun with the Great Trek, and saw this occurrence as a "prelude"; and he provided for the inclusion of all those who spoke Afrikaans. Their common origin was brought to the fore and answers were supplied to such questions as who they were, how they had come to be dispersed over the country and what factors had governed their lot. The manifesto deals with all these points and so does J. D. Weilbach and N. J. du Plessis's *Geschiedenis van de Emigranten-Boeren en van den Vrijheidsoorlog*, (1882) ("History of the Emigrant Boers and of the War of Freedom"). The latter is a eulogy of the victory and great heroic deeds – designed to foster national sentiment. Its purpose was to reveal to "posterity" how "their forefathers had suffered and struggled for freedom and independence" and to enlighten foreigners. Its content and presentation may be summed up in the phrase "all that they had always had to endure at the hands of England and the English". The "just cause" was demonstrated; "the despicable and cowardly deeds" and "mendacious language and alarming policies" of the British were presented in emotional and exaggerated terms. The "volk" found their achievements mirrored in this book and it had the effect of emphasising their common lot. In the Transvaal too there came a demand that national sentiment should be stirred and strengthened "by a thorough and inspired teaching of the history of the Fatherland". "Then the children will re-live the deeds of their ancestors and draw courage and inspiration from these recollections; then they will stand firm in the hour of danger".[31]


5

If we consider the whole development within which Afrikaans historical writing had its "beginning", we are struck by the fact that the dispersed groups of Afrikaans-speaking people had not become nationally minded before the seventies and eighties of the 19th century and did not develop an assertive "nationalism" before 1881. They lacked a historical awareness of themselves and the cohesive forces that could supply an inner unity and provide them with a common future, past and present were absent. After 1881, however, we find between Cape Town and the Zoutpansberg a people that had become largely united in sentiment.

The ideas of a common home and close ties of affinity had become collective and conscious "facts" that crossed all geographical or political boundaries. The feeling that they were bound together and had a future in common, is evidence of the spiritual metamorphosis that had come about. A young and developing nationalism was aware of its own strength, dignity, uniqueness and future. For these reasons it was an attractive and a conservative force; for these reasons too (and the frustrations encountered in the search for a home in which self-realisation could be achieved), this nationalism could be defensive, aggressive, addicted to polemics and sensitive to criticism. The change must be put down to the reaction to the goad of the British challenge; this brought a crisis into the lives of many Afrikaners and set a question-mark over their future that led them to turn to their past.

After 1881 they did have "a history", a common sum of recollections of illustrious achievements of which the "volk" had become aware and which would serve as a backcloth for the future. Awareness of history was inseparable from awareness of self. The process of becoming nationally minded presupposed that they had become aware of their history – and that is where the Afrikaner first became conscious that he had a history of his own. The contemporary struggle and period was extended "backwards" and the nation's existence was "stretched back" into the past. Historical dimension was first obtained in the process of their becoming nationally aware; it was projected into the events of the past to focus on unity; the combination resulted in the appearance of a "national" history. National consciousness resulted in a demand for an account of the past; since this could throw light on the origin and development of the "volk" and since they envisaged a particular future, history was called into play, although it was not always written. From history the people could learn who they were and what was expected of them. A historical awareness of themselves meant that they enjoyed a common knowledge of their allotted place and it bore witness to their inner unity. Their insight was based on a survey of history in its course and unity, its direction and the situation in which they found themselves in their time.

The demands of national consciousness for a knowledge of self led to the investigation of sources and their collection, to contemplation and absorption in their origins and the reasons for their existence. In the threat to their existence they found solace and inspiration in history; it made transparent what had happened to them, gave perspective and distance and provided a "spiritual" breadth in which they could the more easily grasp the purpose of their existence and history. In brief, it led to their becoming aware of the essence of their very being. In the uncertainty of their new life in its relation to the future, history provided a sheet-anchor and links with their newly-acquired insight; it was the only weapon that young nationalism could summon to its own defence. History

43

would bring awareness to them and foster nationalism from which strength could be drawn for the struggle that lay ahead. In addition, history had to serve the purpose of countering defection and signs of weakness. Since this history was so especially their own and bore witness to their sufferings in the passage of time, the Afrikaners would be particularly sensitive about it. And so we encounter the demand that their history should be written "correctly and with accuracy" and their irritation at supposed English misrepresentation. Since its other function was to foster nationalism the historical consciousness and historical writing were likely to be defensive, sketchy, delineative and aggressive. Their own existence was justified and defended in this way. The circumstances of the times undoubtedly contributed to the first Afrikaans historical writing falling into the category of apologia. Did not this very cloak reflect the essential features of an awakening national self-consciousness?

1. Minutes of the Volksraad of the Orange Free State, 9.6.1877.
2. *Vide* my *The Awakening of Afrikaner Nationalism* (Cape Town, 1961).
3. Published by O.F.S. Nieuwsblad Maatschappy, Bloemfontein, 1883.
4. *De Express*, 9.10.1888, 6.8.1889 and 14.10.1890.
5. *De Express*, 13.10.1881, leading article.
6. *De Express*, 30.6.1891; The correspondent obviously put the case in exaggerated style. See note 19.
7. *De Express*, 18.11.1886, 4.11.1886, 21.2.1888.
8. *De Zuid-Afrikaan*, 20.1.1868, 11.3.1869.
9. *Het Volksblad*, 28.3.1872.
10. *De Zuid-Afrikaan*, 13.1.1881.
11. *Ibid.*
12. *De Zuid-Afrikaan*, 12.2.1881.
13. *De Zuid-Afrikaan*, 29.5.1880.
14. *Die Patriot*, 12.3.1880.
15. *De Zuid-Afrikaan*, 25.9.1875.
16. *Het Volksblad*, 17.2.1876.
17. *De Zuid-Afrikaan*, 25.9.1875.
18. *Die Patriot*, 15.6.1877.
19. *Die Patriot*, 1876, pp. 44, 87. The writer probably referred to A. Wilmot's *History of the Cape Colony for the Use of the Colony of the Cape of Good Hope* (1869) –, and W. Holden's *History of the Colony of Natal* (1855), etc.
20. *Die Patriot*, 7.6.1878.
21. *De Express*, 6.7.1882.
22. *De Zuid-Afrikaan*, 28.7.1875.
23. *De Zuid-Afrikaan*, 24.11.1875, 30.6.1875, 19.6.1875.
24. *De Zuid-Afrikaan*, 19.6.1875; it is clear that the opinions expressed were a reaction to Holden's rather hasty conclusions on the Afrikaners of the Republics. His book – especially the section on the Orange River Sovereignty – was meant as propaganda against the abandonment of that territory. See footnote 6 of my essay *Interpretations and Trends in*

*S.A. Historical Writing* in this volume.
25. *Die Patriot*, 13.6.1877.
26. *Die Patriot*, 6.9.1878.
27. *Die Patriot*, 30.3.1877.
28. *Die Patriot*, 9.8.1878.
29. *De Volkstem*, 29.6.1880.
30. *De Volkstem*, 15.6.1881.
31. *De Schoolgids*, 1895.

# THE AFRIKANER'S IMAGE OF HIS PAST

## I

It is as a historian and not as a philosopher that I make my appearance before you.* You will probably find little in my address to justify its inclusion in the "Philosophy of History" section since the latter takes a separate place alongside historical science and answers questions that no longer belong to the sphere of historical science. The philosophy of history deals with thoughts on the nature of history and not with matters arising out of the body of history. It is possible, however, that in my lecture you may find certain premises that will serve to introduce problems of a theoretical kind.

As you know, the word "history" has various meanings. In the first place it can mean history as reality or history in an objective sense. Secondly, it can mean history as a science or history in a subjective sense – the narration of history or knowledge of historical actuality: The latter is related to the image or presentation of the former by the historian's intellect. It is with this image that I shall mainly concern myself but possibly in a way other than you might expect.

I shall not be dealing with Georg Simmel's problem – how the material of past actuality gives rise to a theoretical image in the mind of the historian to create what we term history. What I have in mind is the background to the genesis of the *traditional* historical image of the Afrikaner. You will agree with me that after reading many Afrikaans history books, it will be possible to define an image with certain characteristics that could be termed the typical historical image of the Afrikaner; this particular image would not depend on theme and language alone. My experience as a historian enables me to assert this. A study of national historiography does not hinge on a study of history *per se* but on a comprehension of the *image* that a people forms of *itself*. For that reason one does not limit oneself to a study of history books only but extends the survey to other

* This lecture was delivered at the Fourth Congress for the Advancement of Philosophy on the 6th February, 1958; it was published in *Communications of the University of South Africa* (B.6, 1958) and has since been revised.

writings that have a bearing on history. A typical Afrikaans historical image is not merely the sum of different individual images but something that had a separate existence before the various books saw the light of print; it manifests itself in individual Afrikaans historical writings and is recognisable in them. It is a ready-made image that precedes historical writing – a primary factor while the history books occupy a secondary position. Behind all the different interpretations lies the typical Afrikaans historical image that gives the books their particular hallmark and classifies them as works of "Afrikaans" historical writing.

I shall endeavour to explain the origin, growth, essence, structure, characteristics, background and shape of the Afrikaner's historical image and its practical application; we shall commence with the present time to show that there is such a phenomenon as an image and then undertake a few excursions into the past, and indicate the grounds on which my conclusions are based for this address is primarily the result of research.

2

If I should assert that the Afrikaner people are a people who lean heavily on their past, and, as it were, lives in it, I do not think that I should be exaggerating. It will be sufficient to remind you of the large national celebrations of recent years, of the unveiling of large monuments, of periodical gatherings at national shrines, of addresses by leading men and of the establishment of a South African Historical Society. We need only think of the Day of the Covenant that commemorates the Voortrekkers and of Heroes Day on which the Anglo-Boer War receives ample attention; in these two events we have the kernel of our interest in history and in them the boundaries of the Afrikaans image of history are circumscribed for I may say straightaway that the vision does not extend much further than the Great Trek in one direction and hardly further than the Anglo-Boer War in the other. What happened before or after these two landmarks lies beyond the field of vision of the average Afrikaner man-in-the-street. You will appreciate all this from the annual commemorative addresses to which you have doubtless listened.

You will also be aware of recent apprehensions in a wide circle that interest in history will diminish or that it will disappear as a school subject since it is not a compulsory one. Complaints are made that history books lie unsold on the stationers' shelves[1] and that only approximately three in every five matriculation students take history as a school subject. In its essence this means that there is fear of the Afrikaans vision of history fading and that its practical effects will be lost. National and cultural leaders feel that there should be a lively interest in history; it should not merely be "dead" history that is resurrected on Heroes Day or the Day of the Covenant to be "buried" again immediately after these occasions. They wish it to become a compulsory school subject and this has been pleaded by politicians[2] and educationalists,[3] at political party congresses[4] and even in Parliament.[5] But it is especially in the columns of newspapers that members of the public have given vent to their feelings. All this gives us some impression of the historical image that persists in the mind of the public.

In taking note of the value that is at present attached to the past we can gain an indirect impression of the Afrikaner's views on history. A letter from the Johannesburg Cultural Liaison Committee contains the following sentences: "A people that disregards its history runs the risk of losing its identity" and "we accept the fact that our history is a powerful weapon in our hands for arousing Afrikaner consciousness."[6] At a conference of history teachers that was held in 1954 one heard such utterances as: "History strengthens a national sentiment" and "the fostering of patriotism and of a healthy nationalism are ideals that we should pursue and promote at all times and with all the practical means at our disposal."[7] A speaker at a Cape political congress declared: "If we continue to allow history to be an optional subject, we shall be committing national suicide."[8] And we read the following in a letter to the press: "History must needs be an inspiration to national pride and a source from which strength can be drawn so that we shall stand firmly and steadfastly in our allegiance and devotion to our own nation . . . It is high time that we should teach our children the whole truth of the history of our country and people irrespective of whether it pains the enemies of our nationalism or not, for otherwise its effect is completely diluted or lost."[9] The opinion of one of our Members of Parliament expressed in the House is particularly illuminating: "Apart from religion, history is one of the most powerful factors that has led the South African people along the right path . . . I say that next to religion it is one of the mightiest forms that we possess for building our nation."[10] That will suffice.

From these typical views it will be clear that history is regarded as an instrument to serve a particular aim. As its background it has a particular historical image that will become clearer to us when we consider the views of the English-speaking population group.

The English-speaking section are also displaying anxiety over the subject of history teaching at school. Numerous leading articles in their papers have been devoted to such topics as "History in the Schools", "Truth in History", "Two Histories?", "From Legend to History", etc. There have been complaints that history teaching is "biased"[11] and that school-books contain "twisted history" that makes the English-speaking element "foreigners" in their own country. One of their spokesmen said: "I regret that the twist of interpretation in many of our history books is being used as a powerful instrument of policy. And that instrument of policy is driving our two European sections further apart every year."[12] Another said: "An impression is given that the Boers went into the unknown areas and that foreigners followed them, growing fat by living on what the Boers provided them. This needs to be corrected."[13] In a spate of complaints, it was said that all the heroes were arrayed on one side and the villains on the other,[14] that history was bringing "disruptive forces" into play,[15] that the share of the English-speaking in building South Africa was being belittled and that since history was being taught purely from the Afrikaans angle it was unbalanced, and that into the bargian it was redolent of legend. The statement of an Afrikaans history teacher that "history must be used to build the action and carry on the struggle"[16] evoked many protests. Warnings were voiced at a "fatal dualism" that might arise if history were taught as "an instrument of nationalism and group patriotism".[17]

Under the heading "Two Histories?" a leading article in a well-known paper saw the problem in these terms: "One set of schools will be taught about the struggles of the nation against wicked imperialists who tried to grab its country and denationalize its people. The other will learn about the struggles of enlightened pioneers and administrators against obscurantism and reaction in an effort to make South Africa the modern State it eventually became." But the paper proceeds, neither of these images will be "true". A third image of general validity will have to be found for both white sections for, if history is to fulfil its social purpose, it should unite rather than divide "and if it is not to be a destructive force, its aim must be to build one nation, not two".[18] The matter was even brought to the attention of Parliament in 1957 by an English-speaking M.P. who asserted that we had *one* history that was the property of both white groups. But, he complained, "we do not always obtain the same interpretation". He wanted experts to be sought, some of whom who stood in the Afrikaans tradition and some of whom stood in the English tradition, so that they could undertake a joint approach to the history of the country and thereby lay the foundations of a united South Africa.[19] This desire was expressed in other quarters too.[20]

Remarks of this kind did not fail to evoke a response on the part of the Afrikaners. With regard to the demand for a revision of history books for schools one paper declared – I quote: "The red hot element of Natal are afraid to tell their children the real facts of South African history, such as the annexation of the Natal Republic, the seizure of the Orange Free State diamond fields, the Jameson Raid and the Concentration Camps."[21] A remark concerning the concentration camps led the same paper to reproach an English paper for trying to obliterate "their own trail" and of "twisting the past".[22] A reference to Slagtersnek evoked the response that those executed there would always be regarded as "martyrs" by those who were acquainted with the "true" history of South Africa.[23] Quite recently one read that: "Those English-speaking South Africans who even today try to justify the acts of their forefathers in South Africa have indeed an unenviable task".[24] And so the unbroken controversy continues.[25] As one English paper put it – with the aid of history the Anglo-Boer War is still being fought.

These quotations are sufficient to show that history has become a political issue for both white sections in South Africa. It shows the inner relationship existing between political ideals and the image of the past. The historical image has a practical application – firstly in the political sphere and secondly in the educational field. For that matter the teaching of history at school does depend on a historical image. Without that image it becomes a mere recital of facts and dates.

4

Before one arrives at the origin, essence and structure of the Afrikaans historical image and its manifestation in Afrikaans history books, it is necessary that one should take a glance at the 19th century British historical image that was mirrored in the "Cape History" of that time.[26] To some extent the Afrikaans image was a reaction to it, just as the historical image of the English-speaking nowadays is a reaction to that of the Afrikaner.

In Parliament last year an English-speaking member declared that fifty years ago there had been a "Cape History" that, in fact, was definitely not a history of South Africa; it seemed to him that at the present time they were veering over to the other extreme.[27] What he meant was that the Afrikaans historical image is dominant at present whereas in the 19th century it was the British image that held sway.

What was the British historical image underlying some of the "Cape Histories"?[28] Briefly, it amounted to the fact that no freedom of action was conceded within which a separate South African history could operate. South Africa was a British colony and a part of the Empire. "British History" was the focal point and the purely South African history was "Colonial". The latter commenced with the "purchase" of the Cape and the beneficent influences the British had extended to non-whites and "backward" whites. The liberal, enlightened and democratic ideas behind British rule had freed the "oppressed" non-whites from the "injustices" inflicted on them by the "Dutch". The Boers were depicted in unflattering terms as a lawless and turbulent community retreating before the advance of civilisation.

A few lines sufficed to deal with the Great Trek. The Voortrekkers were described as people who spread into the interior in the natural course of events but yet who had had the intention of evading the slave emancipation act so that they could continue unhindered the "enslavement and oppression" of the non-whites. The Republicans were sometimes described as "rebels" and as "slave traders". They were denounced for barring the entry of British initiative and progress into the interior. The "uncivilised" Boer was compared with the "civilised" Englishman.

5

Up to a certain point there was no opposition to the "Cape History" image. It was only during the last quarter of the 19th century that resistance set in; the intellectual change that led to this is described in another essay so that I shall only discuss this resistance to the extent of which it throws light on the line of thinking that led to the creation of the Afrikaans historical image.

In or about 1874 C. P. Hoogenhout became aware of the image in the English history books used by Afrikaans children. It was then that he discovered that "as yet nothing" had been written in Dutch on the history of South Africa. He expressed the need for a book of this kind so that one-sided histories like those of Hall, Wilmot and Chase that "abused" the Afrikaner could be replaced.[29] The Rev. S. J. du Toit felt that it was a public scandal that there was no book in the language of the country and criticised the English versions for their bias and twisted presentation.[30]

Hoogenhout found Holden's *History of the Colony of Natal* to be full of envy, hate and mendacity.[31] It was also discovered that the English mentioned matters that were to their advantage and kept a discreet silence on others.[32]

These were two lone voices crying in the wilderness but they did point the way that developments would take. The state of the Afrikaner in the Colonies and particularly those of the Free State was such that this "Cape History" dominated the field of history teaching until the end of the 19th century. Resistance to it continued too until the turn of the century. It is necessary that we should take note of some of the typical pronouncements that cast light on the Afrikaans vision of the past.

One of the objections to "Cape History" in the Free State was that it always viewed the Afrikaner from the darkest angle.[33] Such presentations could hurt peoples' feelings and inculcate wrong ideas in the children.[34] Even the Free State *Volksraad* was put on its guard against such misrepresentation. Another warning voice from the Republic found it wrong that the history of England should take pride of place in the teaching of history to Free State children, "yes, even before they know the history of their own land and people in South Africa."[35] "Een Afrikaner", a burgher of this Republic, added: "At school the Englishman has taken care to ensure that the history of the Afrikaner and of his heroic forefathers have not been brought to the fore which might have resulted in national pride and self-esteem being aroused."[36]

There was a complaint from the Cape "that names of the English kings and their nieces and nephews have to be learned by rote while heroes like Sarel Cilliers, Pieter Retief, Pretorius and many more . . . remain unrecognised."[37] The English historical image, it was felt, extinguished all "national sentiments",[38] developed among them a sense of false modesty"[39] about their own forefathers and alienated the children from their people and church.[40] The consequences of this process of denationalisation via "Cape History" were well described by Dr. O'Kulis in *Eselskakebeen* ("The Jawbone of the Ass"). And so there were often demands that history should be presented accurately and correctly,[41] and not by any teacher "contaminated" by English contacts,[42] but by "sons of the country" only.[43] The books of Theal, an English-speaking historian, were often praised by the Afrikaners since the latter considered his work to be "the plain truth".[44]

During the 19th century anxiety was expressed time and again at the Afrikaner child's lack of knowledge of his own country and the cold official attitude of indifference to it.[45] This state of affairs was attributed to the harmful influence of "Cape History" and the absence of Dutch books written from "our own" Afrikaans point of view. Each new history that appeared that was representative of the Afrikaner side, was welcomed. The publication of C. W. H. van der Post's *Piet Uys* was hailed as "an event of national importance."[46] At the end of the century D'Arbez commenced his *Historie-Bibliotheek* with a view to familiarising children with the history of their fatherland.[47]

What was it that the 19th century Afrikaner wanted to see as the content of his history by contrast with "Cape History"? That his national history, and not that of England, should take pride of place,[48] that there should be a counterweight to "the false impressions" conveyed by "Cape History"[49] and that there should be a "faithful and unadulterated" version of "their own" history — a "true" history of "the land of their birth".[50] An historical image of this kind would acquaint the youth with the privations of their forefathers in the country from which "foreigners" were now seeking to oust them.[51] This impression of their history would make their own heroes, domestic life, morals and customs, character and nationality, past and future clear to them and would enable them to uphold their language and rights against "foreign intruders".[52] They wanted to know all about the fortunes and misfortunes, courage, patriotism and especially "the simple, honest faith" of their "revered ancestors".[53] The "Afrikaans spirit" should be invoked out of the past.[54]

As the content of their history they also wished to see a record of all the "reprehensible actions" and "unjust acts" of the British authorities in South Africa against the Afrikaners,[55] for without that there would be no "true" history. It would have to show what the Afrikaners had had to endure through the years; what sacrifices of blood and possessions had been made to secure freedom and independence; how they had been deprived unjustly of their dearly-won gains in Natal and the Free State; in fact, the sum total of the cost of South Africa to their forebears.[56] The "oppression," "persecution" and "slights" to their forefathers were not to be ignored.

What aim did the 19th century Afrikaners have in mind with this content of an "own" history? J. H. Hofmeyr considered history to be the strongest of national ties — stronger even than language.[57] A Free Stater observed that history could serve to arouse national feelings in those who lacked them or whose sense of nationality had weakened.[58] In 1897 the Chairman of the *Taalbond* (Association for the furtherance of the Afrikaans language) encouraged an interest in history since "a people that does not know its own history can have no national feeling or self-respect".[59] History would open their eyes to the true state of affairs and would be a means of fostering bonds of affection that would draw the people closer together.[60] History should teach them that they had a "right" and a "goal" – that of assisting to foster "national pride". In the Transvaal the school principals considered it their task to arouse and strengthen national sentiment "by teaching the history of the Fatherland in a thorough and inspiring fashion". The youth would then draw inspiration from past memories that would give them courage in the face of future perils.[61] We see therefore that in the 19th century history also had to fulfil a purpose in serving the needs of an Afrikaner nationalism.


6


From what I have already said, you will appreciate the close affinity that this historical image had with the early manifestations (1868–1877) and actual origins (1877–1881) of Afrikaans nationalism. This nationalism was largely a reaction to the British imperial factor in South Africa. Imperialism made its impact there at a time when the Afrikaans people had little conception of national identity; they were dispersed over the British colonies and the Boer republics. The Great Trek had mainly been responsible for this dispersal; that event had left as its legacy deep emotional and painful recollections among the Afrikaners, particularly of the clashes with the British and the non-whites. They remembered treatment they had experienced at the hands of the British government in terms of "grievances", but with the latter's recognition of their independence (1852–'54) and the withdrawal of the imperial factor, memories of these grievances gradually grew dim. Republican North and Colonial South were to some extent remote from one another too; the bonds of unity – group consciousness and conceptions of common lot and awareness of a common past – were lacking. As yet there was no vital awakening to the existence of a common fatherland nor to their identity as a people. In the absence of national consciousness, there was hardly any historical consciousness. The renewed thrust of the imperial factor in South Africa (1868–1881) confronted the Afrikaans people with a great crisis. This period commenced with the annexation of Basutoland and of the Diamond Fields and concluded with the hostilities that involved the Transvaal Republic. The Republicans had felt that their freedom and right to an independent existence were threatened. Answers were needed to certain vital questions: What was to be their fate? Would the independence of the North be maintained or would the Afrikaans people be submerged in the English stream?

The British threat resulted in the constituent elements of the Afrikaner people in the Cape, the Free State and the Transvaal being thrown back on their own resources. Across the territorial borders the upper strata "discovered" one another and were united in their sympathies in the face of the great danger. An awareness of a common lot, of ties of blood and of a common fate, arose from the resistance to pressure and so the constituent parts of the Afrikaans people became united in spirit and sentiment. They realised that they shared a common fatherland; patriotic feelings entered into their lives and they gave voice to nationalistic utterances. In the political field the ideal of a united and free South Africa emerged; in the cultural sphere the Afrikaner in the Cape made the discovery of his own language. There was thenceforth a common aspiration to achieve a future unity and a common determination to safeguard rights against threatened dominance.

National consciousness was but a short step to an awareness of a common past. From a preoccupation with the future in store for him, the intellectually minded Afrikaner turned to an investigation of his past and of his origins. How were the *volk* dispersed? Who were the Afrikaners? Where did they spring from? These enquiries into their own nature and origin, the sum total of common recollections, became a "national" history; it led to a mutual "discovery" and to the creation of an historical image that was "closed" (comprehending all the Afrikaans-speaking), thereby bridging the gap that the Great Trek had brought about. We may term this historical "discovery" the historical dimension of their national awareness. Examples were sought from the past to throw light on present trials. New grievances resulted in the discovery of old ones. Grudges that had been latent at the time of the Great Trek were activated and given their place in a version of history that comprised little more than a tabulation of national grievances; this was history that had been lived through and the process of thought of a generaion that had become aware of the significance of its own experience. The distance in time between the Great Trek and the Crisis of 1877–1881, permitted of review and it was in that assessment of past events that the process of historical image-making took place.

When we investigate the process of image-making, we find that the Afrikaners' sense of awareness of the past had a three-dimensional aspect. In the first place there was his very recent experience of the impact of British policies; this experience led him to think back to a second and more remote level, the recollections of similar circumstances in earlier periods. Combined, these two led on to the third dimension – thoughts on the still living history in the present. It is obvious that in point of time a considerable distance separated the second dimension-experience acquired of earlier generations by tradition from the third, but it is in the latter dimension particularly that national legends and myths are apt to emerge.

A legend of this kind grew around Slagtersnek. At the time of the Great Trek the episode had practically been forgotten; contemporary witnesses did not list it among the actual causes of the Trek.[62] It was approximately in 1868 only when the British pressure on the North was mounting, that Slagtersnek was "discovered". Slagtersnek came to symbolise the way in which the British treated the Afrikaners. Anyone wishing to arouse feelings had merely to hark back to the Slagtersnek affair. The more remote the event became in point of time, the more vehement were the views expressed on it. And it was put to more intensive use, especially after the Jameson Raid and again on the eve of the Anglo-Boer War. That which was a reproach in 1868,[63] had become a symbol of oppression and tyranny by 1877;[64] by 1899 it was seen as "bloody murder" – "such as would always be an irritant in every Afrikaner heart".[65] Practically every history book in Afrikaans of the time featured the Slagtersnek episode prominently and in such terms that a correspondent of 1896 was moved to ask whether any Afrikaner could read it "without setting aside his book to allow his feelings to cool".[66] The unfortunate men of Slagtersnek had been transformed into "martyrs" for Afrikaans freedom and victims of "British cruelty".

After the Afrikaans historical image had taken shape in and about the years 1868–1881 its growth ran parallel to political development. Each new crisis added its quota of grievances to the existing ones and the scope of history was gradually extended. The new crisis of 1896–1902 revived nationalism throughout South Africa; with the intensification of nationalistic sentiment went a clearer evocation of the historical image. We see this reflected in the great public interest in Dingaan's Day shortly before the war.

After the catastrophic years 1899–1902 the Republicans had lost their independence. In books and papers we read interpretations of the reasons for this and accounts of struggles and suffering. Few themes have been given as much attention as the Anglo-Boer War. After the war the concentration camps assumed the importance in the historical image that Slagtersnek and the sufferings of the Voortrekkers in Natal had in that context before the war.

The Concentration Camps captured the imagination of the people in a way that very few other occurrences had ever done. The Concentration Camps too were to become a symbol and produce their martyrs.

7

We have already remarked that the traditional historical image of the Afrikaner hardly extends beyond the Great Trek and does not approach our own time much beyond the Anglo-Boer War. These signposts reflect its limits and mark off its content. Why is it that the historical image should revolve around these two poles? It was a dynamic period and a peculiarly romantic one; it was the period of great epic achievements by the Afrikaner people; it was a time during which momentous national events took place -- events that had lasting consequences for South African history. The Afrikaners saw the Great Trek as the central thread of their history; all events after 1806 led to it and the Anglo-Boer War was the Trek's ultimate sequel. A chain of causality linked the Great Trek – the axis of Afrikaans history – with the war of 1899–1902. The Trek divided them and the war united them; in both cases the imperial factor was the determinant. The period 1836–1902 gave South Africa its present shape.

What was the central issue in this period and therefore a fundamental part of the Afrikaans historical image? Contemporary observers had no doubts about it. In 1891 one of them observed that "the history of South Africa from A to Z teaches us that the Imperialists, without exception, have always sought to undermine the Afrikaners' position" and to wreck the idea of an Afrikaans nationality.[67] The central issue was the British Government's line of action and the Afrikaners' resistance to it. In 1875 it was said that the history of South Africa was "an uninterrupted struggle between the Englishman and the Afrikaner".[68] In 1883 an historian asserted that our history was an account of all that the Boers had had to endure at the hands of England and the English.[69] One has reason to believe the Afrikaner man-in-the-street of to-day has an impression of an historical image that is substantially the same as this one. In this image the Bantu only had a place as "barbarians" – in relation to the sufferings of the Voortrekkers in Natal and in subsequent wars.[70]

In this historical image the British filled the role of perpetrators of wrong and injustice; the Afrikaner was deprived of his rights, his language, his country and his freedom. Here is one utterance made after the Jameson Raid: "Think of Natal, Boomplaats, the unjust occupation of the Diamond fields, the unjust intervention in the Basuto War . . . the unjust annexation of the Transvaal and many other instances."[71] After every crisis these summaries of grievances were repeated.[72] The impression they gave was one of British oppression, persecution and injustice. In this historical image there was no place for an explanation of motives. The Afrikaners' struggle for liberty was sketched against the background of English actions; this battle for freedom constituted one of the central threads in the historical image. The account that history provided was one of suffering and struggle for freedom on the part of martyrs for the cause. And that brings me to the basic shape of the Afrikaans historical image. It is formed largely by political ideals like the maintenance of freedom and the achievement of an "own" Republican form of government. The Republicans had to be on constant guard against British actions "so as to justify and defend our acts and intentions" and had to take up arms to sustain their beliefs about the country's future.[73] Consequently they viewed the past as an etching in black and white – on the one hand the British whose acts had to be exposed, on the other the Afrikaners whose existence had to be justified and whose innocence had to be reiterated – the accused and the accusers. This is one of the reasons why it was that only the most blatant differences between Englishman and Afrikaner received notice while periods of unobtrusive development were left untouched by the 19th century historian. It is also one of the reasons for the prominent place that Transvaal assumed in the image for, indeed, it was over that Republic that the conflict between Imperialism and Nationalism took place.

8

The Afrikaans historical image is based on national-political values and on Biblical foundations. That is perhaps the reason for its ethical and moralising note. To the Boers freedom was the greatest of all assets. They saw their whole history as a struggle for freedom; for the sake of their freedom and independence they waged great wars with a world empire on two occasions. Freedom was essential to the continued existence of the Republican form of government; it was a national asset and deprivation of it had a profound effect on their state of mind.

The Boers were known to be a religious people. The treatment they received at the hands of Imperial rulers ran counter to their sense of justice; consequently there was no lack of ethical or moral judgement in their image of the past. In their history books the British government was given its place – in the dock of the court.

As we observed, this historical image rooted in the Afrikaner's nationalism. In the face of the threat to their national heritage they discovered their identity in the pages of history. History could reveal to them who they were, where they had come from and what their destiny was to be. They rediscovered the contemporary struggle in the past and the conflicts of the past were viewed therefore with contemporary eyes. Adulation of the Voortrekkers that has played such a large role in the life of the Afrikaners, commenced at this point – between 1881 and 1899, but with an intensification in the years immediately preceding and following the Anglo-Boer War.

All the virtues were epitomised in the "forefathers". On Dingaan's Day occasions, in particular their "courage", "sense of freedom" and "endurance" were praised and precepts were sought in their deeds.[74] As the pressure of the contemporary struggle increased so did the glorification of the Voortrekkers. Each Voortrekker became a hero. It was among the Voortrekkers that the true "love of freedom" and the true "republican spirit" were to be found. The Afrikaners were "deeply moved" by the Voortrekkers' trials in Natal[75] and one can understand why they entered into the spirit of those years. The cry that went up from the people's heart was often: "What did they not have to suffer and endure!"[76] The Great Trek was interpreted as *the* event that opened the whole country to the influence of civilisation.[77] And when the Afrikaner bethought himself of the reasons for the Exodus he was overcome with great emotion.[78] A book that could evoke such a reaction was obviously written in a particular spirit and had produced a touching image. The image was based on out and out nationalist sentiment.

The Afrikaans historical image was determined by the Old Testament too. We know that the Boers were firmly attached to their Bible; it was the book from which they sought counsel and guidance; and whatever fortune might overtake them was interpreted in Biblical terms. If there is one theme that predominates in their utterances it is the idea that God had summoned them to spread civilisation and Christianity to the interior.[79] They believed that the Voortrekkers had had "the calling of Providence". On many occasions the Voortrekkers were compared with the people of Israel. M. W. Pretorius addressed some of his aged countrymen as "fathers of Israel" and compared them with "the Lord's chosen"; they had fled from the English in the Colony just as the Israelites had escaped from Pharoah and Egypt.[80] To one Republican at least, the Great Trek was evidence that God had summoned the Boers to the same mission as Israel of old.[81]

The idea of special election and consciousness of a mission was emphasized by the annual renewal of the Blood River vow – a ceremony that drew the bonds closer between Voortrekkers and their successors. At these commemorative occasions history and religion mingled. A Free Stater came to the typical conclusion that all that the Voortrekkers had done had been by the Lord's will.[82] One recalls such expressions as the "devout forefathers" and their "hallowed memory", "altars of the people" and "martyrs".

It was Paul Kruger especially who revealed God's leadership in the history of the Afrikaner people; whatever happened to them was His will; He was the Sovereign of history and its central theme. Kruger's conception of history as it concerned the Afrikaner people was based on the compact of the Old Testament. The history of the people was the history of its faith in or alienation from God. This Biblical conception was of great importance in the Afrikaans historical image.

9

The historical image of the Afrikaner that we have disclosed to this point has been based on the private letters and other documents of ordinary people. Before any books had been written on their history, this image of the past was already alive in their minds. These primitive historical thoughts – that created an image in the mind's eye of the people – predated historical writing; it was a spontaneous creation and not a deliberate one. The historical image was there as a token of the awareness of the people of their experience. Perhaps one might refer to it as a people's self-consciousness or the impression that the people had acquired of themselves.

This image also manifested itself in historical writings and was responsible for the spirit in which various books were written as well as for their content, form and particular traits; the reader would realise immediately that such books fell within the category of Afrikaans historical writing. The historical image, however distorted and slanted it might have been, was recognisable – and here we are referring especially to the products of the period before scholarly historical writing became the norm. There were close ties between the writings of the "pre-scientific" period and the actuality that had brought the image to life. The relationship between the historical image and "pre-scientific" historical writing can be more easily discerned than relationship of the former to the "scientific" writings. It is this basic relationship that enables us to appreciate something of the spirit and character of the later and more scholarly works.

Books of the period of crisis, 1868–1881, that saw the Afrikaans historical image emerge and grow, include the following: H. J. Hofstede, *Geschiedenis van den Oranje-Vrijstaat* (1876), C. P. Bezuidenhout, *Geschiedenis van het Afrikaansche Geslacht van 1688 tot 1882* (1883) and the well-known *Die Geskiedenis van ons Land in die Taal van ons Volk* (1877). One might also mention Dr. E. J. P. Jorissen's *Wie zijn wij* (1881), C. N. J. du Plessis's *Geschiedenis van de Emigrante-Boeren en van den Vrijheidsoorlog* (1882), Dr. J. A. Roorda-Smit's *Het Goed Recht der Transvaalsche Boeren* (1881) and the Rev. F. Lion-Cachet's *De Worstelstrijd der Transvalers* (1882).

The crisis of the period of the Jameson Raid and the Anglo-Boer War was productive of much writing e.g. N. J. Hofmeyr's *De Afrikaner-Boer en de Jameson-inval* and C. N. du Plessis' *Uit de Geschiedenis van de Zuid-Afrikaansche Republiek*. J. F. van Oordt's *Paul Kruger en de Opkomst der Zuid-Afrikaanse Republiek* appeared in 1898 and in the following year the well-known *Century of Wrong*. The war gave rise to a flood of literature. – Here we need only refer to Dr. W. J. Leyds's *De Eerste Annexatie van de Transvaal* (1906) and his *Het Insluiten van de Boeren Republieken* (1914). Gustav Preller's *Piet Retief,* 1908, should also be mentioned.

The titles of some of these books are indicative of their content. Anyone who has read one of them would appreciate the spirit in which the rest were written. The historical image and its features that I have sought to depict are clearly reflected in these writings.[83]

10

After 1902 the independence of the two Republics had been lost and the republican form of government existinguished. The burning questions of the day for a conquered people were: what does the future hold? What place will the Afrikaner people have in their country's future? Circumstances had altered radically. Under the new dispensation "Afrikaner" people and state had ceased to be practically synonymous terms as they had been under the Republics. An English-speaking community shared the country and it was a case of having to live with them within national boundaries that were common to both groups. What was to be their attitude towards the British Government and the English-speaking people?

Conciliation? Absorption in the English stream? That would have meant wiping the slate of the past clean. Or would the stricken Afrikaner succeed in keeping his identity within the new South Africa and continue his existence as member of a separate group in the population? Yes, that was to be the ideal for the years ahead. They should sustain their language and culture and, who knows, they might then again secure political power one day. So the "state" of Republican days was transmuted into "political party"; "state" and "people" were no longer practically interchangeable terms, but "political party" and "people" were close to one another. The inevitable consequence was that the political structure in South Africa followed "racial" lines.

The Afrikaner people desired to maintain itself as an entity. What was to keep it together? There was the quickened sense of nationalism and the aspiration to an eventual political victory. Both nationalism and political aspiration were to draw stimuli from the past. At that time history was *the* great reality of the Afrikaner people for it provided them with an explanation of their present state. It was history that could tighten the bonds that held the Afrikaners together and the source from which their ideals sprang. President Kruger's last message had not been a vain one: "whosoever wishes to create a future, may not overlook the past". The recollection in common of a great but painful past was to provide new stimuli. At the root of the memory of a people was the historical image: fundamentally the Great Trek and the Concentration Camps.

This image was indestructible. It was to have the greatest influence in shaping the active political moves and actions of the Afrikaners. It was a bulwark of nationalist politics and could provide fresh impulses for the political front. The more the Afrikaner saw and identified himself with the past, the more powerful were the stimuli for the struggle of the day. And so the historical image of the Afrikaner was converted with a political force. It would be the factor that would hold the Afrikaners together and which would provide them with the "weapons" necessary to combat "the enemies of the people". When it was necessary to arouse feelings against adversaries, "the people" had merely to be reminded of their past: had they not suffered and fought them – would they allow themselves to be "trapped" again?

And so we see how the historical image was put to use at political level. It could hardly have happened otherwise. There is an existential relationship between man and his history. There are few other people who have shown such an attachment to their past as the Afrikaner and it was at this time that he had embarked on his phase of romantic nationalism. This has perhaps been a feature of all young peoples. But the isolation of South Africa had much to do with it. In Europe rapid transformations of the political scene are apt to take place. In our country the "foe" of yesterday was seen as the "political enemy" of to-day. Even if those who were responsible for the disasters that overtook South Africa, had long since passed to their graves, reproaches were heaped on their descendants as if the latter bore full responsibility.

This historical image that the Afrikaner had conceived before the Anglo-Boer War retained its hold after the war.[84] "Voortrekker worship" secured an even greater adherence. In the pages of their histories, and through their use, the Afrikaner people was to sustain itself and maintain the justice of its cause. One thinks of the writings of Dr. W. J. Leyds that we discussed elsewhere in this volume – also of the works of G. S. Preller whose historical writing was devoted to the service of the national ideal. In his *Piet Retief* he interpreted the Great Trek in terms of the Afrikaners' destiny and their nationalism.

The number of reprints of *Piet Retief* testifies to the great historical interest current among the Afrikaners. History evoked visions that offset the reality of loss. We need only recall the revival of enthusiasm over the Great Trek that marked the Centenary year to appreciate what an asset the historical image was for the nationalist and the politician.

In the course of time school history books appeared in Afrikaans and the historical image that evoked was the Afrikaans one.[85] Their rendering of South African history was based exclusively on the Afrikaans viewpoint. The instruction of history at school became a formative force in the life of the Afrikaner people. In more recent times we have noted the concern expressed at the decline of interest in history as a school subject.

II

We have spoken of the Afrikaner's historical image and considered the form it took and its content without giving any precise definition of an image. Historians are generally apprehensive of definitions and I am no exception. It is far from easy to reduce a phenomenon of the intellect to the limits of definition. History as an actuality in a period of self-experienced past is devoid of form or figure, fluid – and incomprehensible. It is only when a person or group becomes aware of what has happened to him or it, that the actuality is translated into an image by the intellect. This can only occur when there has been some lapse of time; otherwise the experiences of historical actuality cannot be reviewed and assigned their limits. Once one has created the image, one then has a grip on or hold over the past; it can then be mapped in a particular way, its limit and lines and contours drawn in or around it, so that it becomes a comprehensible rounded-off unit.

The shape and content that the image assume hinge on a matter of choice by the individual; from a limitless horizon and a multiplicity of events he selects those particular items that seem to have real cogency, usually those that have made an impression on his life or those that will be of decisive importance to his future. His experience of life and his ideals are the determinants of the form of the image. As one who peers through a telescope from a fixed position, he is unable to include the whole of reality in his view. What he does see, depends on his point of vantage so that the image is bound to have a certain perspective and consequently show a particular distribution of light and shadow.

An image of the past is far more than a series of chronicles or facts. It is not merely a depiction of a portion of past reality but its transformation – just as an actual piece of nature, is transformed on the artist's canvas. A point of vantage is necessary to the creation of an image of the past and this position is arrived at by an enquiry that extends back from the present. Time does not stand still and with the passage of events new questions arise to which answers are sought. As time goes by interests change and the type of questions asked – and with that the image changes too.

It is quite true that every historian creates his own image of the past. If six writers of different nationalities were to make a study of the same period, the knowledge that they amassed would give rise to six differing images. Each of them would have its own particular stamp but that does not imply that they would therefore be "false" images. Personal factors like character, circumstances of the time and the social milieu, will be combined in the image that is formed. At most, chronicles and facts, will be the only generally valid strata of knowledge, that are common to all six versions. As soon as the facts are interpreted the images will begin to differ from one another. The "truth" of the image will not lie in the facts and dates that are furnished but in the relationship of the image to the object of study. And here one is not concerned with general validity but "objectivity" which unavoidably contains elements of an inevitable subjectivity. The historian who wishes to evoke an image cannot aspire to more than that. But a false image can be evoked if it includes elements of a conscious or avoidable subjectivity, if the writer deliberately sets himself to harness a portion of the past to church or party, thereby falsifying it and reading into it that which he wishes to see with a view to a fulfilment of his present ideals.

All these considerations apply to the individual image, and to the collective image as well, for the latter emerged as a kind of primitive historical consciousness and a collective frame of mind that was unaware of the emotions. Why should it be that the individual images of historians of the Afrikaner people display similar traits – to such a degree that one can include them unhesitatingly in Afrikaans historiography? I have already remarked that a general Afrikaans historical image was formed that was a collective possession of the people, and was used consciously and unconsciously, to mould its impress of the past. It is these features that the images have in common and which are made manifest in them, even if the impression may sometimes be a distorted one. The Afrikaner's spirit was nurtured from this general image and it has shaped his way of historical thinking. The image has remained constant over a long period despite changes in its form. Is this general and collective Afrikaans historical image liable to change? And, if so, what is likely to bring the change about?

12

As we observed, the Afrikaner's historical image was the product of particular circumstances of the past. Its application later to the political sphere meant that, it could live on without undergoing any drastic alteration. Since then the conditions of the particular time when the image was formed, has changed. New social and economic factors have emerged. Problems have altered and relationships. Yet the traditional historical image, with its elements of myth, has remained substantially unaltered. Politicians have done much to keep it alive artificially.

Is it possible to revert to the original situation in point of time from which the image grew and developed, or will the image be changed to conform to the new set of circumstances under which we now live? Obviously the first is impossible. It is only logical to affirm that an image that is attached to a remote situation in point of time, becomes anachronistic in new circumstances. Past reality that gave rise to the image and present reality are no longer interchangeable terms. An image of this kind has become petrified and can only be kept alive artificially in the belief that it will serve the same cohesive function that it once served. But is that feasible?

It has to be remembered that the generations that participated directly in the image's creation, are no longer with us. There are no longer *oupa's* and *pa's* at whose feet children and grandchildren will sit to acquire these impressions at first-hand. The present generation is at a distance from the actual events that went into the making of the "poles" on which the image rests. Furthermore it has no longer the reasons to act as aggressively towards its adversaries that the previous generation had. The struggle for freedom, to the present generation, is not the reality that it was for past generations.

And, in addition, the way of life of the Afrikaner has altered. He has become urbanised to a great extent. In the early stages of urbanisation there was still a romantic yearning for the wide open spaces and life in the old Republics, but this sentiment was transitory. Is it possible for the industrialised Afrikaner to have the same attitude towards relations between the White language groups as his agrarian forefathers? Surely his interests differ?

It must also be said that in general, the Afrikaner people have reached maturity, or, at least, is well-advanced towards that state. The emotional nationalism of former years will gradually be reduced to rational terms; the aggressive political contest will gradually disappear for has the Afrikaner not shown for many years at the ballot-box that he is able to rule the country?

But there is more to it than that. The world in which the Afrikaner lives to-day is totally different from the world of half-a-century ago. To-day the world is really one and the Afrikaner has to seek a new orientation to fit present realities. A world that is one demands viewpoints of universal validity. In addition, we have the omnipresent colour problem that has grown into an international issue before our very eyes. New questions have arisen as to the country's future and the answers to them, will cast new light on the past. In the face of the rising non-white tide and the interference of the outside world, the politicians advance the theory of unity of the two white language groups.

So what impression does one have of the Afrikaans historical image in the light of these changed circumstances? It seems to be an oversimplified one and it is deficient in universal points of view. It reduces to absolute terms and enshrines a particular group of our forefathers who figured in a limited period of the past. One may term it Afrikaner-centric for it is conceived from the Afrikaner standpoint. The antitheses it displays follow a rigid pattern. It over-emphasises the military and dynamic side of history. Generally the Afrikaner's approach to history is introspective, and apologetic. The Bantu has no real place in his image of the past other than as the foe during the Trekker and Republican periods, whilst the role assigned to the English-speaking is much more that of the persecutor of the Afrikaner than that of builder of the country.

Forces are at work that will slowly alter this traditional impression of history. Scholars are steadily making new contributions – among them G. D. Scholtz who has extended the dimensions of the image widely in his *Suid-Afrika en die Wêreldpolitiek. But in the first instance I had the image in mind that is that of the average Afrikaner – the-man-in-the-street.* Many years may elapse before scholarly work enlarges or changes the impression of history that the ordinary citizen carries. The teaching of history can make the best contribution here.

Naturally the fixed and determined facts of history will not alter; we are not concerned with them. It is the judgment of the facts that will alter in the light of new problems and ideals. What we need today is a historical image with aspects of universal validity. It should account for the place of the Afrikaans people and of the whole of South Africa in the modern "one world" of to-day. It should assist the Afrikaans people to find their bearings in this new world and promote unity between the two white language groups. It will then accord with the situation of our time and the ideals held out by the political leaders at frequent intervals. When the realities of past and present no longer fit the same frame and when the traditional historical image remains unchanged in the new circumstances, it can become a disruptive rather than a constructive force.

1. *Die Transvaler*, 7.10.1953, leading articles and letter from H. Roux under "Readers' views"; see also the same paper's leading article of 10.10.1955.
2. *Die Transvaler*, 10.11.1955, address by a cabinet minister, Mr. De Klerk; *Transvaler*, 12.11.1955, address by Dr. Nicol; leading articles in the same paper d.d. 7.10.1953, 14.9.1954, 10.9.1954 and 10.10.1955.
3. See minutes of conference of history teachers held at Boksburg, 11 and 18.10.1954 and also many articles in *Die Onderwysblad* (educational journal).
4. *Die Transvaler*, 23.10.1954, report of National Party Congress at George, Cape Province.
5. *Hansard* No. 19, 5th session, 11th Parl., 3.6.1957, col. 7339.
6. *Die Transvaler*, 7.10.1953.
7. *Vide* 3 above.
8. *Die Transvaler*, 23.10.1954, party congress.
9. *Die Transvaler*, 22.9.1954, "Readers' views".
10. *Hansard* No. 19, 5th session, 11th Parl., 3.6.1957, col. 7339.
11. *Rand Daily Mail*, 9.3.1957, view of the S.A. Council of Education.
12. *Rand Daily Mail*, 2.12.1957, address by J. S. Fotheringham.
13. *The Star*, 4.9.1956, address by N. E. Coaker.
14. *The Star*, 28.2.1952, leading article.
15. *The Star*, 8.10.1956, leading article.
16. *The Star*, 29.6.1954.
17. *The Star*, 21.5.1956.

18. *The Star*, 7.9.1955.
19. *Hansard*, No. 19, 5th session, 11th Parl., 9.3.1957, col. 7331.
20. *Rand Daily Mail*, 9.3.1957, conference of the South African Council for English education, *Rand Daily Mail*, 18.10.1954 recommendation of a commission of enquiry appointed by the Natal Provincial Administration to investigate educational problems. During the period August – October, 1957 the *Star* featured an experimental series of articles on South African history – later published on a brochure. The facts embodied had to be generally valid and acceptable to both white language groups. An interesting publication that gives the historical image of the English-speaking in relation to S.A. history is A. C. Martin's *History in our Schools, Mutual Respect or Antagonism* (Durban, 1953).
21. *Rand Daily Mail*, 18.10.1954 and *Die Transvaler*, 22.9.1954.
22. *Die Transvaler*, 2.12.1957.
23. *The Star*, 5.9.1957, "Ex-Standerton Concentration Camp" – readers' views.
24. *The Star*, 18.4.1956, from "South African" – readers' views.
25. For an explanation of the attitude of the English-speaking towards Afrikaner school history books see my essay "Interpretations and Trends in South African Historical Writing", in this volume and *Historia* September 1962, *Probleme by die Skrywe van Skoolgeskiedenisboeke*, p. 147–163.
26. This aspect was dealt with more fully in a book of mine on the theory and method of teaching history. (*Teorie en Metodiek vir Geskiedenisonderrig, Johannesburg*, 1960, pp. 92-94, English translation 1964: *Theory and Method of History Teaching*.
27. *Hansard*, No. 19, 5th session, 11th Parl., 3.6.1957, col. 7331.
28. Wilmot and Chase: *History of the Colony of the Cape of Good Hope* (1869); Wilmot: *History of the Cape Colony for Use in Schools* (1871); Henry Sidwell: *The Story of South Africa* (1888); Whiteside: *A New School History of South Africa* (1897); Leith: *A Metrical Outline of Cape History* (1855); Holden: *History of the Colony of Natal* (1855); Russell: *History of Natal* (6th ed. 1899); John Noble: *South Africa – Past and Present* (1877); *Cape Monthly Magazine* (New Series, Vol. III, p. 207).
29. *De Zuid-Afrikaan*, 1.7.1874 and also 28.7.1875.
30. *De Zuid-Afrikaan*, 25.11.1874; also 30.6.1878, 27.3.1875.
31. *De Zuid-Afrikaan*, 19.6.1875.
32. *De Zuid-Afrikaan*, 30.6.1875 and *Die Geskiedenis van ons Land in die Taal van ons Volk* (1877), p. 137.
33. *De Express*, 9.12.1898, a reader's objections to Whiteside's *New School History of South Africa* (1897) which he calls a "concoction".
34. *De Express*, 2.6.1899 and 15.8.1896 – readers' views.
35. *De Express*, 14.6.1898, reader's view.
36. *De Express*, 21.10.1898.
37. *De Express*, 17.9.1897. Dr. Hoffmann on the occasion of the Taalbond's prize distribution at Wellington.
38. *De Express*, 6.7.1882, reader's view.
39. *De Express*, 6.12.1895, leading article.
40. *De Express*, 30.6.1891, reader's view.
41. *De Express*, 13.9.1887, reader's view.
42. *De Express*, 14.6.1898, reader's view.
43. *De Express*, 6.12.1895, leading article.
44. *De Express*, 6.12.1895, leading article; also issues of 13.9.1887, 22.8.1887, 2.7.1889, 15.9.1891.

45. *De Express*, 2.7.1889, leading article and J. H. Hofmeyr's concern in his speech at the closing of Victoria College; *Express*, 17.9.1897, reports of chairman and secretary at Taalbond prize distribution at Wellington; *Express*, 3.5.1898, review of C. W. H. van der Post's book *Piet Uys*.

46. *De Express*, 3.5.1898.

47. *De Express*, 9.11.1897.

48. *De Express*, 6.7.1882, reader's view.

49. *De Express*, 18.10.1887, reader's view.

50. *De Express*, 2.7.1889, reader's view; see also issues of 15.9.1881 and 6.7.1882.

51. *Die Geskiedenis van ons Land in die Taal van ons Volk* (1877).

52. *Die Patriot*, 7.6.1878.

53. *Die Patriot*, 30.3.1887, reader's view.

54. *Die Patriot*, 30.3.1877.

55. *De Express*, 18.10.1887, reader's view.

56. *Die Patriot*, 9.8.1878.

57. *De Express*, 2.7.1889; J. H. Hofmeyr's address at the closing of Victoria College.

58. *De Express*, 30.6.1891, reader's view.

59. *De Express*, 17.9.1897; speeches by Taalbond's chairman and secretary at Wellington.

60. *Die Patriot*, 30.3.1877, reader's view.

61. *De Schoolgids*, 1895.

62. *Cf.* C. F. J. Muller, *Die Britse Owerheid en die Groot Trek* (1948), p. 50; *De Express* 20.9.1891, article by the Rev. J. D. Kestell on the Voortrekkers: "We never learned from any Voortrekker himself that it was listed as a cause of the trek."

63. *De Tijd*, 22.8.1868 and 4.11.1868.

64. *Die Geskiedenis van ons Land in die Taal van ons Volk* and other contemporary publications. See the essay on "History and Politics" in this volume.

65. *De Express*, 26.7.1899.

66. *De Express*, 4.2.1896.

67. *De Express*, 27.10.1891.

68. *De Zuid-Afrikaan*, 25.9.1875.

69. As stated in C. N. J. du Plessis', *Geschiedenis van den Emigrante-Boeren*.

70. See my "Biographies of the Great Trek" in this volume, p. 79, 89.

71. *De Express*, 14.2.1896.

72. *Vide Die Patriot*, 15.6.1877; "We had practically forgotten old grudges but now England is again continually pricking us – just think of the partiality for the Basutos; our deprivation of the Diamond fields and the annexation of the Transvaal. Who can forget such things? No, we think of them; we shall remember them and our children will learn of them in their infancy from their mothers." In *De Express* 14.2.1896 we read: "Forgotten grievances, Slagtersnek, Boomplaats, Basutoland, Natal, the Annexation of the Transvaal, Amatongaland, are revived in our recollections."

73. *De Express*, 10.4.1884, leading article.

74. See *De Express*, 5.5.1891. Examples abound in the newspapers and it is not necessary to detail them. One need merely refer to reports in *De Volksstem* and *De Express*, at the time of Dingaan's Day celebrations.

75. *De Express*, 4.2.1896.

76. *Ibid.*
77. *De Express*, 21.10.1890.
78. *Die Geskiedenis van ons Land in die Taal van ons Volk.*
79. *Voortrekker-Argiefstukke*, p. 120, Natal Volksraad to Governor Napier, 14.1.1841; *Express*, 17.4.1884, review of C. P. Bezuidenhout's *Geschiedenis van het Afrikaansche Geslacht.*
80. *De Tijd*, 9.2.1871 and *The Friend*, 16.2.1871.
81. *De Express*, 27.12.1895.
82. *De Express*, 13.3.1896.
83. On re-reading this essay in 1961 I realised that there could have been more references to Afrikaans historical writing after 1902. To supplement the text refer to "Interpretations and Trends in South African Historical Writing" in this volume.
84. This is true of the historical image that lingered in the people's recollections. It was also an underlying factor in the case of the scholarly writings that appeared in Afrikaans after the First World War.
85. An objective inquiry into the historical image and nationalistic character of South African school histories would serve an urgent need.

# BIOGRAPHIES OF VOORTREKKER LEADERS

*"As long as a history of South Africa exists, the names of Retief, Pretorius, Potgieter, Maritz and other heroes among the old Voortrekkers will stand inscribed in golden letters in it. Why should that be? Because they were the leaders of a great popular movement that was brought into being by injustice, tyranny, oppression and deceit."*

De Volksstem, 2nd April, 1885 (Translation)

I

1884: *Andries Wilhelmus Jakobus Pretorius de Held van Zuid-Afrika* (22 pp.) – U. G. Lauts.

1897: *Piet Uijs of Lijden en Strijd der Voortrekkers in Natal* – C. W. H. van der Post.

1906: *Piet Retief, Lewensgeskiedenis van die grote Voortrekker* (2nd edition, 176 pp. 10th issue, 1930, 409 pp.) – G. S. Preller.

1913: *Chronicles of the two leaders of the Great Emigration, Louis Trigard* (sic) *and Pieter Uys* (In *Willem Adriaan van der Stel and Other Historical Sketches*), pp. 253–294 – G. M. Theal.

1917: *Dagboek van Louis Trichardt* (400 pp.) – G. S. Preller.

1919: *Sarel Cilliers die Vader van Dingaansdag* (3rd ed., 1925, 169 pp.) – G. B. A. Gerdener.

1932: *Louis Trichardt's Trek across the Drakensberg, 1837–1838* (Van Riebeeck Society, No. 13, 163 pp.) – C. Fuller.

1937: *Andries Pretorius, Lewensbeskrywing van die Voortrekker Kommandant-generaal* (2nd ed., 1940, 493 pp.) – G. S. Preller.

1938: *Kommandant-generaal Hendrik Potgieter* (263 pp.) – Dr. Carel Potgieter en N. H. Theunissen.

1938: *Die Epos van Trichardt en Van Rensburg* (68 pp.) – M. Nathan.

1941: *The Northern Transvaal Voortrekkers (Archives Year Book,* pp. 67–170) – B. H. Dicke.

1947: *Die Lewe van Gert Maritz* (284 pp.) – H. B. Thom.

1949: *Piet Retief se Lewe in die Kolonie* (571 pp.) – J. L. M. Franken.

1953: *Louis Trichardt se Laaste Skof* (254 pp.) – W. H. J. Punt.

1959: *Karel Landman op Trek van Melkhouteboom na Bloukransrivier (1837–1838) (Communications of the University of South Africa,* C.13, 33 pp.) – C. F. J. Muller.

## 2

These books are not all biographies.[1] They have been listed however to show the events of the Great Trek and the names of its
leaders have been interwoven. In the nature of things it has not
been possible for a full biography of each leader to have been
written. In the case of Trichardt, Van Rensburg, Uys and Landman sources that might furnish personal particulars were lacking
and writers have had to limit themselves to short biographical outlines or to descriptions of individual trek movements.

One of the leaders who has received a full measure of attention
is Louis Trichardt, not so much because of his life and career, but
due rather to the diary that he left and the *geographical* interest
that stimulated inquiries on the part of many research workers e.g.
Dr. Punt, B. H. Dicke, C. Fuller and M. Nathan. I shall not deal
with their dissertations in this study nor with those of Theal and
Prof. Muller since they cannot be classified as biographies. The contributions of Lauts and Van der Post merit reference because of
their historical significance. It is therefore mainly the biographies
of Piet Retief, Andries Pretorius, Hendrik Potgieter, Sarel Cilliers
and Gert Maritz that fall to be considered – for, as *De Volksstem*
noted in 1886, these men were the leading figures.

3

A reconnaissance[1] of the field of Afrikaans biographical writing
shows that the biographical distribution is rather like that of iron
filings around a bar magnet; the filings are concentrated around the
poles but between the pole and along the sides the concentration is
thin. In this case the "poles" are the Great Trek and the Anglo-
Boer War – a reflection of the importance of these two occurrences
in Afrikaner eyes. One might support this contention by pointing
to the fact that, with the exception of the studies of Theal, Dicke
and Fuller on Trichardt, the English-speaking section has produced
no biographies of Trek leaders at academic level. It is true, however, that English-speaking South Africans have written monographs dealing with the whole Trek movement.[2] No such monographs have emanated from the Afrikaners who have mainly used
the biographical form of treatment in presenting the history of the
Trek. This is some indication that the Trek did not have the same
emotional value and significance for each language group. The
English-speaking were interested in the Trek as it affected *South*

*Africa* (and especially its bearing on the Native question); the interest of the Afrikaners centred mainly on the Trek's positive value in moulding their national identity.

A glance at the titles listed will show that each of the important Trekker leaders has at least one biography or biographical outline. That is not the case with all the Afrikaner leaders of the Anglo-Boer War. This difference may possibly be due to the nearness (historically-speaking) of the war to us and to the fact that all the 20th century documentary sources on the lives of prominent men who took part in the war are not yet available. By contrast, the Great Trek is a more distant event and the bounds of its source documentation have been determined and are readily discernible.

The dates of publication show that the 19th century produced little in the way of Great Trek biographies. The brochure of Lauts is nothing more than a biographical outline; Van der Post's little book is a mere "narration". The biography in Afrikaans belongs to the 20th century. It is only in comparatively recent times that professional historians have devoted their attention to the leaders of the Trek. The centenary celebrations of 1938 gave rise to a renewed interest in the Great Trek.

The titles listed and what I have said already, raise a number of queries. Why does the Afrikaans biography hinge on the Great Trek and the Anglo-Boer War? Why is it that the history of the Great Trek has been cloaked in biographical form? When did the Afrikaners begin to feel that the lives of their leaders should be recorded and why? What are the attributes, defects and merits of the Great Trek biographies? What was the link between the history of the Afrikaner and his historical writing? What growing image was evoked by the successive Trek biographies and, inversely, how did these biographies mirror the progress of historical studies in Afrikaans?

4

To commence with the first query – both the Great Trek and the Anglo-Boer War were great historical crises that reached to the depths of the Afrikaner people's existence. Just as the Great Trek witnessed a concentration of the historical forces in South Africa, so did the Anglo-Boer War too. The further course of events was influenced by these two occurrences. Each of them provided a stage on which the historical actors would perform. The Great Trek divided South Africa and resulted in the Republican North and Colonial South being set off against one another; the Anglo-Boer

War was a complementary process; in its essence it was an attempt to undo the Great Trek by force and to unite North and South within the British political system. From this in turn there emerged a united South Africa in which geographical antithesis gave way to political party antithesis.

Both the occurrences I have mentioned were popular movements that produced leaders of eminence. It is not surprising that a "Day of the Covenant" and "Heroes Day" were adopted. Both these eventful occurrences were essentially dramatic and romantic and their content of valiant deeds, sorrow and suffering gripped the imagination of the people. To the Afrikaners these were great national epics – a source of inspiration and of lofty values. It is for those reasons that the Afrikaans biography has found most of its heroes among the political and military leaders who figured in these two great crises.

In fact, the leaders of the Afrikaans people make their first appearance on the scene during the Great Trek. In that movement they made their "own" history. The leaders were the cause of the events but the events brought forth the leaders e.g. Retief and Pretorius.

The precedent and pattern whereby Afrikaners adhere to leaders rather than set principles dates from the Great Trek. The farmers of the Eastern Frontier left the Colony in small groups under separate leaders and established themselves in the interior on a regional basis under the influences of their leaders. Much of the history of the pioneering period is made up of clashes among the commanders. One can appreciate this when one thinks of the vast expanses and their attendant dangers. Small groups pinned their hopes and faith on local leaders and "believed" in them, for these leaders provided focal points in a wide world in which there was no state authority.

After the Anglo-Boer War too the former military commanders were the men round whom the people rallied. In both instances – the Trek and the War – the authority of the leaders was derived from their importance in the struggle i.e. it was rooted in tradition. The part played by the leaders of the people in the life of the Afrikaners and the relationships of people to leader and leader to people are subjects deserving of attention but they are not cogent issues in this essay.

As to the Great Trek, four of its leaders, Retief, Uys, Maritz and Trichardt (1838), died during the migration whilst Potgieter and Pretorius lived until 1852 and 1853, respectively and contributed to the Trek's consolidation and the establishment of independent republics. Cilliers and Landman were still alive in the seventies but neither played a significant role after 1838. To a certain extent one may speak of parallel lives. As they all took part in the exodus one might expect a certain similarity in the structures of their biographies. That offers an opportunity of contrasting the biographical presentations.

5

When and why did the Afrikaners feel a need to know more of their heroes i.e. become aware of the latter's stature? These are further questions that we have to answer. It was in the next generation after the Trek (about 1877–1881) that they began to ask that their dead leaders should receive their measure of notice. A cultural and political climate provided the conditions. In the Colonial South a handful of nationally-conscious Afrikaners stood fast against a tide of anglicisation i.e. at cultural level they began to plead for the retention of their langue and national identity; in the Republican North they fought at political level for the maintenance of their independence that was threatened by British imperialism. In the resistance in common to internal and external pressure, the intellectual and political leaders of North and South found one another and a common image of present, past and future crystallised; at its centre was the Great Trek.

With the dawning of national self-consciousness and the beginning of Afrikaner nationalism there came the need for historical foundations. The Afrikaners were in search of binding forces, precepts and examples and found them in their forefathers, the Voortrekkers, for prior to them there had been no "leaders of the people". It was only with the national awakening that the Trekker leaders were consciously revealed as "heroes" and their fine qualities of perseverence, piety and yearning for liberty were extolled. Feelings of admiration and gratitude found expression in the desire to commemorate them in the form of monuments and in the written word. There was an appreciation of the Voortrekkers' calibre – as the founders of independence and of a separate national identity and as the pioneers of civilisation and Christendom in the interior. A deliberate attempt was made to arouse respect and affection for the "famous men" of the nation whose memory had become "sacrosanct".[3]

In the Republican North the youth found inspiration in those leaders who had sacrificed their all for the attainment and maintenance of independence; in the South efforts were made to orientate the young towards their "own" national heroes of the Trekker period. This was because the history taugh at school was "British"

75

history with English kings as its heroes. It was for that reason that in 1878 Dr. J. W. G. van Oordt pleaded for a history in which William of Orange, Prince Maurice, Frederick Henry, Piet Hein, Tromp and De Ruyter could figure as the heroes of Afrikaner youth.[4] So too we find the Rev. S. J. du Toit proposing in 1878 that the subject of a heroic poem in a competition should be Piet Retief. "This man's character, aims in life and history surely provide the most suitable material for an epic poem that one can think of."[5] This hope was not to be realised until 1906 but it was the first time, so far as can be established, that anyone gave thought to a Retief biography.

The need for knowledge of the Voortrekkers was expressed right until the end of the century. In 1897 Dr Hoffmann complained that children had to learn the names of English monarchs and their connections by rote whilst "heroes" such as Sarel Cilliers, Piet Retief, Pretorius and many more went unrecognised.[6] After the war of 1899–1902 "Afrikaner" of Heidelberg, Transvaal expressed his concern at Lord Milner's policy of anglicisation in government schools and went on: "What are our children likely to hear in these schools of the great men produced by the Afrikaner race? Of those men whose names should be inscribed forever in golden letters on the historic scrolls of this country, of men such as Piet Retief, Piet Uys, Andries Pretorius, Potgieter, Paul Kruger, Piet Joubert?"[7]

6

Despite all these references to the Trekker leaders the 19th century Afrikaners were incapable of biographical writing. There were published documents available e.g. Chase, *Natal Papers* (1843) and Bird, *Annals of Natal* (1885) but the archival records were unclassified and practically inaccessible. But a more substantial reason was the uneducated state of most of the Afrikaners. In 1878 dr. Van Oordt wrote that he considered that a relatively high educational standard was the prerequisite for any people that wished to recall and record its history.[8] The Republican Afrikaners had not attained that level. They were often semi-literate pioneers who had had to devote all their energies to self-preservation and development of the country. The academic Afrikaner was to be a product of the 20th century. A few who turned their attention to historical writing in the 19th century were either Cape Afrikaners or Netherlanders e.g. the Rev. S. J. du Toit, C. N. J. du Plessis, Nico Hofmeyr, F. Lion Cachet, J. W. van Oordt and U. G. Lauts.

For historic reasons it is necessary that we should pause to take note of the first "biographies" of the Trek leaders. M. C. E. van Schoor places Van der Post's *Piet Uys* (1897) at the start of Afrikaans biographical writing.[9] One may well trace it further back still to U. G. Lauts's biographical sketch of Andries Pretorius that appeared in 1854, a year after the latter's death.[10] Lauts was a professor of maritime history at Medemblick in the Netherlands. He had close contacts with the Voortrekkers. In his *Andries Wilhelmus Jacobus Pretorius, de Held van Zuid-Afrika* he outlined the importance of the Great Trek as a popular movement and introduced his dauntless "hero" to his countrymen. The sketch covers the whole of Pretorius's life – his birth, marriage, farming activities, his trek and his military and political actions in Natal, the Orange River Sovereignty and the Transvaal. It gives the first outlines of a life that was to be expanded on by Preller in later years. South Africa remained practically unacquainted with this pithy review of the life of Pretorius.

Van der Post's *Piet Uys* is not a biography but a "tale" based on recollections of Voortrekkers and historical works available at that time. Uys commands the scene in this book from the time of the Great Murder until his death along with that of his son Dirk. The narrative is smooth and a picture is conjured up of the dramatic period of the "suffering and struggles" of the Natal Voortrekkers. The story is not coupled to facts but is a free narrative within the framework of the actual events. The author regrets that the deeds of the Voortrekkers are not being recorded. He appeals to the youth of South Africa: "You have a right to take pride in your forebears. Within you lies the nucleus of a great and noble people. You possess all the attributes from which a nation can be born. Build upwards on the foundations laid by your worthy ancestors and see that you do credit to them. May the examples of Piet Uys, modest, honourable and courageous Christian and warrior and of Dirk Uys, the young lad who loved his father and preferred death with him – remain forever in the memories of South Africa's sons". Van der Post was a foreigner (Netherlander) who had married an Afrikaner and identified himself with them. He was an attorney and member of the Free State Volksraad.

It is not surprising that *De Express* hailed the advent of the book as "an event of national importance" and pleaded that fatherland history should not be neglected; it was the paper said, "fallow ground" that should be cultivated. Its opinion that the book was "an important contribution to the literature and history of the fatherland" was an exaggeration but it reflects the need and national sentiments of the time.

## 7

The "fallow ground" of historical investigation of which *De
Express* wrote was not to be tilled until after the Anglo-Boer War.
In 1905–'06 a regular feature on the life of Piet Retief written by
G. S. Preller, appeared in *De Volksstem*. In 1906 these articles
were published in book form as a second edition.[11] Subsequently
eight editions appeared. The seventh edition of 1911 was amplified
and expanded on the basis of new data but Preller's conclusions
remained unchanged. By 1930, when the 10th edition was printed,
the 15,000th copy had been sold. This was surely the most successful sales record of any Afrikaans history book in South Africa.
Why was that the case?

The publication of Gustav Preller's book coincided with the
cultural awakening of the Second Afrikaans Language Movement
*(Tweede Afrikaanse Taalbeweging)*. Just as the Rev. S. J. du
Toit's *Geskiedenis van ons Land in die Taal van ons Volk* (1877)
had been one of the first fruits of the First Language movement, so
Preller's *Piet Retief* was a product of the Second Movement. There
was a great thirst for knowledge of the past and for that there was
a reason too.

The experiences of the Anglo-Boer War were the background of
Preller's books. (And also of the first Afrikaans poetry.) Before the
War there had been a strong national consciousness in the Transvaal, based on history, but what was lacking was an ideological
foundation; this would be provided by Preller's book.

A confused people that had lost its independence, sought historical, and national sheet-anchors. Preller's book conveyed a message
– the loss of independence was not the end of the Boer people but
a new beginning: And so Preller sought links in history that would
be of support in the rebirth. Since there were many similarities the
sufferings of the War gave him a better understanding of the
Great Trek. For that reason he laid emphasis on the *significance* of
the Great Trek for the Afrikaners and especially on Retief's part in
it.

In the Great Trek he saw "the emergent history of our nation
and rooted within it the problems and vital questions that confront
us daily".[12] It is not surprising that the needs and problems of his
time were projected back to the Great Trek and Piet Retief for the
book was really more concerned with the contemporary period than
with the past. According to Preller the Afrikaner people would not
have come into being without the Great Trek. He saw Retief as
the man who had given rise to a new nation, "the free Afrikaner
nation of the future".

The book was written in a nationalistic spirit. To Preller the Great Trek was "a national movement"; its purpose was "freedom from the oppressor" (p. 148). The author felt that world history offered "no greater spectacle of human sacrifice and perseverance, of suffering and of heroism, then that displayed by the Voortrekkers in progressing towards their goal" i.e. "freedom" (p. 290).

Preller's writing had a romantic touch. Where the events lent themselves to colour, there he was at his best. It was then that his work was most compelling e.g. one recalls his description of the crossing of the Drakensberg by the Voortrekkers. This quality makes the book very attractive and readable.

However, Preller also had his limitations. The first defect relates to technique and method. He was aware of the fact that his bio-graphy provided scant information on Retief's earlier life in the Cape Colony. In fact, his book really covers three years of Retief's life only, from the beginning of his Trek until the massacre at the hands of Dingaan. In the early editions his sources were limited but he supplemented them in course of time. This process of supplementation really needs a special study in itself. Printed sources form the greater part of his critical apparatus.[13] He made uncritical use of documents, particularly of those concerning Retief in Natal. His method of linking long series of letters of Retief, with a brief "running commentary" leaves much to be desired.[14] He does not evolve the narration from the sources nor give the account in his own words, and the biography tends to become a collection of sources. His narration remains superficial. We perceive little of Retief, the man, or of his character or of the motives underlying the actions of historical personalities. He describes too much and explains too little. His material is not subjected to sufficient intellectual probing.

Retief is depicted as the first and only great Afrikaner of his time. Potgieter and Uys are belittled whilst Maritz lurks in the shadows and is seen as a source of dissension. Retief's significance and importance are overestimated. His actions are always vin-dicated. Preller sees no wrong in his hero and waxes lyrical in his adulation e.g. "faithful, valiant Retief, honest upright Afrikaner, soul of the future Afrikaner nation". The book contains anti-British and anti-Zulu sentiments. He cannot conceal his distaste for "the pot-bellied barbarian" (Dingaan), his "devilish treachery" and "refined cruelty". His hostility also extends to the missionaries, Gardiner and Owen, on whom he squarely lays the blame for Retief's murder. His analysis of Dingaan's motives is unconvincing. Retief is exonerated of charges of "carelessness" and "misplaced confidence".

As a biography the book is a failure. The hero does not always remain in the centre of the stage and the description at times is nothing but ordinary historical writing. The impression that we are given is that of hero-and-villian. The author is uncritically disposed towards his hero. Preller acts as the judge of Retief's opponents and condemns them accordingly.

One can see why this book's appearance during a period that was barren of historical writing was like the vision of an oasis. It was to be one of the sources that would foster Afrikaans nationalism. Just as Eugène Marais's *Winternag* had shown that Afrikaans could be a language of culture, so Preller's Piet Retief showed that the Afrikaner possessed a national history.

## 8

Gustav Preller was destined to be a zealous recorder of the Great Trek. He had a particular interest in the period that was second only to his interest in the Anglo-Boer War. In 1917 his *Piet Retief* was followed by the *Diary of Louis Trichardt 1836–1838 (Dagboek van Louis Trichardt)*. The publication was made at the behest of the S.A. Academy for Language, Literature and Art. (S.A. Akademie vir Taal-, Lettere en Kuns.) It was only in 1891 and 1894 that it became known that Trichardt had kept two diaries in which he had made notes on his trek routes, the topography, the state of the weather, personal relationships among members of his party, details of the party's livestock, etc. The matter received special publicity at the time of the opening of the Delagoa Bay Railway in 1895. Since then Trichardt's route has aroused more interest than that of any other Voortrekker. Many research workers e.g. Fuller, Dicke and Punt have been inspired to trace the route by means of the diary, particularly the trek over the mountains to Delagoa Bay.

Gustav Preller's interest in the diary was based especially on its value as a source of information about his "own people" – their "proud sense of freedom", "philosophy of life and nobility of soul", "racial awareness" and "the supremacy of their European blood" or the "superiority of the white man" to the native. He describes Trichardt's trek as a "reconnaissance of the Afrikaner – in search of Freedom and the Sea", "and also sees in it" the freely chosen Destiny of his nation.[15] Weighed against their deliberate and persistent persecution from one generation to another at the hands of the British, is the "inherent urge for freedom" of the "Boer nation". According to Preller, national consciousness can only be rooted in history and tradition.

Preller included a biographical outline of Trichardt in the diary;

it was based on very limited data and referred mainly to Trichardt's earlier life in the Cape Colony. He clears his hero of certain libellous charges made by British officials. (Theal's outline of Trichardt's life is also incomplete.)

## 9

The need for more knowledge of the Great Trek is also reflected in Prof. G. B. A. Gerdener's, *Sarel Cilliers die Vader van Dingaansdag*, first published in 1919 with a third edition appearing in 1925.[16] It was a biographical outline of "the father of the Voortrekker's Church". Prof. Gerdener considered Cilliers to have been "a dauntless pioneer of civilisation, a brave fighter for freedom, a noble patriot and a pious man of God". He felt that Dingaan's Day should be understood correctly and celebrated in the way that the victors of Blood River had intended. This was the most important point in the introduction to this biography. But there was more to it than that. It was also intended to help sustain feelings of veneration towards heroes and quicken the sense of national consciousness that had gradually been gaining ground since 1919.

In the Great Trek Gerdener sees the epic period of the Afrikaner's history. Monuments were few and far between and so biographies of the nation's heroes had to aid in "arousing interest in and love of the past". In his eyes Retief was the martyr, Pretorius the warrior and Cilliers the prophet of the Trek. For Potgieter he had little respect and Maritz is barely touched on. He wished the life and struggle of "valiant" Voortrekkers to be learned and the "soul" of the events to be perceived. His aims were associated too with the period of intenser nationalism that followed the Rebellion of 1914–'15.

Prof. Gerdener undertook no easy task. Drawing on limited information he had to evoke the stature of an "ordinary" man. Cilliers's importance as an historical personage lay in his participation in the actions at Vegkop and Blood River, but more particularly in his share in the *Vow* (*gelofte*) that preceded "Dingaan's Day". Furthermore he performed spiritual duties among the Voortrekkers and later in the neighbourhood of his Free State farm. Shortly before his death he compiled a journal that forms the basis of Prof. Gerdener's account.

In the absence of personal details, the author, for the better part, provides a "framework", i.e. he describes the situations in which Cilliers was an actor and occasionally, where the journal or other sources permit, gives an indication of Cilliers' role. The lack of documents precluded the biography being developed around Cilliers as its central figure but his description of events is lively. The book bears the imprint of strong influences exercised by Preller's *Piet Retief* and Cachet's *Worstelstrijd der Transvalers*. In his chapters on his hero's service to the Church and his "message", Gerdener mounts the pulpit to expound lessons drawn from the devout career of Cilliers.

The author holds the view – nowadays rejected – that Cilliers was the leader and "hero" at Vegkop since, according to him, Potgieter was supposed to have been further north at the time of the clash. He sees the Great Trek as the consequence of the people's urge for liberty and the summons of Providence. The Trek, as far as Cilliers was concerned, was "a matter of conscience" – he had to go. He calls the account of the heroic death of Dirkie Uys a "fabrication", maintaining that the boy had died earlier at the battle of Italeni. He blames Potgieter for the death of Uys. To Cilliers he awards the distinction of being the man responsible for the vow – hence the sub-title of his book. The book gives a lucid survey of the Trekkers' history from Vegkop to Blood River and supplements Preller's *Piet Retief* that terminated with the Great Massacre. The book made its mark in determining the future shape of Dingaan's Day celebrations; as a biography it was unsuccessful for the various reasons we have given.

10

Not until 1938, the great centenary occasion of the Great Trek, did the next biography of a Trekker leader appear. The centenary occasion inspired many writers to make a study of the Trek period. Gustav Preller followed up his biography of Retief with *Andries Pretorius, 'n lewensbeskrywing van die Voortrekker-kommandant-generaal,* that went to a second edition in 1940. Preller thought that there were only two really great leaders – Retief and Pretorius. To him the latter was the most significant personage to emerge from the popular movement. Pretorius surpassed Retief in historical importance since, consciously or unconsciously, he built on the foundations of the ideals that Retief had cherished – and he lived to see their full realisation with the recognition of his people as a free and independent one.

The book's title shows that Preller deals with the period 1838–1853 – from Pretorius's arrival in Natal to his death, a long period during which the foundations of the Republic's independence were laid. Preller needed some 500 pages to describe the life of Pretorius. He starts with his hero's life in the Cape Colony, deals with the Natal period, the interference in Trans-Orangia and his actions in the Transvaal. The highlights are his military achievements at Blood River, Congella and Boomplaats, and his political ventures such as the formulation of a native policy in Natal, his pleas on behalf of his people to Pottinger, party relationships in the Transvaal and notably his attainment of the Transvaal's independence at the Sand River Convention.

Although the book purports to be a biography, it is not that at all. This perhaps is due to Preller's conception of history – that great men do not make history but that the masses do and that great men only lend their names superficially to events "and these names make very suitable headings of chapters" (p. 3).

The book is linked with Preller's earlier views in *Piet Retief*. What emerges that is new in his interpretation of the Great Trek is that he now sees "freedom, space and movement" as its purpose. In *Andries Pretorius* "freedom" is the central theme and Pretorius's life is a struggle to gain or maintain it. He also tries to see the Great Trek's link with the Teutonic tribal migrations and the biography lays emphasis on *race*. He was undoubtedly influenced by the racial theories of National Socialism in his time, by the struggle for "segregation" of the thirties and by "the poor white problem". His biography is interlarded with signs of contemporary influences.

Preller writes as an Afrikaner from the Afrikaner point of view and for Afrikaners. The book abounds in subjective views, moral pronunciations and condemnations, especially as regards opponents of Pretorius – whether they be Napier, Russell, Potgieter, the Natal Volksraad or English historians. Captain Smith, he finds, was "an intransigent hater of the Boers"; the "injustice" perpetrated by Napier on the Boers is exposed in emotional terms without any penetration of the motives underlying Napier's policy. There are sneers at "Afrikaners in English service against fellow-Afrikaners", "hirelings of the conqueror" (261, 264–265) and at "Handsupper-Boers", etc.

Preller justifies Pretorius and gives battle with his adversaries. In this biography too we note that he yields himself up to his hero and is unable to regard him objectively. Hendrik Potgieter, in particular, suffers in the process. As far as Preller is concerned, Potgieter's importance lies in the fact that he agreed to a reconciliation with Pretorius in 1852. Preller shows no appreciation of Potgieter's part in the history of the Great Trek. His departure from Natal at a critical time and his opposition to Pretorius and the *Volksraad* of Ohrigstad, leads Preller to underestimate him. When

Pretorius takes an oath of allegiance to the British, Preller justifies it as "acquiescence in the inevitable".

Preller made particular use of printed sources. He did not make a thorough study of the career of Pretorius in the Cape Colony – a considerable defect in the book. (A dissertation will need to be devoted to that.) As he did explore the Cape Archives, he ought probably to have found much material that would throw light on the first forty years of his hero's life: However, he was over-hasty. In his biography there is too little on the years 1843-1847 that Pretorius spent in Natal. His use of the documents in the Transvaal Archives is unsatisfactory. This becomes clear when one studies his confused impression of Transvaal political relationships.

Preller was uncritical in his use of sources too. To give two examples: on p. 318 (1940 edition) he forces the contents of a document of 1849 to fit into 1847 since he failed to apply internal criticism and allowed himself to be misled by an archival official's inclusion of the document under an incorrect year. On p. 332 he fits the content of a document of 1849 into 1847. We have therefore in both these instances faulty chronology of factual content.[17]

In this book Preller follows the same system he employed in *Piet Retief*. He includes lengthy documents in the text and follows them up with short sentences by way of commentary. His method lends itself to repetition and extends the text unneccessarily. In fact, that is one of the main weaknesses in his work; in many respects Preller is overwhelmed by his source material. He does not extract history from the sources and reproduce it in his own words and therefore fails to evoke an image for us. In a book of this kind all sorts of items are mentioned that have no particular relationship to the subject under treatment. Preller's book is overloaded with material, lacks intellectual penetration and is apt to be superficial. And there is a lack of balance. The author frequently drifts away from his main topic to dwell on various side-issues, thus overloading his text unnecessarily; this renders his work clumsy and prolix. The hero of his book is not kept in the centre of the arena; the period is described rather than the man. The divisions of the book are not related to those of Pretorius's life. Unity and broad lines of development are lacking. Neither is clarity a feature of this book. Vagueness and uncertainty reduce its value. The sketch we see has no clear contours and Pretorius disappears among the mass of material. His real importance in South African history is not reflected in Preller's text and the book does more harm than good to the reputation of that statesman. A new biography of Andries Pretorius is urgently required. To my mind he was the greatest Afrikaner statesman of the 19th century.[18]

Preller's journalistic talent is all too apparent in this work. We recall his heading "A Mosquito brings union" (p. 398). He strives after effect. Where an event lends itself to description Preller is at his best e.g. in his accounts of the Congella and Boomplaats battles. When it comes to natives and party relationships, his work becomes incomplete and weak. As in his *Piet Retief*, he gives preference to events of a dramatic hue so that the text tends to become unbalanced. The book is far from being a well-devised one and is a failure as a biography.

We should bear in mind, however, that Gustav Preller was self-taught and not a "schooled" historian. His importance lies in his pioneering work. He succeeded in arousing the Afrikaner's interest in history. Despite the deficiencies in his work, he did contribute to our knowledge of the Great Trek but more especially he gave it a place in our hearts.

II

1938 also saw the appearance of a biography of *Hendrik Potgieter* written by Dr. Carel Potgieter and N. H. Theunissen.[19] As its main object this biography sought to present a misjudged man, one whose quiet pioneering and civilising work had not received as much attention as the Natal leaders. As the authors rightly point out, the "blood and tears" period in Natal had received more prominence than the "more sober tale" of Potgieter whose spade-work in the interior had gone unseen and unappreciated but which had yet laid the foundations of "Afrikanerdom" (pp. 262–263).

According to the authors Potgieter was the custodian of an "Afrikaner ideology" and he achieved his "greatest ideal" of "a powerful Afrikaner state". It was Potgieter who decided the fate of the "white man in the North; with him begin" the real Great Trek; Trichardt's trek had only been a "precursor" or a "reconnaissance". In their view that Potgieter never received sufficient recognition for his "cleaning-up" work the authors are correct. The action of Kapain has the same significance for them as Blood River had in Natal. According to the writers Potgieter put a "glorious ideal" before "Afrikanerdom" before Pretorius achieved the independence of the Transvaal. The authors commence with Potgieter's early belief that Natal would prove unsuitable for a settlement since the British would never leave them alone there in peace; they feel that Congella justified this conclusion. Later the Natal Trekkers were to intrude as "the first Outlanders" into the region into which Potgieter had penetrated.

The book sets out to restore a "misjudged" Potgieter to a place of honour – historically as well as historiographically. The authors emphasise the positive virtus of their hero and absolve him of the historical verdict that he left the Natal Voortrekkers in the lurch after Italeni, that he was responsible for the death of Uys, and that his "obstinacy and perverseness" caused trouble in the Transvaal. They show how he was "personally shunned and cast aside" in his own life and how posterity acquired a wrong impression of the man.

The authors also carried on a controversy with the historians. In their book they denounced the old historical disapproval of Potgieter expressed by Preller, Gerdener and others. Men such as Maritz, Retief, Pretorius, J. J. Burger, Napier and Livingstone are "demolished". In belauding the "greatness" of Potgieter, the authors sought to reduce the historical stature of other contemporaries. Retief, for instant, is reproached with having exposed hundreds of people to danger – something that the authors assert that Potgieter would never have done. Pretorius is reproached for having remained in Natal after 1842 for "personal gain" and for having taken an oath of allegiance to the British – a mortal sin in the eys of the writers. As their standard they take the attitude of "true Afrikaners" towards the British – pure and great in Potgieter's case, but very suspect in the case of Pretorius and the Natal Voortrekkers. Pretorius, whose praises had been sung by Preller and other writers, comes in for particularly harsh treatment. The authors also censure the new arrivals from Natal at Ohrigstad for their "campaign of slander", "intrigue" and "servility". J. J. Burger was guilty of "venomous hatred"; Napier was "a lover of Kaffirs and a hater of the Boers"; Dr. Philip had "hangers-on", etc.

The authors are particularly hard on Preller's *Andries Pretorius* in their footnotes[20] and are correct in many references to points of fact. They restore Potgieter to a place of distinction and absolve him of any blame. They let us view a more or less perfect man who was quite aware that he was an Afrikaner – a man who emerges from a "purification" process at the hands of the authors, free of faults and great.

This biography has more substance than Preller's *Andries Pretorius*. It makes easier reading, it is less long-winded and is a well-written account. However it tends to be superficial; at certain points it diverges from the main theme and in other places the faint documentary trail is followed sedulously. We do not get an accurate analysis of motives and background outline is often lacking. As in Preller's case it lapses into the category of "general history". We do not see Potgieter as the central figure throughout. Relationships in the Transvaal are imperfectly mastered and there is vagueness about the movements of leaders coupled with certain factual inaccuracies.

The use of the expression "Afrikaner ideology" and words such as "fusionist" and "process of fusion" are suggestive of National Socialism and the political scene in 1933–'34. The authors view their hero uncritically and as a biography the book is unsuccessful. The value of the book lies in the revelation of the importance of Potgieter among the Transvaal Voortrekkers. But the significance of his role is over-estimated. There is a projection into Potgieter's life of material that belongs to the contemporary setting of the authors. He is *their* creation, an idealised being.

12

In 1919 Prof. Gerdener expressed the hope that a future historian would describe the history of the Great Trek, not so much for the purpose of giving the dry facts "but to enable us to see the lives and struggles and deaths of the indomitable Voortrekkers. Let us see into their laagers and into their covered wagons, and if we may, into the hearts of these people. Let us feel something of their experiences, of their stout-heartedness, perseverance and bravery on one hand, and of their sorrows, pains and trials on the other. If it can be achieved, let us see into the soul of these events."[21]

These words of his reflect, in my view, Prof. H. B. Thom's achievement in his *Gert Maritz*, published in 1947.[22] The book is the work of a scholar and to my mind the finest product to date of scientifically written history and biography in Afrikaans. There was room for this work. Biographers of the Great Trek had neglected Maritz, underestimated his importance and even belittled him. Prof. Thom who made a thorough and exhaustive study of the source material of the Great Trek, introduces a man who had to be rescued from oblivion. He presents Maritz as one of the most significant figures in the beginning of the Trek concept, in the organisation of the Exodus and in the conduct of governmental and civic affairs. He shows us one who could be a source of inspiration in times of depression. Contrasted with Preller who considered Maritz to be the cause of much misery, even of civil strife among the Trekkers and later Republics, Prof. Thom produces quite a different image. We are shown a man of democratic convictions and one who was conversant with law-books.

From the papers of Gert Maritz it becomes evident that Preller overrated Retief in his uncritical adulation and that Maritz had a longer and more correct vision, especially when it came to dealings with Dingaan. If Maritz's advice had been taken, the massacre would probably never have taken place. The author lets us view Maritz as the central personality among the Trekkers. His achievement at the battle of Mosega is assessed and the importance of this clash is shown. We also gain a new impression of the relations obtaining between one Trekker leader and another; and the relationships differ somewhat from the picture painted by other historians; this is particularly the case in the relationship of Maritz to Potgieter, Potgieter to Retief, and Maritz to Retief. Some of Retief's weaknesses as a leader become apparent; there is therefore, a re-evaluation of the latter's life. The fact that he was previously overrated historically was mainly due to his aura of martyrdom.

This biography does show us the Voortrekker *life*. Precision is brought to the movements of leaders, to treks, places and dates. Prof. Thom weighs his material critically and corrects the conclusions of other writers. His footnotes too are often corrective so that from his pages we obtain the most certain image and clear contours of the Great Trek of any writer to date. The author uses his sources critically and leaves the way open for improvement, where lack of sources produces any uncertainty. He reveals an impressive critical apparatus.

As a biography the book bears the hall-mark of success. By applying strict self-discipline the author was consistently able to keep Maritz in the centre of the arena. Everywhere we encounter signs of a careful, considered, well-founded and balanced judgment. The author is unemotional; we are given perspective and depth with which to view the scene. Each step is explained logically but only after an analysis of motives has been applied. On every occasion he lets us see the circumstances and motives underlying personal decisions. The character of his leading figure is depicted convincingly and he has made a deep psychological study of Maritz. We understand Maritz from this ''inner'' insight and see him as a man whose good qualities and weaknesses developed in his environment. The sources had their limitations. Thom does not condemn, he adjudicates; he does not reproach, he explains. He has a keen eye for detail and makes us see the interaction of his hero and his surroundings. He etches his main lines of deployment clearly and yet succeeds in showing us more of the everyday life on trek. His narrative tone is restful and his style rich in imagery without being as compelling as that of Preller.

Prof. Thom too was not independent of the particular stamp of his time and of his national affiliations. We find that contemporary terminology is transferred in his presentation of history. In the Voortrekkers he discerns ''racially pure Afrikaners'' who acted with a conscious sense of responsibility towards posterity. He calls them "the first real Afrikaner nationalists". Afrikaner nationalism, however, dates from the eighteen eighties only. His comparison of equalisation with "trusteeship" – the latter a word that was foreign to the period 1836–1938 – reflects the political conceptions of our day. Terms such as "Afrikanerseuns en -dogters" are also present-day forms of usage. Like Preller he has an aversion for "the Afrikaner in English service".

The book is written throughout from an Afrikaner's point of view. It reflects a certain form of condemnation of British policy as indicated by the use of such words and phrases as "wretched" and "lamentable inefficiency and myopia and so much vexatious injustice" (p. 69). When it comes to relations with non-whites we read that Silkaats was a "bloodthirsty tyrant, devoid of conscience" (p. 121) and that Chaka was a Zulu tyrant without peer. The emphasis falls on the opening of the hinterland to the "European" or "the white man". Dingaan's action is stigmatised as "barbarous murder and bestial blood-thirstiness" (p. 218).

13

Prof. J. L. M. Franken's *Piet Retief se Lewe in die Kolonie*[23] that appeared in 1949 bridged a gap that was apparent in Preller's *Piet Retief*. Whereas Preller needed more than 300 pages to deal with Retief's three years on trek, Franken required 571 pages to explain Retief's life in the colony. He does not proceed beyond 1836 since he feels that he has no more to offer than Preller on the Trek period. However, on the basis of intensive research in the Cape Archives he could present new material on Retief's life in the Colony. This shows us immediately how incomplete Preller's research was. If an historian can find so much material on Retief, it is quite clear that there is still much more to be said about the earlier life of Andries Pretorius.

Prof. Franken is a scholarly research worker who has produced a learned book. In using his documentary sources he tried to be as impartial and objective as possible so as to give "a reasoned description of Retief's career in the "mother country", dealing with his private affairs as well as his activities as a civil servant and as a leader of the people". The book commences with Retief's forebears and parents and concludes with his departure from the Colony. Franken made use of much source material and we obtain a new impression of Retief's early activities – his farming and business transactions; the conditions at that time; commando life;

89

the move to the Eastern Frontier and his bankruptcy and imprisonment there. Franken gives precise information on Retief's movements and places of residence, his personal possessions, his building contracts and the court cases in which he was involved. We see Retief as a man who acted in the interests of his fellow-citizens and who was constantly giving  thought to the current state of affairs.

Franken proves that Stockenström was not so insulting to the Boer character as has generally been accepted and that he became a "scapegoat". He sees the Great Trek as a "peacable freedom movement" by means of an "Exodus" (p. 438). He feels that it was "fundamentally a movement to escape from the yoke of the British Government with its immediate and most important cause the absence of security on the frontier". As with previous writers he emphasises "the urge towards freedom" although that was not a general phenomenon. Franken feels that it was rooted in the "Dutch national past" of the Trekkers and couples it with the Patriot and Slagtersnek episodes.

This book is not a successful biography; in fact it can hardly be called a biography. But it does contain the material for a biography. Where he quotes Retief's letters *in extenso,* Franken himself says that the book falls "within the realms of source publications". It consists in fact of a chain of documents, or of extracts from them, interspersed with Franken's comments and interpretation. The method – one we have noted that was also used by Preller – does not lend itself to the creation of an image that has unity and form. It is a kind of microscopic investigation that produces chronicles rather than historical writing.

Sometimes the author delineates the circumstances of the time without admitting Retief to the scene i.e. his participation in the commando of 1812. Since Retief was fortuitously a member of this commando, commando life is described. Franken seldom emerges from the documents. For that reason he fails to produce a clear and simple impression of Retief's life. The text is over-loaded with unexploited source material. The author fails to see the wood for the trees. Moreover the book makes stiff and dry reading. One wonders whether Retief's early life justified an investigation of this kind. It contributes little to our knowledge of his role during the Trek. It is only from 1832 onwards that items occur that cast their shadows ahead to the Migration. To my mind Franken reads too much into Slagtersnek when he associates it with a sense of national consciousness being aroused among the frontier farmers.

When the biographies of the Great Trek from Lauts and Van der Post to Franken and Prof. Muller's essay on Karel Landman are reviewed, a growing image is disclosed; this began with simple delineation, incomplete data and bits of imagination and ended with involved and detail-laden presentations that gave greater certainty and presented more acceptable relationships. The growth of this image coincided with the increase in and availability of new sources one one hand, and on the other, with the application of scientific standards, to method and refinements in the technique of historical writing. Where the "historian of the people" took the lead in the beginning, the scholar followed to give a more precise rendering. The latter approached more approximately to reality since the romantic writer sought to arouse feelings and addressed himself to the people's power of imagination.

The evolution of the image also runs parallel to the needs of the time. It is not surprising that Preller's book ran to many editions, while more recent works of a more scholarly kind do not find a ready market. "Technical" writing of history draws less attention than romantic and details do not lend themselves to fantasy.

Each of this biographies embodies new elements and has therefore contributed to an enlargement of the image of the Trek period, of its leaders and of their relationships; it has enabled this image to be reviewed from time to time and established with greater certainty. The books also reflects a growing image of the leaders – their actions, calibre and place in history. The involved nature of the complicated result shows how the science of history developed.

Furthermore the biographies point to the existence of a certain relationship between a people and its historical writing. The contests among the leaders, for example, are prosecuted by their biographers. The defence employed by the Trekker leaders against attacks by the British is also taken over and employed by their biographers. The characteristics and structures of the history of the Afrikaner therefore have a certain parallel to his approach to and treatment of historical writing. The historical image that has come into being has fulfilled a social function in this way. It has contributed to the defence of the Afrikaner's existence as a people and so has helped to promote their historical continuity. In that sense the Afrikaners' national historical writing has also been nationalistic.

In dealing with these biographies certain defects have been pointed out. That brings us in conclusion to the biography as a species of historical writing. Modern historians have given particular attention to it. The best book on the scientifically prepared biography is Prof. Jan Romein's *De Biografie*.[24] J. A. Garraty's *Nature of Biography* (1957) and S. Dresden's *Structuur van die Biografie* are also important works. We refer now to the requirements of a modern biography set forth by Romein.

It is generally accepted that biographical writing imposes onerous requirements on an author. In the first place since it calls for detachment on the writer's part. But he has to practically identify himself with a man long since dead and use that intimacy to give life to the dead. There is always the danger that the author will associate himself too closely with the historical figure and that he will identify himself with his hero to such an extent that he will be unable to keep him in perspective and arrive at objective conclusions.

In the second place the modern biographer should be able to summon psychological penetration to his assistance; he should be able to fathom his hero's psyche, understand and explain him. The writer should be able to recreate his hero as a *person*. It is only sufficient sources, especially private letters, that make this possible.

Thirdly the biographer is required to expose the complexity of the psychic image of the historical personality. These are exceedingly difficult conditions for historians for they demand complete sources and these are often lacking. The modern biography is a combination of history and psychology. It is not history alone, nor biology alone nor politics alone. It deals not only with human *life* but with human *fate*. To use an expression of Grillparzer, the former is so small, the latter so great.

A biography does not call for description only but evaluation as well. It should not be restricted to adulation or condemnation, but should contain judgments based on an objective study of facts. It is only after the death of an historic figure that his life can be viewed as a whole within the framework of his time. The emphasis therefore does not fall on the framework but on the *judgments* passed on the historical figure within the events of his time; how the events affected his life and conversely, how he affected the turn of events. In the biography the intellectual development of the hero should be shown; the author is expected to lay bare the essence of his subject's life and show us its structure. Biography is not just history but a combination of science and art. Our historians have still much to learn in this respect.

1. This study is a by-product of a more comprehensive work on the image of the Great Trek in South African historical writing, *vide* my *Die Beeld van die Groot Trek in die Suid-Afrikaanse Geskiedskrywing.* (Communications of the University of South Africa C 36 and C 42.)
2. E.g. M. Nathan, *Voortrekkers of South Africa* (London) 1937 and E. A. Walker, *The Great Trek* (London) 1938.
3. See too my *Die Afrikaner en sy Geskiedenis* (1959).
4. *Z. A. Tijdschrift,* II nr. 7 (new series), Aug. 1878, p. 23.
5. *Die Patriot,* 7.6.1878.
6. *De Express,* 17.9.1897.
7. *De Volksstem,* 6.4.1904.
8. See footnote 4.
9. *Historia,* March 1959, p. 5, in his article on the biography in Afrikaans historical writing.
10. It appeared originally in the *Camper Courant* in 1854. See the brochure in the Lauts Collection (T.A.), 13, vol. 9, no. 1342.
11. See *Standpunte* (new series), No. 33, pp. 69–70, notes by Prof. T. H. le Roux. I have adhered to the reprint numbers shown in the books. According to Prof. Le Roux the newspaper articles represented the first edition.
12. *Piet Retief,* 10th ed., 1930, p. 348. Subsequent references are taken from this edition.
13. E.g. Chase, Bird, Erasmus Smit, Theal, Stuart, etc.
14. *Vide* e.g. pp. 40–71, 74–76, 92–95, 138–141, etc.
15. *Dagboek* (Bloemfontein 1917), p. XI, CXXVI–CXXIX.
16. J. L. van Schaik, Pretoria. The last edition is discussed.
17. Compare the pages mentioned of the 2nd ed. 1940 (A.P.B.) with *Voortrekkerargiefstukke,* pp. 256 and 289.
18. Cf. my opinion of Pretorius as a statesman in *Die Eenheidstrewe van die Republikeinse Afrikaners* (1951), p. 18 and *Die Konvensie van Zandrivier* in *Tydskrif vir Wetenskap en Kuns,* Oct. 1951, (Part XI, No. 2), p. 199.
19. Afrikaanse Pers Beperk, Johannesburg.
20. Cf. *inter alia* pp. 149, 169, 170, 175, 196, 215, 223, 225, 372, etc.
21. G. B. A. Gerdener, *Sarel Cilliers,* p. 11.
22. Nasionale Boekhandel, Cape Town, 1947.
23. J. H. de Bussy, Cape Town, 1949.
24. Amsterdam, 1946, p. 237.

# THE ANGLO-BOER WAR AND THE HISTORICAL WRITINGS OF DR W. J. LEYDS*

> *A war in South Africa . . . would be a long war, a bitter war, and a costly war: and it would leave behind it the embers of a strife which I believe generations could hardly be long enough to extinguish.*
>
> Joseph Chamberlain, May 1896

## I

"It is my intention to provide the Afrikaner people with a vade-mecum, with a collection of documentary items of evidence that have hitherto not been availale. I have in mind those documentary items that have reference to the way in which the English always acted towards the Boers. And that is something the Boers should not forget or lose sight of if they wish to safeguard their existence in future and their own interests – They must not let themselves be taken in by friendly appearances!" These remarks were made by Dr. Leyds about his book, *Eerste Annexatie (First Annexation of the Transvaal)*[1] in a letter to H. C. Bredell on the 7th September, 1906.[2] In December of the same year he wrote to E. von Hoesslin of Cape Town: "He who wishes to improve conditions and to lay the foundations of a better future, has to be cognisant of the earlier situation and the unfavourable background that has given rise to the present sorry condition of South Africa. An ostrich-like policy is of no assistance."[3] He informed General Beyers that President Steyn had expressed thanks for the book "on behalf of the whole people". The President had also said that the old grievances should not be overlooked – "lest we forget" and had concluded by saying: "Your book must become a vademecum for every Afrikaner."[4] Leyds continued later: "Our leading men have expressed their approval of my book recently published and all of them want it to be distributed among the people."[5] If the book "should serve to arouse the Afrikaner spirit, then that would be my richest reward" was his concluding observation in a letter to F. S. Malan and A. Fischer.[6]

These avowals are reminders of the period after the Anglo-Boer War when the Afrikaners were confronted with a chill reality and thrown back on their own resources. There had been a widespread collapse in the greatest catastrophe and national disaster that had ever befallen them. The independence that they had prized was

*First appeared in *Tydskrif vir Wetenskap en Kuns*, April, 1954.

gone, their homes destroyed and thousands of graves, row upon row, or widely scattered, testified to their suffering. In this critical situation with its sense of despair and groping, there arose the great problem of reconstruction with all the heart-searching that went with it. Over their "devastated" condition, in the chaotic present, hung the question mark of the future: what place would the Afrikaners have in the future South Africa? It was evident that the war had brought about a state of affairs that was similar to the period 1806–1836 (pre-Great Trek) a juxtaposition within common territorial bounds of victorious English and Afrikaners. The Trek had brought about the division of South Africa into Republican North and Colonial South, two poles around which events were to revolve until 1902. Now no further "flight" to the open spaces was possible, as in the case of the Trek, and the Afrikaners would have to continue to exist as a people within British territorial limits or "disappear" in accepting the theory of "the clean slate" that proclaimed "conciliation" and "fraternisation". "State" and "nation" would no longer be practically interchangeable terms as in Republican days and of the Afrikaner it could thenceforth be said: "Not a state, but a nation". This view would be the key to their political future but would also determine their vision of the past. Dr. Leyds wrote: "Whosoever wishes to estimate what the future relations between the Boers and the British Government are likely to be, should make himself fully conversant with their past relations." The theory of "the slate that has been wiped clean" is "valueless to anyone who has drawn on the experience of History".

In this time of crisis Leyds looked ahead; he created an ideal for the future and from that position returned into the past. The Afrikaner people should remain united as a separate group; "they must not let themselves be taken in by friendly appearances" and old grievances should not be forgotten. And so he commences his history with a vision of and plans for a *future* that would lend significance to the past. In that way he sought to "make" the history of the Afrikaners, give it meaning and draw from its armoury the need of the times – weapons for the coming struggle. So that to Leyds knowledge of the past and the dawn of the new era were linked and history was to serve as a function of the political ideology of the day. He realised that the Afrikaners of the pioneering era had not yet achieved a highly developed culture; that there was no literature of quality or products of the fine arts; the Afrikaners had their history as their achievement, and had their heritage to cling to and certainty was to be found in them whereas there was perhaps an uncertainty about the future. With the past as their greatest "reality" and as the fundamental factor of their existence, the Afrikaners had something to clutch at and were shown the way in which they might advance into the future. In the situation to which they were inextricably bound and in the recollections on which they lived, those who had suffered injustice, could take stock of themselves and establish the basis for a renaissance; then self-esteem could be restored and they could justify and defend the idea of their right to an existence of their own. In this way the past became closely associated with their everyday circumstances. Dr. Leyds would give the rendering that would justify their continued existence as a people; he would show them where their destiny lay and what their place in the world was and explain the significance of the events that had overtaken them. Gustav Preller was also to have a hand in this work after the war — witness his *Piet Retief* of 1908.[7] It was a natural implication of such books that the history of South Africa was to be presented in them from an exclusively Afrikaner point of view.

Leyds would also investigate those malevolent influences that had brought about the catastrophe and expose these dark forces; he would provide an arsenal — "a collection of evidential papers" — from which ammunition could be drawn to discharge at the "enemy", and on which armoury they could draw in times of need. He would provide an activistic history that would consciously nurture the nationalism that he foresaw. He told a certain Schultz of Hamburg that he had compiled a vademecum from the English sources as the English, when in conversation with Afrikaners or others on the subject of British actions in South Africa, roundly asserted that certain charges were "untrue" or else demanded "proofs".[8] He finds the First Annexation (of 1877) "most instructive";[9] it gives a good idea of "the bearing that recent events will have on the future", and it is not without reason that he chose as the moral of his work: "That which was, that is now".[10] "The course of the annexation can therefore not be passed over by anyone who takes South Africa's future to heart." The "proofs" are taken from English writers and should shed light on the "real bones of contention of the day". In discussing *Het Insluiten* he remarks: "I only wish to provide material. I have given no place to my own feelings of indignation. But those who review the book may assail the British in the light of the facts that I have adduced."[11] That Leyds realised the purport of his book is apparent from his intimation that he withheld *Het Insluiten* from publication during the First World War since: "there is already enough bitterness in the air and it goes against the grain to fan the flames of hatred still more". Leyds, in fact, regarded his work as "purely historical". And that brings us to his historical presentation.

Since the war had been a desperate struggle between Afrikaner and English and was at the root of Leyds's investigation, he undertook an enquiry into relationship of the races after 1795 with the intention of carrying it through to 1899. His *Eerste Annexatie* covers relations until 1884 and *Het Insluiten* proceeds to the period 1894–'95 dealing with the ways in which England thwarted the expansion of the Republic in its effort to gain access to the sea. He intended publishing a further volume that would have been devoted to British interference with the internal autonomy of the South African Republic during the years 1895–1899. He did not do so, probably because Dr. P. R. Botha worked on the subject in his *Die Staatkundige Ontwikkeling van die Suid-Afrikaanse Republiek onder Krüger en Leyds.*[12]

The writings of Dr. Leyds do not really deal with "relations" between the two races; to a greater degree they are a study of the imperialist methods by which England achieved her goal of annexation. According to Dr. Leyds a chain of events took place during the period 1884–1900 of "so excessive a kind that one can scarcely find their equal anywhere in modern history". In the Transvaal the Republicans were to suffer from "a policy of animadversions, criticism, vexations, rebukes, warnings and insults", leading to "threats" and culminating in war. The author's bitter indignation was aroused by the Second Transvaal War of Independence and it is easy to see why he wished to reveal "how the Boers had been treated by the English". He is convinced that the war could have been avoided and therefore goes on to investigate the *question of guilt*: he has however determined in advance who the guilty are. And so he lays a *charge* against the English and plays the part of the "crown prosecutor". It was for that reason that the *Spectator* of the 6th October, 1906 noted of the book: "It is the case against Britain"; the *British Weekly* of 8th November, 1906 stated: "It does not make pleasant reading". Dr. Leyds himself observed: "Some have termed my book more of an attack than a history. That is the case. But these accusations have to be put at the Boers' disposal, and not merely the evidence."[13] We can only refer to a few examples here.

In dealing with the pretext that bankruptcy was a sufficient reason for the annexation of the Transvaal in 1877 Leyds remarks: "Could they not have afforded the Republic temporary financial support? If they had done so they would have made friends of the Boers and spared South Africa long years of misery" (p. 230). The English were unable to put themselves in the position of others and it was this that "brought on the greatest difficulties in South Africa" (312). The British lacked "magnanimity" after the first war of liberation; otherwise they would have restored the absolute independence of the Republic. "Once again they could have made a firm ally of the Republic" and brought "an abiding peace" to South Africa – "simply by acting with probity and undoing the wrongs that had been inflicted. Instead of that . . . (404). He then accuses: "They chose to dictate rather than arbitrate [shortly before the Anglo-Boer War] and preferred the rule of the sword to that of law and order. They could have ensured the amicable co-operation of the independent republics. Yet instead they would not abandon "the right of the strong" so that on every possible occasion they could endeavour to translate the independence [of the republics] into a state of subjection and dependence. It was a fatal error, as events have shown with increasing force, from that day to the present" (409–410). The English are furthermore charged with not keeping their word. (I, 91); of turning deaf ears to appeals for good-will and co-operation (II, 175); of aspiring to possess the riches of others. Even the phrase "instead of supporting and bolstering a young and weak neighbour . . . " amounts to an accusation. (II, 48). Eventually he depicts the lamentable position of the Republic: "Cut off from the sea, robbed of a harbour, filched of territory that was rightfully its own, deprived of territory that had been offered to it in good faith" (II, 312). "With criminal intent" England had "robbed" the Republic of its "hard-earned independence". (II, 118 and 130).

Dr. Leyds's book is not only an accusation but also an *exposure* of English actions in South Africa. He shows how all her promises were "heedlessly broken" right from the beginning (9) and how British policy was made up of "a series of broken promises and hard dealings" (14). At all times they were intent on hurting the feelings of the burghers in the Cape and of undermining the latter's confidence" (22). "On the part of the English incredible blunder followed blunder" (23). "The Governor, in his wisdom, saw fit to trample the Dutch colonists underfoot rather than win their allegiance" (24). Their lot was "endless vexation and harassment", "distrust and defamation" (34), "persecution and assault" (181), "oppression" and bad treatment (121) – all this at the hands of a nation that "trampled on the rights of others" (212). Natal was "palmed in" wrongfully (57) after the Afrikaners had cleared the way; the conventions were violated "with baleful consequences" (98); the Diamond fields were "stolen" (156); the Natives were armed to fight against the Republics (246) and Shepstone never fulfilled his promises.

Dr. Leyds is also to be seen in the role of a sleuth who *unmasks* and *reveals guilt*. This applies especially to the pretexts under which the true policies of the English towards the Republics were concealed. He tells of the "sedulous way" in which so many English writers avoided mention of the Sand River Convention without which a comprehension of Anglo-Boer relations was impossible. "Their silence speaks volumes." The English people were "deliberately fed" with such "parodies" of history. Where South Africa was concerned the British had a "befogged vision" overshadowed by an image of "the bloodthirsty and cunning Boer" (138). This applied to the annexation of Basutoland and the Diamond fields which he regards as "the setting of the South African stage" (156). All the "false pretexts" are exposed. In the case of the Keate award he shows that territory that was denied to the Transvaal whilst it was a Republic became part of the Transvaal when the latter was a British possession (174). The Diamond Fields annexation comes under heavy fire. "There is no period in South African history in which so many misconceptions were current and it seems therefore more than ordinarily necessary to record the facts and in addition to show what became of the grievances that existed before the annexation, after it had actually taken place" (185).

It is at this point that there is an exposure of writers such as Conan Doyle,[14] J. Bryce,[15] R. Haggard,[16] P. FitzPatrick[17] and J. Nixon[18] who had all made accusations and depicted the annexation of the Transvaal as "a generous sacrifice" on the part of the English. His censure applied too to the *Goldfields Mercury* and British bluebooks – "models of adroitness" with their "preparatory slander", "complaints and accusations" – as well as to the official papers of Shepstone and Governor Frere with their "misleading information."[19] Phrases such as "nothing was less true" (219), "all these presentations [of the facts] were untrue" (233), "how unfounded this view was" (293), "and what was the truth? (260), "appearance of veracity" (233), "deliberately presented in a false light" (227), etc. are used to unmask the false, untrue and twisted versions of the British on the Annexation. The underlying mood is – reverse the roles, point out the guilty and put the injustices to right. Superficial reasons for the annexation are also exposed e.g. that Sekukuni was supposedly unconquerable, the "Zulu peril" (242), the "inherent weakness" of the S.A. Republic, the wishes of the majority (211) – the method of approach being "before and after" (185)[20] or "therefore . . . yet" (227) etc.

Leyds makes special use of footnotes to correct erroneous impressions. The following footnote item is a typical example of his

99

method. The Boers were accused of using the Swazis against Sekukuni. The English used the Swazis for the same purpose on five occasions. "Once again therefore: that which was wrongful and regarded as a criminal act before annexation becomes a rightful and an appropriate action after annexation" (228). When the Republicans fought a seven month campaign against the Bapedi they were charged with being unfit to rule themselves and had therefore to be annexed. When the English subsequently fought the Bapedi for twenty months "they posed as rulers par excellence and as victors to whom honour and distinction were due" (227).

As well as being a "Sherlock Holmes" Leyds was also the barrister whose task it was to *defend, clear* and *exonerate* the Republicans against all the "accusations"; "defamation" and "denigration" of English writers and officials in South Africa, and to justify the Boers' position in South Africa. He writes, for example, of the "many misconceptions" about the Afrikaners of the Eastern Frontier, of the "even more erroneous way in which they were represented" (26) and of "the torrent of malicious slander" (33) concerning their treatment of slaves, the Hottentot and the Bantu (40). He justifies the "escape" of the Trekkers from such treatment (22, 44) and exculpates them of charges made against them (49, 92). The slanted versions dealing with "slavery" in the Transvaal are denied (162) and he shows that what was called "slavery" when the Boers were responsible ("booking in" system of Native children) was referred to as "charity towards one's neighbour" by the English immediately after the annexation. The "slander with design" (197) that the Transvalers used explosive bullets against the Bantu is refuted (198); the allegations of infringement of the rights of the Zulus are unmasked (240, 232); he refutes the claim that the Afrikaners were "great cowards" (328) and exposes the scandalous and libellous cry of "treachery" that was used in the case of the Bronkhorstspruit battle. "Fictitious horror stories" such as those of FitzPatrick on Afrikaner "barbarism" in the Transvaal war of 1880–'81 are exposed and the Republicans freed of all responsibility. These tales, says Leyds, were told "with the intention of lowering the Afrikaners in the esteem of the world" e.g. General Cronjé's "treachery" (336, 342); the charge of murder in the Elliot case (348); the Green affair (344) and the Barber case (350). He goes on and asks: "Do not the actual facts of these cases make an impression, far different from FitzPatrick's story?" (344). Phrases such as "these insinuations are too contemptible to warrant refutation" and "to besmirch the whole Boer people" reflect the mood of the book. *Het Insluiten* is written in similar strain.[21]

As well as being the advocate in the case Leyds plays the *judge,* finds those in the dock guilty and passes sentence. The following verdicts show us how his historical writing is that of *moral* condemnation from the bench, more or less as Schiller put it in the sentence: "Die Weltgeschichte ist das Weltgericht": "It was a succession of astounding blunders (23); "the way in which the crime was carried out (referring to the annexation of the Diamond fields) (156); "could have spared South Africa long years of misery" (230, 312, 404), "wanted to break the neck of Afrikanerdom whatever the cost" (231), "brought on most of the troubles in South Africa" (312), "sensible rule lay beyond the realm of the attainable" (392), "they could have ensured the continuance of friendly co-operation", "it was a fatal error" (40) and "criminal intent" (*Insluiten* II, 313).

The author's indignation brought in an emotional element of personal participation and marked preference for the object of his sympathy. Words and phrases such as "the English paid little heed to such a triviality" (156), "robbed", "trampled down the rights of others" (212); "shameful slanderous clamour" (334), "a jingo and fanatic of the worst kind" (*Insluiten*, I, 170) point to this. Due to the nature of the documentary material he does succeed to some extent in clamping down on his own indignant feelings in *Het Insluiten*.

### 3

When we seek to characterise the historical presentation evoked by Dr. Leyds we note that on one hand there is a narrative in the negative – "suffering", "embitterment", "dissatisfaction" and "oppression" of the Afrikaners and of wrong inflicted on them; on the other there is a catalogue of the "wrongful acts" and "crimes" committed by the English between 1795 and 1899. And so the past is divided into two sharply defined and absolutely separate spheres into "friend-foe", "white-black"; "what was" and "what might have been". Many "proofs" and "examples" are adduced to illustrate the relations. This method of Dr. Leyds resulted in his history of relations between Englishman and Afrikaner failing to qualify as a true "history". The presentation tends to become a mechanical assembly by the author on a schematic pre-conceived arrangement. The material has to produce "proofs" to fit the predetermined purpose. A piecemeal method of construction like this can hardly reflect unity or coherence. In dealing with the Transvaal War of 1880–'81, he by-passes the "relations" and gives sporadic examples with the result that no cohesive and total image is discernible. The book actually is an account of what "they" did to "you" in "such and such ways" but are the motives ever enquired into? Is there a serious attempt to understand past relationships or the "manner" of dealings with one another i.e. does he reveal the factors underlying the act or explain the background? Where the English really always lurking in ambush with depraved motives and evil intent? Were there not perhaps understandable motives (even if their consequences proved unpleasant for the Afrikaners) which would explain why they acted as they did?[22] Where he deals with the annexation of Natal (57) we read: "But then . . . as soon as it was known in England that the Boers had subjugated the Zulus and made Natal habitable, the British Government took steps to grab [the territory] that the Boers had won." He indicates what obstacles barred the road of the Afrikaners but does not explain why the obstructions were put there. There is an accusation in the use of the word "grab" that implies avarice and a low motive. If he had discussed motives he would have had to mention the strategic factor, with the underlying fear of intervention by foreign powers. The same criticism can be applied to his condemnation of the British incorporation of the territories of Zambaan and Umbegesa in 1895 (Northern Natal). One assumes that he was familiar with the political situation at that time, yet he fails to see that fear of German intrusion could have motivated the English action (*Insluiten* II, 147).

The result of this method is a superficial simplification that is intended to be the historical foundation for a political programme – and that leads us back to our point of departure. The book is charged with an emotional content; as Dr. Leyds puts it, Englishmen who read it will feel the scourge whilst it will supply the Afrikaners with "weapons for the struggle". It would therefore be quite superfluous to have included motivation since we have a "compendium of evidential material" or "vademecum" that is calculated to arouse and consolidate sentiment. History is seen as a political weapon to keep alive feelings of injustice.

We again see the part that the *future* plays in his time-bound vision of the past. Did he not declare that he was in search of "instruction" (138, 327)? Although Dr. Leyds declared that the book was intended for an English-speaking public, he had to admit privately that the content was such that it was not impossible that the British Government might place it on the banned list.[23] The English would not like to see themselves "exposed" by a "foreigner",[24] so that the book was really intended more for the Afrikaners than the English, as the author himself admits.[25]

There is wishful thinking in the "utility value" that he attaches to the past. The war should not have taken place; the British should not have acted as they did towards the Republics but should always have upheld and supported them (404); they should have done it in Natal (58); they should have returned the Diamond fields (156) and supported the South African Republic financially in 1877 (230); they should have permitted a restored South African Republic to expand in all directions, particularly towards the sea, without restraint. (*Insluiten* I, 58, 74, 290, II, 5, 48, 311.) His judgment is influenced by "the might have been" on one hand and by the events of his own time on the other. It is for these reasons that he projects a national consciousness among the Afrikaners from 1902 back to 1795 presupposing that the Afrikaners had a highly developed sense of national awareness throughout the period. On p. 14 he says: "Their recollections of the first British occupation with its series of broken promises and acts of harsh treatment was no less bitter".[26] One wonders whether this is the author imposing his feelings on the past rather than weighing the meaning and importance of the events against their actual historical results. Were the insurrections occasioned by "broken promises" alone? With Dr. Leyds there was no question of extracting the motives without any other considerations, no attempt to "understand" the past as well as possible. He remains throughout prosecutor, detective, advocate and judge — advancing his "proofs" clearly and logically – but at the cost of violation of the principles of scholarly historical writing. He harnessed history to immediate national goals.

He undoubtedly did the Afrikaners a service in shattering the impression of the past that had been created by English writers and in stripping the English and their representatives in South Africa of their pretensions; this was intended to make them a little more modest in their approach to the problems of co-existence with the Afrikaners. Dr. Leyds achieved something that no Afrikaner could have done at that time; he searched the past and put useful information at their disposal. It was not only serviceable and activistic material that was amassed; valuable knowledge of the 19th century was accumulated. It bore the stamp of the war and was compiled with the future in view. That accounts for its peculiar form of construction. We can appreciate why the *Volkstem* of 8 September, 1906 considered that the book "had all the qualities that entitled it to be included among the standard works on the nineteenth century history of South Africa". It can be understood too, why this "vademecum" set a standard and remained the ideal model of historical writing in some Afrikaner circles for such a long time; it cannot be denied that it had a great impact. It is clear that the book interpreted the sentiments of the Afrikaner at that time. The time has arrived however when these methods of presentation that have become traditional and standard practice with some historians, should be viewed critically and in perspective. This form of approach to history is unsuited to present times and circumstances. A new approach to the works of Leyds will enable us to unravel the discardable elements and recognise its subjectivity and to view the appropriateness of the image afresh by considering it as a work of its time and appreciating the purpose behind it. And we can then place this historical presentation back in the setting of the period from which it sprang.

1. *De Eerste Annexatie van de Transvaal* (Amsterdam 1906). The First Annexation of the Transvaal (1906). *Het Insluiten van de Boeren Republieken* (1914). (The Transvaal Surrounded 1919.)
2. Leyds Archives (Pretoria) 235, p. 301.
3. Leyds Archives 236, p. 38.
4. Leyds Archives 235, p. 416, 23 Nov., 1906.
5. Leyds Archives 236, p. 17, to H. C. Bredell, 14 Dec., 1906.
6. Leyds Archives 234, p. 257, 19 Nov., 1906.
7. See my article, *Biographies of the Great Trek* in this volume.
8. Leyds Archives 235, p. 258, 28 Aug., 1906.
9. Leyds Archives 235, p. 105.
10. Vide *n* 8.
11. Leyds Archives 239, to Dr. Kiewiet de Jonge, 26 Aug., 1913.
12. The methods of Dr. Leyds are followed in this book and it has the same characteristics.
13. Leyds Archives 235, to a certain Mr. Hiemstra, 10 Oct., 1906.
14. *Eerste Annexatie*, p. 186, referring to a brochure in this case.
15. *Impressions of South Africa* (1899).
16. *Cetewayo and his White Neighbours* (1882): *Eerste Annexatie*: 232, 240, 350–51.
17. *The Transvaal from Within* (1899): *Eerste Annexatie:* 336, 337, 339.
18. *The Complete Story of the Transvaal* (1885): *Eerste Annexatie*, 460.
19. E.g. pp. 186, 197–8, 232, 240, 269, 314, 327.
20. Practically all the writers after Leyds do this.
21. Cf. I 145, 148, 168–9, II 147–177, 188–9, 199, etc.
22. Similar enquiries might well be put in the case of some of the English historians who sought to understand South African history from the point of view of "imperial" or "colonial" motives only without regard to the true motives underlying the actions of Afrikaners and Natives.
23. Leyds Archives 234, p. 257, to F. S. Malan, 19 January, 1906.
24. Leyds Archives 236, p. 8, 3 December, 1906.
25. Leyds Archives 235, p. 301.
26. That Leyds was unable to stand aloof from his subject is borne out by his remark: "Practically every day in my work I am reminded of the days when I was privileged to work with President Kruger". (Leyds Archives 236, p. 17.)

# HISTORY AND POLITICS*

This topic is not a new one. We find that political views had a strong influence on South African historical writing during the 19th and early 20th centuries. It was even more noticeable in the case of the former century than in later times and perhaps more evident in English historiography – one recalls W. Holden's *History of the Colony of Natal* (1855), John Nixon's *Complete Story of the Transvaal* (1885), A. Wilmot's Story of the *Expansion of Southern Africa* (1894) and F. R. Cana's *South Africa from the Great Trek to Union* (1909). Since 1948 historiography in English has shown many signs of strong political influences, I do not intend giving a general survey; that would extend the study unnecessarily. I shall confine myself rather to one example taken from our own time and contrast it with the post-1902 period and the work of Dr. W. J. Leyds. My investigation is concerned with the principles at issue.

I have nothing but respect for the content of Dr. Breytenbach's book, *Die Tweede Vryheidsoorlog*, in so far as it introduced new material on the diplomatic prelude to the Anglo-Boer War of 1899–1902. It is a particularly valuable contribution to our history and few historians in this country can match the author's ability to write history in such a pleasing style. Anyone who reads the book of Drs. Leyds[1] and Breytenbach[2] cannot fail to notice the similarity (to a greater or smaller degree) of the spirit animating them and approximate resemblances in their methods of construction. Dr. Leyds was principally concerned with the encirclement of the Republics, Dr. Breytenbach with the diplomatic struggle that hinged on the internal sovereignty of the South African Republic and resulted in the Anglo-Boer War "in so far as Dr. Leyds left it incomplete". Both lay claim to the conduct of a "thorough, detached and impartial" investigation into the conflict between Boer and Briton, between "Imperialism and Nationalism". In the previous essay I have referred to the work of Dr. Leyds, this work carried the stamp of his time; it was a release of his anguish of mind and appeared at a time when the Afrikaners seemed to have absolutely no future in store, at a period when they sought a foothold and an outlet for the

* First appeared in *Standpunte*, December, 1953; subsequently revised.

future. These circumstances and the time-determinant gave Leyds's work a strongly subjective quality.

But time does not stand still. The Afrikaners who had been struck down, remustered their ranks throughout South Africa; at first they were apologetic, showed signs of having an inferiority complex and behaved aggressively as a people in opposition; but gradually they matured politically and culturally. It was in this time that Dr. Breytenbach's work was published. Did the circumstances of the years 1948–'49 bear any approximation to the years immediately following 1902? Life in the present is naturally a consequence of former days and past deeds exercise a powerful influence on it so that prejudices do linger. But, one might ask, do such influences – for the better part acquired unwittingly – keep pace with altered circumstances? The later historian is able to weigh the past calmly and soberly and use an intellectual rather than an emotional approach in the unravelling of causality. When a later writer reveals the same attitude as Leyds to the past, one wonders whether it was possible for his writing to be equally inspired by the gravity of the actual events that weighed so heavily with Leyds. Is it not rather the case that Leyds's apologetic method of approach had become a tradition and prescribed this particular vision of the past? If tradition has prescribed a certain vision and method of approach but the situation that gave rise to the vision has receded into the past i.e. if the realities of past and present are no longer complementary, then a perilous gulf will yawn between tradition and reality. It is here that the impress of an inevitable subjectivity – which as imperfect beings we accept as being part of our earth-bound lot – is apt to give way to an avoidable form of subjectivity. The latter, however, may have an *appearance* of being unavoidable or of "objectivity" and is justified in the name of "the cause".

Historical writing that results from this type of approach can only be seen as an expression of the political views that inspired the writer. Political passions have always been barriers to a true comprehension of the past, especially in a country like South Africa where memories are long – in Europe, on the other hand, the foe of to-day is the friend of to-morrow. The situation in South Africa arises from isolation and the fact that kinsmen of the aggressors lived and remained in the country; it was not merely a case of the conqueror ruling for a while and then disappearing from the scene. A nation had to be built of two language groups living within common territorial bounds. It was in this period that "state" and "people" were no longer interchangeable terms. "People", political party or "race" would be equated so that party politics would really be *racial* politics and each white language group would be anxious to secure political power.

The "political" struggle becomes in its essence a "racial" struggle and in addition to the usual differences of principle, includes the *historical* element; the historical acts of the English in the past are brandished in the faces of "the English" (a vague and abstract term) of today and this association provides a powerful weapon to arouse sentiment with certain objectives in view. It is in this way that historical writing can serve as the handmaid of politics. Before we investigate the dangers inherent in this type of writing, we shall discuss Dr. Breytenbach's book by way of example.

2

My methodological analysis hinges on the premise that the author was unable to free himself from the hold of his political passions; his emotional participation in the events serves to reduce the value of his work. He entered into his work so wholeheartedly that he could not set himself at a distance from it and take a detached view or see that this historical experience, acquired vicariously, had resulted in an image being formed, that both in its structure and the approach to it, failed to coincide altogether with the bounds of historical reality.

Before we embark on the subject of avoidable subjectivity, I should like to discuss some technical aspects of this book. Firstly, there is the way in which material was assembled in the narrative; it amounts to a compilation, a chronicle and the sum total of a series of despatches and official papers; the majority of these latter are reproduced almost in their entirety and are discussed in an accompanying emotionally "loaded" commentary. It is as if the author were unable to rise above his data and view it from a height so that therefore the reconsiderations, remodelling and perspective that would have conferred unity and wholeness on the image are wanting. The work is really a collection of proceedings, the cohesion of which, depends on a temporary order of succession. Subject matter of a divergent nature is grouped together under certain headings but do these headings cover the contents of the chapters (see chapters 2, 3 and 8)? Is the depiction of the period successful? When the image is not derived in clear outline from the sources, the chances of meaningful divisions being evolved, are reduced. Where the problem of sovereignty is dealt with – a subject that constitutes a unity in itself – we do not obtain a clear picture, the writer splits the subject into fragments and scatters them over the pages, merely mentioning the matter because it figured in the official despatches.[3] An assembly of bits and pieces of document-ation does not create a true image in itself nor does it guarantee objectivity.

Coupled with these defects is the absence of an adequate expla-nation of the background. The "diplomatic prelude" is unfolded in a spirit of "this they did to you" that dims the true perspective; niggardly treatment is given to motives and the analysis of factors; there is a tendency to over-simplification and the subject stands isolated from the general South African position and the inter-national situation; it appears to hang suspended in mid air. There is no introduction and a blunt beginning as the reader is plunged into the middle of the commandeering issue of the Malaboch campaign. In this discussion the Uitlanders come under fire – the reader's feelings are aroused against them but there is no deline-ation of the background (p. 2). We are told nothing of the in-judicious action of the Transvaal Government in commandeering British subjects, particularly when agreements had been concluded with practically all the other countries in terms of which their subjects were freed from any obligation to render military service. Nor are we reminded that it was this very issue that created the climate in which the National Union grew and which gave the Uit-landers an opportunity of turning to Britain and for that country to interfere in the Republic's internal affairs. One should seek to "understand" the ulta-nationalistic feelings of the Uitlanders rather than "condemn" them.

The author is more concerned with assailing the British and listing their misdeeds than with the significance of the events. He mentions the policies of federation (pp. 12 and 15) but does not give the background of the British ideal of a South African fede-ration nor does he put the South African Republic in its relative setting in the whole South African framework. Where he absolves the Republic of any blame for the Uitlander grievances issue, it would have been more convincing if he had mentioned the bribes that went with the Selati Railway concession (p. 55). The way in which the Government granted concessions was surely anything but irreproachable; the dynamite monopoly certainly gave rise to grievances – yet the author dismisses it in a line or two by saying that dynamite could have been imported at a somewhat lower price but that this would hardly have been of any benefit to the mines (pp. 58, 252). Nothing is said of the economic difficulties of the period 1895–'98 – with a knowledge of these circumstances the Uitlanders actions can be more readily grasped; there is also little on the political situation in South Africa at the time of the Bloem-fontein Conference.

Anyone who reads Dr. Breytenbach's book might well gain the impression that the diplomacy of the Transvaal was practically flawless. On one occasion he does mention that Reitz, "for inexplicable reasons", presented the British Government with a cudgel with which it could belabour the Republic (p. 283). What, in fact, was the position? After Leyds had gone to Europe the Republics did not have the men to match Chamberlain in diplomatic finesse. Kruger never had much knowledge of international affairs; the staunch patriotism of Reitz itself did not make him a diplomat since he possessed neither insight nor acuity. On many occasions the Volksraad acted in such a way as to dismay the friends of the Republic. President, Kruger, despite all his admirable qualities, was often guilty of errors, of pursuing shadows and, by being obstinate and autocratic, of misdirecting affairs.[4] His mention of suzerainty in 1896, a matter that had not been raised since 1884, gave the British Government an opening that was to be exploited in due course. In season and out of season the status of the Republic was laboured, and was not the postponement in May, 1899 of the franchise question for a further year a shortsighted move? Since Britain treated the franchise issue as a matter of prestige, to what extent did this decision have a bearing on the outbreak of the war?

The author's "prelude" is not drawn against the background of international politics; one might rather term it "an assembly of despatches between Pretoria and London" – so closely is this theme adhered to that London becomes the only outside world of the Republic. The whole matter is therefore divorced from occurrences elsewhere in the world. The author could have discussed the rise and essence of the New Imperialism and the changes it brought in the international scene, its influence on the British attitude towards South Africa; how and why Britain wished to draw the bonds of Empire tighter, the strategic value that Britain now saw in South Africa, the activities of the powers in possessing themselves of the African continent – all matters that were bound up with the "prelude". In a few instances[5] the author does refer briefly to international affairs but only on occasions when other countries are mentioned in Chamberlain's despatches e.g. on p. 25 where Germany is suddenly introduced without his discussing that country's interests in and relations with the South African Republic. He does not state that in 1895 there was considerable tension between England and Germany or describe how the Republic gave backing to German power so as to aggravate the divisions among the great powers. One would also have liked to have read a full account of the Delagoa Bay railway question as an irritant in Anglo-German relations and of its influence on the British attitude towards the South African Republic. One recollects that Britain obstructed the Republic's attempt to secure Kosi Bay through apprehension of German ambitions. According to the author, this was done so as to "clip the Republic's wings and restrain it to an inland captivity". (p. 2). He asserts that after 1896, Chamberlain could use the pretext that the Republic was intriguing with Germany and was a menace to South Africa, or else that he believed certain "lies" since it "suited his purpose" (pp. 159, 69). In the case of South Africa did not Britain have *real* apprehensions on the score of strategic interest? The South African Republic was only one of the facets of the world political scene with which Chamberlain was confronted. It would also have been illuminating if the author had discussed the whys and wherefores of the Anglo-German relations that led to England being given a free hand in South Africa. (Cf. p. 236). It is through the intellect that we seek to understand history and see something of its inner spiritual significance; we shall hardly be assisted to do this by any presentation that is calculated to evoke an emotional response.


3


The absence of an adequate background survey and the failure to evoke a satisfactory image of the period have to be considered in their relation to other aspects – the way in which the material is given form, the grouping of forces and personalities, and the progress of and emphasis on developments in the book's construction. The political predilections of the author result in the compilation of lines of direct contrast – wrong/right, bad/good and foe/friend, without any intermediate lines. As with Leyds, it is a case of expose and exonerate, accuse and justify, condemn and absolve, although the sharp differentiation is probably less noticeable in Dr. Breytenbach's work. The author himself becomes a factor in the historical events under review. The actual presentation cannot be equated with the author's stated aims (I, introduction) since the material has already taken shape before the investigation; guilt has been apportioned in advance. "It was solely and exclusively the fault of the British Government" (I, 349) is not a "conclusion" that he arrived at during the study; the keynote from cover to cover is the "obliteration" of "independence purchased so dearly".[6] The account becomes a marathon of all that "the people" suffered as seen by an indignant historian; he "draws from the inexhaustible source of living water" to provide inspiration for the future and foster the "idea of nationality" or "ideals".[7]

"Accusations", "lies and slander" are refuted in such phrases as "simply untrue", "similarly false" and "how mendacious the assertion is". A sentence such as "It was Chamberlain and not the Republic who harboured aggressive plans" (193, and 279) reflects the defensive character of the construction and the desire to absolve the Republic of all blame. The documents of diplomacy constitute a complicated synthesis of appearance and truth, of pretexts and motives; in them lies a "concealed" actuality. If the historian is to lay bare the truth in them, he has to be doubly careful not to be distracted by his own feelings. In convincing fashion the author shows that Kruger did not strive to unite South Africa under the Republican flag – one of the charges made against him by the English (pp. 277–281), but does he not fail to appreciate the real apprehension there was that the Transvaal might so grow in importance as to overshadow the British colonies in South Africa and become a future menace?

Historical personalities are introduced in a spirit of admiration or of dislike. Kruger is referred to as "the darling of his people" (213), Butler as "a noble and honourable" man whilst Milner has particular attributes, "a dry and impenetrable arrogance" and "a quick-tempered fanaticism" (189). A sympathetic approach probably has one advantage; it enables one to penetrate more deeply into the motives of one's heroes but it has a negative aspect, the danger of one's identifying oneself with them; this renders detachment difficult; there is too close an association between subject and object and an assimilation of the past to the world of the author. The man who is the object of admiration or defence may not be permitted faults. A hostile approach, on the other hand, can never succeed in being penetrative; the motives that guided historical adversaries are passed over and the deeds of the "foe" are frequently depicted as acts of subversion and cunning that require exposure. We need only recall the author's account of the Greene-Smuts agreement (324). Where Loch is reproached with encouraging a rising in Johannesburg, the author omits to add that he denied it (*Vide* C.8159, p. 19). Even if the High Commissioner had spoken an untruth – his defence should have been included. When Milner enters the scene he is always watching the situation "with a sharp eye" so as to "obliterate" the Transvaal's independence – as if this was the only motive concealed in the pretexts that he advanced. I do not seek to justify the actions of Chamberlain or Milner but wish the exalted and responsible task of the historian to be appreciated i.e. to understand the men of the past as well as possible, however reprehensible their actions may be to Afrikaner eyes. These acute statesmen were undoubtedly influenced too by considerations of colonial and international weight, for example the apprehension that the Afrikaans national idea would become the dominating factor if the representations of the Uitlanders were left unheeded; and the fear that their own position in the world would be affected if they could not bend a small and insignificant state to their will.[8] The fact that the Afrikaner has won a "greater" South Africa and a future, should enable him to bring his intellectual faculty to bear on the past and look at it without illusions.

Where the historian departs from given realities and turns to wishful thinking and idealised image-making then the narration runs the risk of revealing one-sided standards of judgment. A statement such as "instead of encouraging and assisting the young state the British Government hindered . . . its development (p. 1) shows that the writer wished to see the Republic expand into a strong state with the support of the Imperial Government. His history therefore resolves itself into an accusation and a denunciation. England, he says too, should not have rejected the Boer ultimatum of 1899 since "its demands were eminently reasonable and their acceptance would not have entailed any humiliation for Great Britain – on the contrary it would have redounded to England's honour" (344). The possibility of the historian becoming the moral arbiter, has dangers implicit in it. A remark such as "what one might expect from a Christian people . . . this they failed to do" (II, 209) is out of place in a scholarly work.

The following circumstances arise from free play being given to the emotions. Firstly, the author selects documents that are loaded emotionally, identifies himself fully with their content and then proceeds to put the adversary "in his place", acting on the assumption that this is a scientifically well-founded procedure for the documents really speak for themselves. Who is it that lets the documents speak, one might ask? Otherwise they would have no message.[9] Secondly one's own feelings of indignation can introduce an element of avoidable subjectivity into the rendering. An example of this is the over-emphasis of the Uitlander mob's behaviour towards President Kruger in June 1895. It can readily be understood that this incident aroused the displeasure of the burghers. It was correct that the author should have said so. But he leaves the impression that it was he who was affronted and that he is "having it out" with Loch in the ring because Loch had sought to put a better complexion on the affair than it warranted (p. 6). The following representative selection of expressions will illustrate my contention: "So the High Commissioner proceeded with his shameless lying" (22); "vociferously" (115); "simply untrue" (53); "lies and slander that called out to high heaven" (100); " to smear as black as possible" (124); "an assiduous seeker" (180); "in shameless fashion" (186), "to see them disappear from the face of the earth" (194); "plagued" (216); "embittered and thirsting for the great day of reckoning" (218); "fling in their face"; "No! They wished to see a Republic that was weak so that they could take it with their cold hands!", "this is a shameless lie" (II, 143), etc.

4

At this point we take leave of the book to discuss the general relationship of politics and the writing of history.

Any historian who becomes the exponent of party tenents usually lapses into a tendentious or nationalistic narration which is not the same as a national-historical approach. He looks for glory and inspiration and idolises great figures from the past, it being his intention to add strength to the present position of his people, to gain comforting assurances for the future and material with which to castigate opponents. He looks back with feelings of piety and affection but without the necessary critical faculty. We need but recall Preller's view: "It is not the unsavoury, the bad, the criminal or the vile in people's acts of commission and omission that makes others happier (therefore) I have simply left aside those things that ought not be published . . . to my mind we are under no obligation to give such unpleasant details as would be detrimental to our own people . . . No . . . I am attached to historical truth but may the hand that types these words rather wither than that I should go out of my way to abuse a fellow Afrikaner in history . . . we are too much of a family; we know one another too well."[10] This view of history was possible shortly after the Anglo-Boer War, but times and circumstances change.

Where the historian – and here we generalise – takes up his cudgels to serve party interests – his work acquires a belligerent character. He uses history as an arsenal against the "foe" of the past (but really of the present), since "the struggle continues". Historical science then changes into an emotional account that has to stimulate sentiment. The "political" historian writes with fire; he clambers into the arena himself, fights alongside his heroes and takes his revenge on "the enemy".

The historian thus supports the struggle for power and loses sight of the many facets of truth. His presentation is not that of people but of "friend" and "foe", ranged as in order of combat and marshalled in terms of his emotions. The danger then arises that "history" becomes an account of the struggles of the past with right and righteousness as the prerogative of one side only. Because the writer is obsessed with indignation of what "the enemy" has done, nationalistic appreciations and moral judgments form important constituents of this type of work.

Many dangers attach to this course. The real process of "understanding" is brought to a halt for the background delineation and indication of motives are not to be found in the "this-they-did-to-you" method of approach. Nationalistic historical writing is always rigid. It does not rest on a synthesis of pros and cons and is not based on a full sense of justice being done since that would not square with the usual political view. As Joachim Wach remarked, the true historian has to set aside his national prejudices, and conceal his personal inclinations as far as possible. Otherwise he will forfeit the great privilege that history confers, that of aiding his fellow-man to move out of the present and to view the past with open eyes. Otherwise the conventional war for justice in a changed world remains the pattern.

In conclusion, a counter to the distracting prejudices of too close a contact with political affairs. One can only really observe the unfamiliar. The historian therefore, like the traveller who leaves his own country temporarily and then views it with other eyes, has to set himself at a distance from the material with which he is familiar, his pet notions and wishful dreams – as in the case of the Anglo-Boer War – and look at it afresh with the eyes of a stranger; thus make a detour from the known to the unknown so that he can make fresh contact with the familiar. In this way it becomes possible to understand the familiar, but at the same time to view it as an extraneous phenomenon.

Without familiarity with the material no understanding is possible and without the historian setting the familiar apart and at a distance, no vision is possible. But vision is necessary to convert the experience that has been relived into an image-at-a-distance.

If this procedure is followed it is the writer's thoughts that will create the structural relationships in his work and breathe life into them. If the historian has immersed himself in one particular sphere only, the chances of avoidable subjectivity, of his identifying himself completely with the object of his admiration, are increased – as are those of his becoming a mere chronicler. It is only distance, the deliberate setting of the intimate and familiar at arm's length, that makes a critical appraisal and perspective possible; it opens the way too to background depiction and a convincing analysis of motives. The historian is then able to evoke a clear, well-defined and total image from his documents. Intellectual probity and scholarly caution are his safeguards against the emotions being given full play. It does not exclude the likelihood that the normal conditioning factors of life will always play a part. But the willingness to set oneself at a distance from the material will greatly assist in eliminating avoidable subjectivity. The ideal of objectivity can only be aspired to if there is a compromise between participation in the events depicted and the perspective of distance from them.

1. *De Eerste Annexatie van de Transvaal* (1906), *Het Insluiten van de Boeren Republieken* (1914).
2. *Die Tweede Vryheidsoorlog* (1948–'49), *Vols.* I and II. *Die Betekenis van die Tweede Vryheidsoorlog* (F.A.K. 1949).
3. See pp. 177, 180, 195, 224, 228, 230, 250, 283, 313, 321, 327, 329.
4. See, for example, G. D. Scholtz: *Die Oorsake van die Tweede Vryheidsoorlog*, II, pp. 53, 69, 76, 79–80, 75–76, 192, 217–9, 223, 244–45, 253, 262 I, 285–86, 288, 290–1, II 324–25, 202, etc.
5. Cf. pp. 25, 30, 59, 62, 69, 84–5, 149, 159, 237.
6. Cf. pp. 110, 183, 186, 189, 228, 266, 230, 330, etc.
7. See Dr. Breytenbach's *Betekenis van die Tweede Vryheidsoorlog* (F.A.K. 1949), p. 67.
8. *Vide* Scholtz: *Oorsake* II, pp. 295–305.
9. See pp. 188-9, 58-9, 53-5, 151-2, 265-6, 292.
10. Quoted by Professor C. J. Uys in *Die Volksblad,* 8 Nov., 1947.

# INTERPRETATIONS AND TRENDS IN SOUTH AFRICAN HISTORICAL WRITING*

## A BRIEF REVIEW OF THE 19TH AND 20TH CENTURIES

I

I do not intend giving a complete survey in this lecture. What I have in mind are the visions of the past that have been held by the most important groups in our South African population and the trends that were revealed in their treatment of the past. Since the field is wide, it will be obvious that one cannot go into detail on the importance of individual historians. It may be thought that I have given overmuch emphasis to the work of lesser writers and insufficient to historians of significance. In dealing with views, attitudes and general tendencies one cannot completely ignore the lesser writers. I have dealt with several of the more important Afrikaans-speaking historians in other lectures and studies.

My material is arranged in the order of the points of view of the Afrikaans, British and Bantu. I should like to give you a glimpse of what South Africans' thoughts were on their own history. It is sometimes difficult to know where to draw the dividing line with precision; some writers who were Afrikaners by birth, wrote in English or found an affinity of interest and vision with the English-speaking and vice versa. One thinks of Henry Cloete and George McCall Theal in this respect.

Since the professional approach to the writing of South African history is a recent phenomenon, it is necessary that we should review the "pre-scientific" period too, for in that pioneering era foundations were laid on which others could build or views be advanced that would evoke a reaction. As was the case in America our first writers in the field of history were not professional historians – men such as S. J. du Toit, William Holden, F. Lion Cachet, W. J. Leyds, Gustav Preller, J. H. Malan, John Noble, A. Wilmot, George McCall Theal and Sir George Cory.

To appreciate the historiography of the 19th century one has to

---

* Inaugural lecture delivered on the 23rd March, 1961 at the University of South Africa.

realise that the first writers were confronted with uncatalogued archival records and an absence of official documentation – in marked contrast to the historians who were schooled in scientific methods after the First World War and had the advantage of good archival facilities. One also has to observe that the year 1900 is not a true demarcation of the division between the writings of the 19th and 20th centuries, the patterns of the 19th century persist until about 1914. I consider that the works of Theal and Cory fall within this cadre.

Our history was not restricted to studies by South Africans; writers who had lived here for extensive periods or who left it as emigrants, immersed themselves in the subject and produced contributions that had lasting value. Where such work has had an influence on our historical writing, it will be referred to briefly. The works of historians such as Eric Walker, W. M. Macmillan and C. W. de Kiewiet who live in Britain or America at present however undoubtedly belong to our own historical heritage.

In undertaking a reconnaissance of the various types of interpretation and trends in South African historical writing one has to remember that history is concerned primarily, with human relationships and that the historian's vision is determined by contemporary circumstances and values – values which have their genesis in the *weltanschauung* of certain groups of people with differing traditions. It is the passage of time – the basis of historical comprehension – that determines which part of the past shall be recalled, and which forgotten, or to which themes and which material attention shall be given and the kind of image of the past that will be formed.

The 19th century saw three lines of interpretation of South African history having as their basis the establishment of the British colonies, the founding of the Boer republics and expanding Imperialism.

2

The interpretation of the Colonial viewpoint hinge on the interests of the Cape Colonists – English or Dutch – but with the realisation that the colony was dependent on and formed a subordinate part of the colonising motherland, Britain. Typical writings of this school of thought are A. Wilmot and J. C. Chase, *History of the Colony of the Cape of Good Hope* and W. Holden, *History of the Colony of Natal*.[1]

The early British writers really wrote in apologetic vein on Britain's colonisation of the Cape. Their historical writing centred on the arrival of the British: the deeds of the Governors, the British Settlers in the Eastern Province and the border wars against the Xhosas. What has occurred during the earlier period under Dutch rule lay on the periphery; so did the history of those colonists who had removed themselves from British rule after the Great Trek. It is noteworthy that it was two writers of Afrikaans origin who gave their attention to such subjects: Judge E. B. Watermeyer in his *Three Lectures on the Cape of Good Hope under the Government of the Dutch East India Company* (1857) and Judge Henry Cloete in his *Five Lectures on the Emigration of the Dutch Farmers* (1856).[2]

Watermeyer who also wrote from the British colonial angle paints a dark picture of the Company's period of rule in contrast to the blessings of British rule and the freedom, relief and progress that the latter brought about. Cloete was the apologist for the Great Trek of 1836 but he entertained doubts as to their future in which they would be without the advantages, protection and civilising influence of British rule. These two books were the basis of the approach by British writers of the Dutch period and the Great Trek until George McCall Theal produced more comprehensive studies based on archival sources.[3]

The writers of the Colonial school were noticeably in sympathy with the Dutch colonists within the colonial boundaries but did not extend this sympathy either to the Dutch colonists who had lived under the Company's rule[4] or to the Republicans beyond the confines of the colonies; the latter were pitied[5] but also criticised.[6] When Republican actions clashed with British interests colonial historiography adopted a more hostile note and the alleged lack of culture in the Republics and the "exit" of law and order were compared with the enlightenment, order and progress prevailing under the colonial government. Unattractive qualities were attributed to the Republicans; their "ignorance", illiteracy and averred "maltreatment" of and "cruelties" towards the natives whose land they had supposedly seized unlawfully, were emphasised. These views, favourable and unfavourable, were put into a more correct perspective by Theal during the last quarter of the 19th century.

Most of the early books of Colonial vintage were instructive[7] and designed to spread knowledge of the needs and requirements of a distant colony in Britain so that interest in emigration could be stimulated and the colony receive greater attention.[8]

To some extent the writers were critical of the "tyranny" of Lord Charles Somerset; they were particularly severe in their treatment of a government in London that frequently allowed itself to be misled by the "incorrect" information of missionaries into formulating policies that clashed with the interests of the colonists e.g. as in the case of Lord Glenelg on the occasion of the Sixth Frontier War.[9] Their attitude towards the missionaries of the London Mission Society was unsympathetic and condemnatory. Dr. John Philip, in particular, came under heavy fire for taking the part of the non-whites against the colonists. A substantial part of their writing is given over to exonerating, justifying and defending the colonists in the face of missionary accusations and traducement.[10]

Much attention was given to the clashes on the border between Bantu and the colonists – these were viewed from the white man's vantage point. The Xhosas were depicted as "barbarians" and "ever encroaching savages" to whom blame for friction was to be apportioned because of their thieving ways and marauding raids".[11]

These writings were not based on archival material and were therefore defective and often inaccurate. Although attempts were made to compile connected accounts of the colonial history of South Africa the results lacked structure and were unintegrated. We are presented more with chronicles and annals than with history.

As regards the practical side: at school "British History" was taught alongside "Cape History" and the former had Britain as its central theme with the Cape on the fringes. The history of South Africa was not "independent" and did not have its own focal point.[12]

Coupled with the Colonial stream of historiography is the name of the most productive historian South Africa ever produced – George McCall Theal (1837–1919), a Canadian by birth.[13] His first work of note, *Compendium of South African History and Geography* (1874) was based on secondary sources and reflected the opinions of his predecessors, particularly in relation to the Dutch-Afrikaner colonists, but after he made a study of the archival source material he began to differ from them radically and in his later works set out to correct their presentation.[14] He too wrote from the viewpoint of the colonists but on a broader plane since he included the Republican colonists in his field of study. He therefore came closer to a real South African viewpoint. With the further lapse of time and the increase in importance of the Republican North, he was able to exercise a broader view than his predecessors whose focal point of attention had been the British colonies alone.

In his writings Theal contradicted prejudiced writers and others who had referred contemptuously to the Hollander-Afrikaner colonists as "retrograded Dutchmen" and set himself the task of recording these incorrect presentations, slanders and slights that had fallen to their lot, rectifying the injustice done by bringing the true facts to notice. He expressed an appreciation of their pioneering work in opening up and developing South Africa, accounted for their qualities and characteristics against the background of their isolation and admired their desire for freedom and their piety. It is not surprising to find that the Republican Afrikaners held him in great esteem as we shall later see.

In the case of the frontier clashes Theal stood for the White against the Bantu; the barbarism of the latter had to yield to the civilisation of the former. Collisions on the frontier, Theal maintained, were the fault of the Bantu. He therefore defended the colonists against attacks by the missionaries and wrote in disapproving terms of the latters' actions.

And so we find that he reproached the Imperial government in London with wrongful intervention in South African affairs, asserting that its acts were based on defective knowledge and incorrect information. This was particularly applicable to native policy which he felt could have safely been left in the hands of the colonists. It was his further view that the colonists – English and Republican – had to conduct a struggle for self-realisation against an uncomprehending and interfering Home Government that brought disaster to the country with its annexations of Basutoland, the Diamond Fields and the Transvaal.

Theal's work had defects; it inclined to take the form of a series of chronicles, it did not pay attention to influences from abroad and it failed to produce a conception of the unity of South African history and give it structure. Nevertheless, it had great influence; it was superior to all the previous works and therefore replaced them as the basis of South African history and of school text-books. Theal covered practically the whole field and, in addition, was responsible for the publication of many volumes of documents.[15] Even during the early part of the 20th century he still had the reputation of being "the historian of South Africa".

His work was to give rise to opposing viewpoints and a process of affirmation, correction and denial of his conclusions followed during the 20th century.

Sir George Cory (1862–1935),[16] who emigrated to South Africa in 1891, was at first a teacher in the Eastern Province and then (1904–1925) Professor of Chemistry at Rhodes University College, Grahamstown. Like Theal he was not a trained historian. His interests led him to record the history of his surroundings, particulary that of the Eastern Province, he made use of memoirs and archival sources. Although his five thick volumes (1910–1930) bear the title of *The Rise of South Africa* they are a history of the British settlers of the eastern region rather than a history of South Africa.[17] He did not carry his venture much further than 1853 and drew on Theal to a large extent. The standpoint he took was that of the white colonists who had experienced the resistance of the Bantu in their expansion. As with other writers of the Colonial school, we find condemnation of the "interfering" politically-minded missionaries in his work. Cory was sympathetically disposed towards the Voortrekkers and Republicans but from a British point of view. His work abounds in detail and, like Theal, he was a compiler of chronicles. In his writing too there is a lack of unity, an absence of structure and the larger outline of a work of synthesis.

### 3

The switch in the Colonial viewpoint in historiography to the *Imperial* direction runs parallel with the changes that convulsed South Africa during the last quarter of the 19th century. As is well known, with the conventions of Sand River and Bloemfontein (1852 and 1854) the Imperial Government accepted a division of South Africa into a Republican North and Colonial South. With the appearance of strong new forces on the scene, the interior of Southern Africa gained in importance and in Britain a changed attitude towards the colonies manifested itself; the policy behind the conventions was condemned and the Republican North was viewed increasingly as a stumbling-block in the path of British Imperial interests. During an Imperialist period the British territory in the Cape Colony was expanded northwards.

Basutoland (1868), the Diamond Fields (1871) and the Transvaal Republic (1877) were annexed; then followed the Transvaal War of 1881 in which the Transvalers achieved success. The subsequent discovery of gold and the growth of Johannesburg came at a time when British imperial policy was fully committed to the scramble for Africa: Bechuanaland, St. Lucia Bay, Kosi Bay and the Rhodesias were annexed. The next objective was a united South Africa under the British flag, an ideal that was unacceptable to the Republican North. The Jameson Raid and the Anglo-Boer War were really attempts of British Imperialism to achieve this unification by force – and although these methods ultimately achieved success in 1910, they gave rise to an intense Afrikaner reaction in the form of emotional nationalism and a spirit that fostered a specific historical vision.

This clash of ideals and the contrasts influenced historiography. After 1881 there was an historical presentation that was conceived from the Imperial viewpoint. It differed from the Colonial trend in so far as its focal point was the *expansion* of the British Empire and that Empire's great achievements. Its ideological basis arose from the conviction that the "chosen" Anglo-Saxon race had been entrusted with a sort of God-given task – of spreading British authority over the globe in the interests of *progress, civilisation* and *humanity*.

This historical writing dates from the restoration of the independence of the Transvaal and defeat at Majuba. A spate of historical works appeared, voicing anti-Transvaal sentiments. The writers condemned Gladstone's liberal policy, bemoaned Britain's humiliation and "exposed" the weaknesses in Imperial policy that had led to the failure of the Transvaal annexation. Books in this category included H. Rider Haggard's *Cetewayo and his White Neighbours* (1882) and John Nixon's *The Complete Story of the Transvaal* (1885). In these writings an unflattering picture of the Republicans was drawn; the authors found justification for the British annexation and recorded charges against the "crimes" which the Boers were alleged to have committed against the non-whites in the interior when the former had ceased to live under British authority.[18] The "War of Liberation" of the Transvalers was a "Boer Rebellion" in their eyes.

The change of sentiment is clearly perceptible in the later work of Alexander Wilmot, joint author of *History of the Colony of the Cape of Good Hope* (1869); he followed this up in 1894 with *The Story of the Expansion of Southern Africa* – an account of British expansion in a country "in which one of the greatest and richest empires of the southern seas is now in course of being built up". He lauded this expansion and the empire-builders but damned those who stood in its path e.g. the Bantu[19] and the Boer[20] and either found justification for or pleaded for their overthrow. He was particularly censorious in referring to the Zulus, the Matabele and the Transvaal Government's treatment of the Uitlanders.[21]

Wilmot's subsequent contributions were *History of our Own Times* (four volumes), 1897–1899, followed by his *History of South Africa,* 1901. These books bore the imprint of the crisis of the Anglo-Boer War period. He flatly refused to recognize that the interests of Boer and Briton were opposed to one another, particularly as far as the Transvaal was concerned. The books registered a strong disapproval of the Republicans as well as of the Cape Afrikaners and their leaders. He placed responsibility for difficulties and for the War on their shoulders and defended the British. He justified the Jameson Raid and accused the Afrikaners of a "conspiracy" against the British in South Africa – a plot, which, had it not been thwarted, would have led to the overthrow of British authority in South Africa and to the establishment of a South

African Afrikaner Republic. His history revealed an acute sensitivity wherever Britain's prestige was in question.

These books which had their origin in South Africa are linked with British historical writings overseas on South Africa – books that announced to an Anglophobe and pro-Republican world[22] why it was necessary that the Republics should be conquered. Propaganda motives dictated the nature of these writings and they were characterised by denigration and libellous attacks on the "foe". The Boer Republics were the accused in the dock and the British historians sat on the bench to pass judgement. The history of South Africa was interpreted in the light of the great collision of 1899–1902 for which President Kruger was blamed. The "backwardness", and "uncivilised condition" of the Boers were emphasised and their "atrocities" towards the non-whites – "crimes against *humanity*"[23] – and all the grievances were listed. In 1901 A. M. S. Methuen observed that during the War the British believed that the Boer was "savage in his habits, a cruel slavedriver, cunning, shifty, unclean, lazy, and unprogressive".[24] There is plenty of published material to support such credulous beliefs.[25]

The anti-Boer tendency found continued expression after the war in the historical writing of those who were admirers of Lord Milner.[26] Even to this day history books published in England that deal with South Africa or with prominent Englishmen associated with the country have an anti-Boer tendency.[27] One has to remember, however, that in Britain there were defenders of the Boer cause too, particularly in Liberal circles, who condemned the policy and wartime actions of the Conservatives.[28]

What strikes one about the writers from the Imperial standpoint is their opposition to the writers of the Colonial trend to whom reference has already been made. Theal, in particular, became the target of their attacks. Because of the views he had expressed in his books, concern was expressed at the great authority his books carried and the use that was being made of them by Anglophobe and pro-Boer circles in Europe.[29] They accused Theal of being anti-British and sought to bring his testimony into disrepute. A comparison of his *Compendium* of 1874 with his later works was intended to show how he had changed from anti-Boer to pro-Boer, being vulnerable therefore to changes of unreliability, prejudice and "duplicity".[30]

Theal's sharpest critics were James Cappon, a Canadian Professor, and E. B. Iwan-Müller. The former was able to find nothing in Theal's work but accounts of "misrule and incapacity, and even arrogance and tyranny on the part of the British government."[31] Iwan-Müller reproached him with "extreme untrustworthiness with the conclusion that his works could not be considered "the best guide in this part of the Empire's history".[32] "He", wrote Iwan-Müller, "passed lightly over the characteristic merits of British rule . . . ; he has misunderstood or misrepresented its highest traditions; he has unfairly emphasized its defects, and made as little as possible even of the economic and industrial advantages which it undoubtedly conferred in South Africa. And he has done this for the sake of setting up traditions of Boer history which are certainly at variance both with these records and a commonsense analysis of facts." This was a condemnation in exaggerated terms. Dr. W. J. Leyds who came to Theal's defence, pointed out that Theal was neither "anti-British" nor "pro-Boer" but on the basis of his study of source material, was "impartial"[33].

And now to refer to the practical side of historiography: After the war the teaching of history and school history books became political matters. Lord Milner felt that the teaching of a purely South African history should be discarded for "everything that makes South African children look outside and *realize the world* makes for peace. Everything that cramps and confines their views to South Africa only (limits their reading, for example, to Slagter's Nek, Dingaan's Day, and Boomplaats and Majuba) makes for Afrikanerdom and further discord."[34] The teaching of history was temporarily suspended and later, as a substitute for fatherland history, Bertha Synge's *Story of the World* was introduced. Attempts were also made to denationalise the Afrikaner child by teaching the history of the British Empire – attempts, as we shall yet see, that aroused resistance in Afrikaans historical writing. Many of the post-war school histories were written from the British angle and were in an anti-Republican and anti-Afrikaner vein.[35]

When the Union of South Africa was brought about, the sharp edges of the Imperial trend were blunted: both white language groups were participants and it was desirable that "sensitive feelings should no longer be wounded". For example, in *South Africa from the Great Trek to Union (London)*, 1909, F. R. Cana asserted that he wrote without bias and had endeavoured "to do full justice to both the great races – British and Dutch – whose past struggles are here recorded." He wrote from the new unified South Africa as his basis and tried to avoid contentious points; however there are many glimpses of anti-Afrikaner prejudice in the book. Similarly prejudiced views are also apparent in Dorothea Fairbridge's *History of South Africa* (1918) although the tone is milder. She too tried to emphasise the "unity" of the two white language groups by pointing, inter alia, to their co-operation during the First World War. One had to be aware of the past because of "a common love for the land and loyalty to the Empire".[36] The British historians at the time of Union tended to pat themselves on the back at the realisation of this project.

4

Side by side with the historical writings of the Colonial and Imperial trends, there appeared *Republican* or "Afrikaans" historical writing during the last quarter of the 19th century, the basis of which was nationalism. It differed from the other two in so far as it laid claim to be "fatherland history" i.e. history that centred on this country and was not a history of the projection of another country or of another part of the world. Whereas the Colonial type of historical writings hinged on the white settler of the British colonies (or of South Africa in Theal's particular case) the historiography of the Republicans revolved around the Voortrekkers or the Afrikaner colonists of the North. The conditioning factors were: the enforced separation from the old Dutch motherland after 1806; the voluntary withdrawal from British authority in the Great Trek, 1836; the establishment of independent Boer republics, 1852–54; the isolated existence in the interior and the continued interferences of British authority resulting in the annexations of Basutoland, the Diamond Fields and the Transvaal and culminating in the Transvaal War of Independence.

The Republican Afrikaners had experienced history as a struggle against nature, the natives and Imperialism. The basis of the image they had formed of themselves lay in the annals of the Jews of the Old Testament; these, after a period of oppression in Egypt (for which read "English in the Cape Colony") had settled in Canaan among the heathen (for which read "Bantu"). They felt themselves called to open the "desert" places to civilisation and Christendom, to curb the "inferior generation of Ham" and to maintain their identity within a closed but independent state.[37]

Resistance to pressure, threats and loss of independence gave rise to an Afrikaner nationalism in the approximate period 1868–1881; this provided the basis for historical writings that were self-contained and introspective. It sprang from a need of self-expression; from a wish to formulate their special identity; from a desire to account for and justify their separate existence and from the need to defend themselves and contradict or correct the accusations and "slanted presentation" that had particularly characterized the historical writings of the Colonial and Imperial trends. In the Cape Colony, for example, there was resistance to "British" and "Cape History" since in the Afrikaners' view it was not "fatherland history" and gave prejudiced impressions of the Afrikaners. The Rev. S. J. du Toit and others published a book in Afrikaans in 1877 with the meaningful title *Die Geskiedenis van ons Land in die Taal van ons Volk* ("The History of our Country in the Language of our People"). It was intended to give the "true" facts and defend the wronged. The book's significance does not lie in its content – it abounded in inaccuracies – but in its nationalistic point of view and the anti-British tendencies it revealed.[38] It is not surprising that *Het Zuid-Afrikaansche Tijdschrift* preferred this book despite all its shortcomings, to a book of John Noble that bore the significant title *South Africa Past and Present – A Short History of the European Settlement at the Cape* (1877).[39]

Much of the Republican historical writing, similar to that of Colonial genre, was concerned with disseminating knowledge of the Republics abroad with a view to attracting immigrants e.g. U. G. Lauts, *De Kaapsche Landverhuizers of Neërlands Afstammelingen in Zuid-Afrika* (1847), Jacobus Stuart, *De Hollandsche Afrikanen en hunne Republiek in Zuid-Afrika* (1854) and J. H. Hofstede, *Geschiedenis van den Oranje-Vrystaat* (1876). After the Transvaal War of Independence it was Netherlanders too, resident in the Republics, who took up the Afrikaner cause, made it known in the outside world and defended it against British imperial attack. Books such as *Het goed Recht der Transvaalsche Boeren* (1881) and *De Worstelstrijd der Transvalers aan het Volk van Nederland Verhaald* (1882) by Dr. J. A. Roorda-Smit and F. Lion Cachet, respectively, are good examples of this.

In the period between the wars of 1880–1881 and 1899–1902 the Republican Afrikaners paid increasing attention to their history. This interest ran parallel to the intensification of Afrikaner nationalism that crystallised around the question of the Transvaal's independence (1881), and was sustained by continued imperial pressure. Patriotic history was emphasised in the schools and the authorities were at pains to compile suitable handbooks.[40] Official celebrations of the anniversaries of Dingaan's Day, Paardekraal and Majuba, conjured up a past that stretched from the Great Trek to the War of Independence.

In 1893 a state historian, G. A. Odé, was appointed in the Transvaal.[41] Theal's books were approved of in the Republics and recommended for use in the schools. The Republicans reposed great confidence in his impartial historical writing and expressed appreciation of his defence of the Boer character and of his corrective approach to their history.[42] The attitude towards the "history of the people" was that it was to be welcomed since it would create cohesive forces and stimulate nationalism. The following is a typical view: "It is good that a nation should honour the brave deeds of its forefathers; it teaches the young people what sacrifices their fathers made in the cause of freedom and of the courage with which they knew how to secure and defend it; it develops a national sentiment."[43]

Books such as *Geschiedenis van de Emigranten-Boeren en van den Vrijheidsoorlog* (1882) *Uit de Geschiedenis van de Zuid-Afrikaansche Republiek en van de Afrikaanders* (1898) by C. N. J. du Plessis, *De Afrikaner-Boer en de Jameson-Inval* (1896) by N. J. Hofmeyr, *Paul Kruger en de Opkomst der Zuid-Afrikaansche Republiek* (1898) by J. F. van Oordt and *Fifty Years of the History of the Republic in South Africa* 1795–1845 (2 vols. 1899) by Dr. J. C. Voigt praised the courageous achievements of the Boers during the Great Trek, the Transvaal War of Independence and the Jameson Raid and gave glowing accounts of the qualities, peculiarities, morals, customs, mode of dress habits and manners with the deliberate intention of preserving the Boer heritage that was being threatened by the inroads of British culture and influences, particularly after the growth of the Witwatersrand. These books were written in stormy emotional language and their central trend was "the way in which the Boers have always been treated by the English".

The basic content of their historical image was "the history of suffering" of the Afrikaner and "the desperate struggle" against British thrust from the Great Trek to the "War of Independence". Their history is recorded as a series of grievances against the British, "the oppressors" and "persecutors" against whom the Afrikaners were forced to wage a struggle for their liberty that cost them bloodshed and material loss.[44] The Bantu is given a place – in relation to the epic deeds that were called for to repel Bantu attacks, or in those instances where the British were in collusion with them. A marked anti-British spirit pervades this historical writing.

On the eve of the Anglo-Boer War all the grievances against the British from 1806 onwards were assembled in *Het Eeuw van Onrecht* ("A Century of Wrong"); in bitter vein the authors pointed out the "calumny" and "slander" from which the Afrikaners had suffered; they proceeded to expose the "hypocrisy", "cunning", "vengeful attitude", "hate" and "covetousness" of the British Government (p. 60). It was an attack on England, designed for overseas consumption and showed the "injutice" inflicted on a small "oppressed" nation – a nation that found itself compelled to struggle for its "freedom" against a world power.[45]

During the War, when the Boers were making history, their

admirers abroad were recording their history assiduously. The Boers then enjoyed the attention of an interested world that marvelled at their efforts to retain their freedom and made much of them. A stream of historical works, for the most part based on Theal's works and *Het Eeuw van Onrecht* rolled off the presses of the Netherlands,[46] Germany and the continental countries to the great irritation of the historians of the British Imperial school.

The Anglo-Boer War provided new material to add to the existing roll – further prodigies of valour, suffering, strife and grievances – the most important of which latter was the Concentration Camp issue. The war was described in memoirs and books with graphic titles such as *Die Stryd tussen Boer en Brit, Vir Vryheid en vir Reg, Helkampe,* etc.[47]

The full value of history was only appreciated when Lord Milner ordered the temporary cessation of school instruction in South African history after the war as he feared that it would foster Afrikaner nationalism.[48] This gave rise to much dissatisfaction as the teaching of history was seen to be the "nucleus" of the people's existence, the "foundation" on which the future of the people would arise.[49] Mothers were appealed to to teach history to their small children and to inculcate affection and respect for the earlier generation who had made such great sacrifices to establish an Afrikaner nationality.[50] The leaders of the people found this theme an inexhaustible one. South African school historians were sharply criticised[51] and renewed demands were made for "fatherland" history written from the Afrikaner point of view. History was ascribed a value second only to that of the Bible – possibly because of the cohesive forces it possessed that would be of use in restoring the body politic and for the inspiration that could be drawn from it for the further struggle ahead. It was required to nurture nationalism afresh. The Republican era lay behind them but it had to remain alive in the people's memory. The historical memory would have to be used to carry the struggle further.

The Afrikaners had to preserve their identity within a greater South Africa that was under British domination and by falling back on their history could offer resistance to liberal and anglicising influences. History was the fortress to which they could withdraw and the storehouse of the ammunition they could use in a political offensive. Intimate links between politics and history were established. One also has to remember that an interest in history coincided with the language struggle and the cultural movement; several histories appeared in the Afrikaans language.

*De Eerste Annexatie van de Transvaal* (1906) and *Het Insluiten van de Boeren Republieken* (2 vols., 1914), were the fruits of Dr.

Leyds's reflections on the "war-guilt" question. They constituted a "vademecum" or collection of evidential material to show how the Boers had been treated by the British from the very start. These books were an attack, an exposure and a condemnation of the foe and a defence of the Boers; Leyds was prosecutor and presiding judge rolled into one.[52] He intended to provide weapons for the future conflict.

The War also resulted in a deeper absorption in the history of the Great Trek. It became the central theme of Afrikaner history. Hitherto it has never been dealt with thoroughly from the Afrikaner angle. Without archival studies the pre-war historical writing on the Trek had been superficial. Although Gustav Preller lamented the chaotic and primitive state of the Archives, this did not deter him from publishing his "classic" *Piet Retief* in 1906 – a work that achieved seven reprints by 1911. The book's importance to my mind lies in its *philosophical* groundwork of nationalist ideology, something that had been lacking before the War.[53]

Preller saw the Great Trek as "the birth of the Afrikaner nation" and Piet Retief as the first Afrikaner to give utterance to his "nationality", thereby assisting to found "a free and independent people". He considered that without the Great Trek there would have been no Afrikaner nation. In Piet Retief's manifesto he saw revealed "the clearly defined awareness of a separate Afrikaner Nation, of a separate People with its own Language, Religion, Moral code, History and Tradition".[54] He investigated the meaning of history in this way.

Preller's message to his people was that the Anglo-Boer War which had cost them their independence, did not mean the end of the Afrikaner nation. Knowledge of the people's past was essential – among other things it could counter and correct the history books of the Imperial trend. To use Preller's own words: "The Afrikaner is jealous of his history, jealous of its genuine truth and he may not allow this history to be taught to him by others."[55] Preller "puts things correctly" and defends or justifies his case in the face of "British misrepresentations". Similar treatment was meted out by J. H. Malan in his *Boer en Barbaar* (1913) – a subjectively written and anti-British book.

When Union was brought about the slogan was "Forgive and Forget"; it referred especially to the historical conflict of Boer and Briton. Prof. Moorrees expressed what was probably the view of the majority of Afrikaners when he said that there could be forgiveness but that they could not forget without breaking faith with those whose "heroic blood had drenched the fields of our beloved country".[56] Preller too was unable to accept a severance of the ties between present and past, or the notion that one generation owed no obligation to another.[57] The Afrikaners accepted Union but it did not stir their hearts. The coming of Union never imposed itself as a focal point on their historical image; that focal point remained the history of the Republics stretching from the Great Trek to the loss of their independence in the "War of Freedom".

The World War and Rebellion of 1914 fanned the flames of the old racial struggle. A typical product of this period is J. A. Smith's *Boer en Brit van Slagtersnek tot Jopie Fourie* (1917), written in the fashion of *Century of Wrong;* it again conjured up one by one all the historical grievances of "a century of oppression". It was a tale of the British villain and the Boer hero and a synopsis of the wrongs done to the Afrikaner, especially in the Concentration Camps where women and children were "murdered" and made "to die of hunger" (p. 63). Eric Stockenström's *Geskiedenis van Suid-Afrika* (1922) embodies a similar Afrikaner-centric vision and anti-British prejudice. The themes were limited to certain national matters only. A change was to come in this method of approach.


5


Scholarly historical writing in the United States was linked with the universities and therefore commenced at a comparatively late date; this too was the situation in South Africa where the work of the professional historian really dates from the third decade of the 20th century i.e. after the First World War. The foundations of professional historical writing in the *Afrikaans* universities were laid by men from Europe e.g. E. C. Godeé-Molsbergen[58] and W. Blommaert both of whom taught at the University of Stellenbosch and Eric A. Walker .[59] Their successors, a younger generation of historians, included Professors S. F. N. Gie, J. A. Wiid,[60] H. B. Thom and P. J. van der Merwe – men who had been trained in German, Dutch or French universities. At the University of Cape Town Professors J. Edgar and Eric A. Walker did substantial work; elsewhere men of distinction were A. F. Hattersley (Natal), W. H. Macmillan and Leo Fouché (Witwatersrand), A. J. H. van der Walt[61] and D. W. Krüger (Potchefstroom) and I. D. Bosman (Pretoria) all of whom had received training overseas. In turn they instructed younger generations of historians who wrote dissertations or published their findings on a considerable scale.

History students are required to base their dissertations for masters' and doctors' degrees on archival research. This was a powerful stimulus in promoting "scientific" historical writing. A further favourable factor was the passing of the Public Archives Act of 1922; it eliminated the "primitive condition" referred to by Gustav Preller and organised the archival records of the Union on a sound footing; research facilities were improved immeasurably in comparison with those that had obtained before this legislation was adopted. Thereafter source publications, edited officially and by private bodies,[62] eased the task of the historian. Before 1922 little had been done to publish such material – the most important publications had been those of the Rev. H. C. V. Leibbrandt[63] and G. M. Theal,[64] from 1926 a modest stream of source publications began to appear and today it has assumed fairly considerable proportions.[65] Wide avenues of publication too promoted historical writing. Purely historical publications took their place alongside the more general magazines.[66] Of still greater significance was *The Archives Year Book for South African History*, an official publication, that owed its appearance to the initiative of the late Prof. J. L. M. Franken and first appeared in 1938. It is a mirror of the activities of history students at the various universities. To date some 35 volumes have been published in this series, they contain 80 dissertations of which number two-thirds were written in Afrikaans.[67]

"Pre-scientific" historical writing concerned itself for the better part with the struggle between Boer and Briton. The coming of the trained historian, by way of contrast, brought with it fragmentation of the old theme and more differentiation and specialisation. Allied and auxiliary disciplines received attention in addition to the approach to history as a basic academic pursuit. Within the limited scope of this review it will be difficult to do justice to the variety of themes that were dealt with or to discuss the most important writings in any detail.[68]

The choice and treatment of themes was largely determined by two factors, the first of which was available sources. University students made use of archival matter that was available locally. Where adequate source material was available, the historical field was explored; where such sources were lacking, the ground was left untilled or studies were meagre – this applies e.g. in the case of our colonial background – the 17th and 18th centuries-source material for which reposes in the Portuguese, Netherlands and British archives. It applies too to the 20th century in respect of which the official records are generally not yet available, except in the shape of newspaper reports or official state publications. For these reasons we find few publications in Afrikaans on our "pre-history", on our colonial background and our contemporary history. *The Archives Year Book* and published lists of dissertations provide sufficient pointers to these gaps. In the North the Archives contain records that date from about 1842 onwards; consequently historians and students of this region tended to concentrate on the 19th century.

The second factor that determined the choice of themes was the line of interest of the Afrikaans historian; this often coincided with his nationalistic philosophy of life and his struggle in the political and cultural spheres to maintain his identity. In this respect the writing of the professional historians did not break continuity with those of the 19th century, and it was therefore a continuation although it displayed a far more moderate approach and spirit. A form of regret revealed itself – regret at loss of independence and for the disappearance of the 19th century way of life that stood in such sharp contrast to the urbanisation of the 20th century. A romantic yearning for the past was apparent and glorification and idealisation of Republican history. The 20th century Afrikaner saw himself reflected in that period – a period of history of pioneering and expansion – that revealed the ideals and peculiarities of the Afrikaners and a time in which their spiritual and political views and their development were shaped. The period on which he concentrated was, in his view, one in which a great national epic had been unfolded. In it lay the keys to his own struggle and strife, to his ideals and his educative mission; it was the fount of his inspiration.

The intellectual approach was of such a kind that *political* history enjoyed primacy. Since the 19th century involved such a variety of relationships – British colonies, Boer republics, the Imperial government and Bantu tribes – it was obvious that the main attention would be directed on this century. Because the South African Republic was the political storm-centre after 1877, Afrikaans historical writing was Transvaal-*centric*.

In exercising their profession the Afrikaans historians seized on two decisive events: the Great Trek and the wars of independence that affected the Transvaal. These two formed the poles around which the writings of the Afrikaans historians were concentrated.

The causes and course of the Great Trek were sifted out but no monographs on broad lines were published. The history of the Trek period was divided up and woven around the "great men" or heroes of the Trek. The historians showed compassion and sympathy in drawing romantic images of the struggle against Bantu and Britain. The centenary celebrations of 1938 gave a great impetus to research into the Trek. However, it is possible to state, that there are still many uncertainties and unsolved problems that relate to the finer points of the Trek period. The romantic image created by the narrative approach has largely been dispelled by the objective studies of Prof. C. F. J. Muller[69] who separated the various factors in the British attitude towards the Great Trek and dealt with its events in a rationalistic way using a type of *verstehende* method. Furthermore the detailed studies of Professor H. B. Thom did much to supersede or correct the stereotype versions of Gustav Preller; Preller's overestimation of Retief's role was put in a more balanced perspective with a sounder estimation of the relative parts played by the Trek leaders. *Gert Maritz* (1947) is one of the most outstanding of the historical products in the Afrikaans language.[70]

The Voortrekker ideal – search for freedom – was projected into the 18th century, a period that received special notice since it could conceivably throw light on the "evolution" of the Afrikaner Trekboers[71] (i.e. the gestation period of the Afrikaner people). Historians investigated the struggle against the Company's officials;[72] the manifestations of ideals of "freedom" and "Nationalism" in the "Republics" of Graaff-Reinet and Swellendam, the Trekboer and the Voortrekker were differentiated and the way of life, character and migration of the former were described. Professor Van der Merwe who had been a student of the eminent Dutch historian, J. H. Huizinga, undertook a most objective study of the pioneering history of the Afrikaner during the 18th century to the start of the Great Trek.[73] His work had links with the earlier writings of Professors Leo Fouché and A. J. H. van der Walt. Connecting links were found between the Patriot movement, Slagtersnek, The Great Trek and the Republics. Nowadays the belief that Swellendam and Graaff-Reinet ever were republics has been rejected[74] whilst the question as to whether the Voortrekkers were nationally-minded people or not remains a subject of debate.

The historians dealt with other themes – the Cape Frontiers,[75] the histories of the republics in Natal,[76] the Transvaal[77] and the Free State,[78] and with subdivisions of such themes such as: border and land issues,[79] relationships with native tribes and with adjoining territories,[80] forms of administration, political institutions,[81] the role of the church,[82] the school,[83] the mission[84] and historical personalities;[85] the history of language and literature[86] also received attention as well as the economic problems of farming, the railways, customs and labour.[87] For the most part, these themes were taken from the 19th century and were specifically *Afrikaans*.

The Anglo-Boer War received scant attention from the Afrikaners on its military side,[88] except for the war memoirs of participants; it is only in the present time that students and lecturers, particularly those of the Military College, have applied themselves to a deeper study of the military issues. The Government too has appointed a state historian to record the history of the War. The "causes"[89] and "diplomatic prelude"[90] to the War were analysed from the Boer standpoint and the Concentration Camp issue was dealt with in somewhat bitter fashion.[91]

As we observed earlier, the coming into being of the Union of South Africa was never really popular as a subject of historical study and it is only recently that students, particularly those of Potchefstroom University, have turned their attention to some of its aspects.[92] No large monograph in Afrikaans has yet been published on it. Political relationships after 1910 have been dealt with in a few biographies of the Afrikaner leaders.[93] The Afrikaans historians have shown no particular enthusiasm for recent or contemporary history but there is now an encouraging trend in this direction e.g. Prof. D. W. Krüger's *The Age of Generals*. (Johannesburg 1958.)[94]

If we try to sum up the main characteristics of Afrikaans historical writing by university students – without losing sight of the dangers implicit in generalisation and omitting exceptional cases – we notice one particular characteristic; the dissertations are so overloaded with minor details that they tend to become compilations – with extracts from sources – rather than true historical expositions with clearly discernible main lines of treatment. Professor W. P. Coolhaas has aptly pointed out that too little distinction between the important and the trivial is drawn.[95] This can perhaps be ascribed to "letting the facts speak for themselves" and further to lack of self-discipline.

In the second place an over-emphasis on the use of local archives has resulted in the appearance of a great number of divergent studies. This has resulted in a loss of contact with the broad currents of general South African and European history. They reveal defects in knowledge of all the branches of historical science and generally of intellectual disciplines. It can also be attributed to a too close adherence to the principle of "stick to your theme".

In the fullness of time specialisation in the subject produced a considerable number of dissertations of which it might well be said: "one could not see the wood for the trees". The process of fragmentation created a need for synthesis but this was not to be undertaken by any single author. In 1951 25 contributors produced *Geskiedenis van Suid-Afrika* (in two volumes) under the editorship of Professors A. J. H. van der Walt, J. A. Wiid and Dr. A. L. Geyer. As a work of synthesis, however, it was not a success; there was a certain amount of overlapping; the chapters varied in quality and the work did not create a unified, integrated image with a balanced relationship pattern. It more or less reflected the multiracial pattern of life in South Africa with its division under the following headings: "the White man in South Africa" (with Afrikaans-English relationships as the main thread), "forms of government", "economic development", "native and colour policies" and "the cultural struggle of the Afrikaner".

On the occasion of the Van Riebeeck Festival in 1952, *Drie Eeue: Die Verhaal van Ons Vaderland* was published in five volumes with Drs. A. J. Boëseken, D. W. Krüger and A. Kieser as its principal contributors. It was a more successful attempt at achieving an integrated history, but it was a "popular" work. We have yet to see a large monograph in which one writer sets forth the unity, structure and integration of a broad South African historical development in all its manifold facets.

An achievement similar to that of the edition of *Geskiedenis van Suid-Afrika* was *Kultuurgeskiedenis van die Afrikaner* (three volumes) that was published in 1950 under the editorship of Professors C. M. van der Heever and P. de V. Pienaar. It is open to similar criticism. However useful the books in these two series may be, they lack the unity, cohesion and structure of a true *Geistesgeschichte*.

Another feature of scientific historical writing in Afrikaans is that the conception of the past is based on the point of view of the *Afrikaner*. We have already advanced reasons to show why that was the case. We now have to show how it influenced the spirit and type of historical writing and what limitations it imposed.

Earlier on Gustav Preller had been convinced that it was only by writing as "an Afrikaner" that he could acquire "a knowledge of our people".[96] In 1938 Professor D. W. Krüger asserted that it was incorrect procedure to examine the history of South Africa and of the Boer people from "outside" as if it was more or less an insignificant subdivision of "British Colonial History"; if studies followed these lines they would of necessity lead to neglect of the internal history of South Africa.[97] He claimed that theirs was "our own Afrikaans view of history" and sought "to live into the past of our own nation, standing on Afrikaans ground in the midst of his people".

In 1943 Professor Thom concluded that historical research brought one into touch "with the heroic figures that were the products of your country and people in the past, and who in their turn help to give direction to struggles and fortunes of your people . . . This study does not lead us away from that which is our own; it actually leads us to it. It does not uproot us from our own soil; it gives us deeper roots in it. It is for these reasons therefore that the research worker engaged on the history of our fatherland . . . always realises that he is serving the spiritual welfare of his people." Professor Thom furthermore felt that the truth should be sought but from "the heart of the people". "We must see that our historical research becomes the property of the people", "The spirit of our people should penetrate our history and, with our people, it should be rooted in the same cultural ground."[98] These views are a general reflection of the spirit and mood of Afrikaans historical writing. One discerns in it resistance to historiography in English, to which we shall return for closer scrutiny, but it also points to a pragmatic tendency that is a characteristic of Afrikaans historical writing and renders it something of a closed unit.

This approach however had limitations, the implications of which have become apparent in our own period of transition. In the first place it created an historiography that was too local and almost parochial – it pursued its course like a lonely planet making its orbit through the heavens. The want of sufficient initiation in or orientation in general European, world or colonial history resulted in the creation of an independent intellectual microcosm with a vision that was directed inwards and which lacked perspective. It was perhaps a token of our intellectual isolation.

The sound advice that Professor Moorrees proffered to the historians in 1911 was not followed i.e. that history should also be viewed from the angle of world history. He then explained the motives behind his suggestion: "Our history does not stand on its own. From its very first pages it brings us in contact with mighty world events that have exercised a tremendous influence on the development of the races. One cannot gain a good grasp of the significance of the first white settlement in South Africa or assess it adequately without ascending the higher rung of the ladder to take note of the events that resulted in a colony being planted at the southern point of Africa."[99] This is equally applicable to later events. It is true that in 1924 Dr. S. F. N. Gie made a laudable attempt is his *Geskiedenis vir Suid-Afrika* to fit our history into the framework of European history; however, his was simply a presentation in parallel and the former was not shown to be an important offshoot of the latter. It is only in our time that historians like Prof. C. J. Uys, Drs. W. J. de Kock and G. D. Scholtz have attempted to bridge the gap. Professor de Kock in his *Portugese Ontdekkers om die Kaap* (1957) made a penetrating study of our early colonial background and put our history into the wider perspective of the voyages of discovery. In his book *In the Era of Shepstone being a Study of British Expansion in South Africa 1842–1877* (1933), C. J. Uys puts the annexation of the Transvaal into the framework of world politics.

The Afrikaner's viewpoint in his approach to history was marked by a deep-rooted feeling of regret at the disappearance of the Republics; he was dissatisfied with the past (a factor that distracted his attention from present and future) and he disapproved of the ways in which English-speaking historians "doctored" the facts. A period of reaction set in that was characterised by corrections of "twisted" facts and justification or defence of his own point of view. It followed that the positive contribution of the English-speaking to the growth of South Africa was generally overlooked, under-estimated or left untouched; "the Englishman" was not seen as a fellow-builder but in fact as a persecutor and as an adversary. One can perhaps conclude that this attitude was due to the fact that English-speaking were their opponents in the political field.

Coupled with this aspect, and also to be ascribed to the excessive devotion to themes that were specifically Afrikaans, was a disregard or neglect of the role of the non-whites as an activating force in South African history. Emphasis fell on white supremacy and the inferior status of the native; the latter was even "segregated" in historical writing; his contribution was not integrated with that of the white man and his history was dealt with as something "apart".[100] Where contacts between the races were described, the interpretation given was that of the white who disdained to investigate the way of thinking of the non-white. Dr. T. S. van Rooyen has pointed to this deficiency.[101] Few books dealt with racial contact situations, and where they did, the treatment was either too broad[102] or too limited[103] in its scope – a pinpointing of beacons. What was overlooked were social consequences, changed patterns of life and the results for both white and black of the juxtaposition of civilised and primitive peoples within an industrialised community.

The fact that the contemporary struggle led to overmuch emphasis on political history, meant that certain other spheres of history were neglected. It was noticeable that there was a dearth of knowledge of our Dutch colonial background and of western cultural values in general. In the field of economic history too, our historians did little more than scratch the surface. Although there has been some praiseworthy work,[104] the time has arrived for comprehensive studies that will bring such aspects into line with the general trends of political history. The significance of our cities and their role should also receive attention. Although both the Transvaal wars of independence are now fairly remote events in time, military histories of them, in the restricted sense, have yet to appear. This applies too to writings on the history of intellectual development.[105] We lack books on the evolution of the Afrikaner's political thoughts, on his democratic views, the Republican ideal, the role of the Bible contrasted with the church's role: At this juncture no "history of the Afrikaans people" is feasible. There has only been partial treatment in the sphere of our moral, social, domestic and religious life during various periods of our existence. In the realm of social history Professor A. N. Pelzer has set a praiseworthy example[106] but there too there is still much to be accomplished.

Although the Afrikaner historians wrote from an Afrikaans viewpoint, it can be said to their credit, that this did not signify that all their writings were necessarily subjective. Historical science can never be devoid of viewpoints or be neutral; objectivity and particular viewpoints can be reconciled provided the writer shows that his contentions are scientifically founded. As the historical strife between Boer and Britain receded into the past, the historian was able to detach himself more from his subject and the principles of objectivity secured greater adhesion e.g. one thinks of the fine achievements of Professors H. B. Thom, C. F. J. Muller, P. J. van der Merwe and G. D. Scholtz. The study of basic principles and the theory of history, in which the younger Afrikaner historians begin to interest themselves after the Second World War, also brought welcome progress in this direction.

In conclusion one can assert that the students of the Afrikaans-speaking community have made a greater contribution in their dissertations, quantitatively and qualitatively (discounting exceptional cases) to historical science in South Africa than students of the English-speaking community.[107] The publications in the *Archives Year Book* bear out this view. Reasons for this lie perhaps in the numerical preponderance of the Afrikaners, in their ability to make use of High Dutch documentary material, in their predilection for their people's past and probably in a difference of attitude and approach towards the M.A. thesis. The Afrikaans universities which follow the continental approach to historical research seem to impose requirements that differ from those of the universities that use English as a medium.[108]

6

The First World War was an occurrence that widened public interest in history;[109] it was after this war that scientific historical writing was adopted by writers of the English-speaking community, as well as by the Afrikaans-speaking community. The English-*speaking* historian's attitude to the past differed from that of the

Afrikaner; he did not seek to carry its burden on his shoulders but rather wished to throw off its shackles. Perhaps it was for this reason that he showed more interest in present and future. The old Colonial and Imperial visions were discarded and many facts were corrected, including those connected with the Great Trek and the Anglo-Boer War.

The smugness of English-speaking historians at the achievement of Union was dispelled in the nineteen twenties. They saw new problems ahead that led them away from the traditional Boer-British antithesis. These were the problems that followed in the wake of the First World War e.g. the emergence of a political awareness among established urban non-whites. New legislation affecting the urbanised native led to the realisation that the racial question was the predominant political problem in South Africa. The English-speaking historians were the first to discern this problem and to institute inquiries into its origin and genesis. Their next step was to review and rewrite history from the angle of racial conflict. In the process many of the traditional viewpoints went by the board.

Professor Edgar Brookes's *History of Native Policy in South Africa* appeared in 1924[110] and J. A. I. Agar Hamilton's, *The Native Policy of the Voortrekkers* in 1928 and his *The Road to the North* in 1937. The last-mentioned author investigated the racial contacts and the beginning of the native problem in the North in an objective way; his work, however, and in particular the second book, is defective in unity and cohesion.

The work of Professor W. M. Macmillan was of great importance. As early as 1927 – and there he was ahead of his time – he realised that the "colour question" was a part of a "world Race Problem"[111] and that the native question could not be isolated and was not without parallel elsewhere in the world. He felt that "the defenders of 'white' civilisation must now plead their case before the Supreme Court – the moral conscience of the world."[112]

His books *Bantu, Boer and Briton, The Making of the South African Native Problem* (1929) and the *Cape Colour Question* (1927) were thought-provoking and laid the foundation for a *liberal school of historians*.

Macmillan came – to use his own phrase – with a "radically new interpretation of known and generally undisputed facts". This applied to the frontier clashes between white and black and racial contacts that hinged on the Great Trek in their political and social but especially their economic aspects. Macmillan adopted an aggressive attitude towards Theal, Cory and the Afrikaans historians; an aggressive tone is often a feature of the enunciation of a new viewpoint; he opposed himself to those writers who had taken the part of the white against the non-white or had criticised the missionaries (Dr. Philip, in particular) or who had depicted the Great Trek as an event of heroic dimensions. He threw light on history from the point of view of the Bantu and saw South African history as a process of subjection of the non-whites and alienation of their land, and the Bantu's conversion into an urban proletariat where they laboured but received no political rights. *Land* and *Labour* are the key words in Macmillan's interpretation. As far as Macmillan was concerned the Great Trek was the result of "land-hunger". The Trek itself was "the great explosion" or a "rebellion" and "a way of escape" from equalisation that was being pursued as a government policy; it rolled up the great flank of the Bantu and in subjecting and dispossessing them sowed the seeds of today's native problem. According to Macmillan the Voortrekkers were not equipped to exercise any civilising influence on the Bantu; that stage was only reached when the diamond and goldmining industries came into being. His interpretation of the Great Trek was that it was "the great disaster" of South African history.[113] He belittled the Republics for their "backwardness" and the "sorry story of petty internal dissensions and of state bankruptcy"; they helped to create the poor white problem and destroyed the unity of South Africa; in these states was preserved the "slave-owning mentality" of the 18th century since the principle of no equality was entrenched as their official policy.

Macmillan, whose views were largely based on Dr. John Philip's private papers, became the latter's apologist. He described Philip as one of the few "statesmanlike figures" of the 19th century. He therefore rejected the belief of former historians that Philip had only been "a mischiefmaker", in which view, incidentally, he is supported by most English-speaking historians nowadays.[114]

The Afrikaners considered that Macmillan's line of thought was absolute "heresy". Nevertheless he succeeded in adding a deeper meaning to the Great Trek and widened our insight into that period. His reaction to existing interpretations, based on one-sided missionary sources, was penned in exaggerated terms and with an inadequate comprehension of the particular coloured problems involved.

Macmillan's pregnant conclusions were not without influence e.g. Professor J. S. Marais' *Maynier and the First Boer Republic* (1944) and *The Cape Coloured People, 1652–1937* (1939). Macmillan had restored Dr. Philip to a place of respect; Professor Marais did the same in the case of that "perhaps most misunderstood figure"; Maynier. Where Macmillan had undermined Theal's authority, Marais demolished and "debunked" it. He pointed out Theal's "bad workmanship", "errors of fact and interpretation" and his "prejudice" towards the non-whites. As he felt that Theal's *History of South Africa* had formed the basis of South African history, he tested Theal's version of the frontier problem between 1778 and 1802. He concluded that as Theal had made so many "errors" in his account of this short period, the rest of his work was also to be held suspect.

Marais wished to pave the way for "a true South African history" that would be free of prejudice. Like Macmillan, his approach to the frontier situation was based on the conviction that the whites were not always in the right and that the non-whites were not always in the wrong. In his book on Maynier his standpoint was the liberal one and his approach to the past that of one who comes to the defence of a cause. He broadened our vision by seeing our history as "the history of the contacts between racial groups of widely differing civilizations and the gradual coalescence of these disparate elements into a single, if heterogeneous society". His *Cape Coloured People* is a valuable contribution to our knowledge of the Coloureds and of the Afrikaner's attitude to colour and colour policy.[114a] The latter has attracted the attention of many English-speaking writers e.g. Professor J. D. MacCrone's, *Race Attitudes in South Africa* (1937).

Perhaps the brightest star to glow in the firmanent of South African historiography is Dr. C. W. de Kiewiet with his *British Colonial Policy and the South African Republics* (1929), *The Imperial Factor in South Africa* (1937) and *A History of South Africa Social and Economic* (1941); he far surpassed his mentor, Macmillan. De Kiewiet set his face against the Colonial, Imperial and Republican trends in our historiography, since he believed that they were either too parochially English or too parochially Afrikaans. He pointed out that two great determinants of our history – the natives and the British government in London – had been overlooked.

De Kiewiet finds that the relationship between white and black is the most important aspect of South African history. "To the black man, not to the white man", he writes, "does South African history owe its special significance" and then continues: "The greatest social and economic fact in the history of the century is not gold nor diamond mining nor even agriculture, but the universal dependence upon black labour."[115] It is not the account of the establishment of the Republics and their struggle for independence that is so important, but the way in which the non-whites changed the nature of the white community after the former had been subjected militarily, their land had been alienated and they had become detribalised as urban or rural labourers. We again encounter Macmillan's basic ideas, *land* and *labour* i.e. an economic interpretation of our history.

De Kiewiet does not separate white and non-white in his writings; histories of the Cape Colony, the Free State and Transvaal do not exist as far as he is corcerned; there is only one history of South Africa, one in which whites, non-whites and the London government are inseparably intermingled. South African history cannot be studied as an isolated phenomenon. In De Kiewiet's view the Cape Colony and Natal were but two of the forty British colonies and the way in which the others were approached from London (which also depended on world events), had an influence on the colonies in South Africa. He shows how the history of the two Republics was influenced by external factors. De Kiewiet's approach broadened historical comprehension. That his work was stimulating, is borne out by the footnote references to it in so many books of Afrikaans historians. De Kiewiet's use of archival sources in London was valuable to many scholars who were unable to consult source material overseas. He gives us another view of the 19th century and shows that our history is a synthesis of the interaction of Bantu, Boer and Briton. De Kiewiet's *History of South Africa* is a brilliant work with illuminating flashes of thought and suggests wide possibilities of interpretation. It is written from a moderate liberal standpoint.

Historiography in English has been favoured by overseas contributions to Empire history and to that of the Commonwealth.[116] The authors of such books were able to use the London sources and put South African events into general colonial or world perspectives. It was an approach to which some Afrikaner historians raised objections; they wished to deal with the history of the Afrikaner people as an isolated affair, as a closed and self-sufficient unit, not as that of a sub-division of the Empire. The British overseas historians for their part lacked a knowledge of Dutch or Afrikaans and did not use the "Afrikaans" sources; these considerations restricted their vision on internal events in South Africa to a one-sided approach. A synthesis of the conclusions of both groups would have provided a more balanced impression.

Where the Afrikaans historians generally applied themselves analytically, it fell to the lot of the English-speaking historians to labour on more synthetic lines. To date no Afrikaans monograph covering all aspects of the Great Trek period has been published whilst it stands to the credit of the English-speaking historians that they have considered the Trek as a whole in terms of synthesis and scholarly description e.g. Eric A. Walker's *The Great Trek* (1934) and Manfred Nathan's *The Voortrekkers of South Africa* (1937).

The synthesising characteristic of historiography in English is apparent in De Kiewiet's *A History of South Africa;* he undertakes one broad sweep of our history, showing its unity and brings perspective and a pellucid judgment to a multiplicity of social, political and economic material. He sustains a high level of objectivity although the vision he brings to bear is a very personal one. He writes in a spirit that is unmarred by prejudice.[117] What is true of De Kiewiet also holds good for E. A. Walker's *History of South Africa* (1928) although there is an element of prejudice in it. The book was conceived from a moderate liberal angle but has one particular weakness – one is left with the impression that the British government never erred in its South African policies. A more recent edition has undergone a change of title to reflect the transformation of the post-war world – *A History of Southern Africa* (1957). In dealing with more recent events Walker has a less sure touch and one notes the absence of his earlier balanced judgments. He has allowed himself to be overinfluenced by the current prejudices against the Afrikaner. Although he used an enormous amount of detail Walker knew how to keep clearly to the main lines on which his theme was developed and he imposed unity, perspective and form on a diffuse field that was not confined to political aspects only. Like De Kiewiet, he broke away from traditional methods in his attempt at a synthesis of the history of western civilisation in South Africa rather than dealing with the constituent parts (colonies, states, native tribes, etc.) separately.[118]

There are other avenues that have been opened by our English-speaking historians – and, to our regret, we must note without any corresponding effort of significance on the part of the Afrikaner community. One of these relates to the tremendous service the English-speaking writers rendered to the non-whites of South Africa from the 19th century onwards in recording their early tribal histories and folklore.[119] This field was traversed not so much by the historian as by the missionary, the administrator and the ethnologist. Much that would otherwise have been lost was preserved for inclusion in the pre-history and history of our country. One thinks of the histories of the Xhosas, Basutos[120] and Zulus[121] and of many other tribes. It is only recently that a few Afrikaners have given their attention to such subjects. This is a field, however, that has still to be covered by the *professional historian*.

Coupled with the foregoing is another field that offers limitless possibilities for research – prehistory. In our day there is a particular tendency among European historians to extend the boundaries of histories into the times of early man. In this field too the English-speaking authors have taken the lead and produced work that stands comparison with any similar studies elsewhere in the world. It commenced in the 19th century. We cannot go into details[122] but one thinks of the *South African Archaeological Society* and its publications such as A. J. H. *Goodwin's The Loom of Prehistory* (1946)[123] and his *The Stone Age Cultures of South Africa* (with C. Van Riet Lowe)[124] as well as M. C. Burkitt, *South Africa's Past in Stone and Paint* (1928), and Revil Mason's *Prehistory of the Transvaal* (1962).

The English-speaking historians have also served our historiography well in taking a lead in studies of our colonial antecedents. While the Afrikaans-speaking writers were disposed to investigate the wrongs of the past, some of the English-speaking writers chose to study the Portuguese background and thereby broadened historical perspectives. One thinks of the works of S. R. Welch[125] and Eric Axelson.[126] I have already mentioned Professor W. J. de Kock's recent work.[127]

The interest of the English-speaking community in local history is striking e.g. Bulpin's work on Transvaal[128] history and that of Professor A. F. Hattersley on Natal.[129] Although not always the work of historians by profession, it testifies to a South African feeling. The Afrikaners, for their part, have done much in arranging commemorative festivals of towns and religious congregations; they have written historical books or brochures on such subjects with the disadvantage, however, that the contributions generally had a local stamp and were not fitted into the framework of wider events in the country.

Lastly, there was a typical contribution by the English-speaking community – biographies devoted to great figures that South Africa has produced, for the most part political leaders such as English-speaking Prime Ministers of the Cape e.g. Merriman, Molteno, Jameson – and also Botha, Smuts, Sir Percy Fitzpatrick, etc.[130] "The Life and Times of . . . " is a typical English tradition; the biography is written by some-one to whom the subject's private papers have been entrusted. The biography always remains as an enduring monument. It is in this tradition that Sir Keith Hancock, an Australian, is at present engaged on a biography of Smuts.

7

We next have to consider the impact of a changed world on South African historical writing. Until the end of the Second World

War it was still possible for South Africans to live in isolation: the colonial world was well-ordered and administered and white authority practically unchallenged. No-one realised that the domination of the whites over the non-white people of the world was a passing phase, and that the white man who had wielded undisputed authority over the coloured races for about 400 years would have to surrender it. The Second World War weakened Western Europe and our generation has witnessed the crumbling of the colonial era. Asia, the Middle East and Africa have risen against their white overlords and forced them to withdraw from their bastions. It is a worldwide revolution of vast dimensions. The period of colonialism has passed irrevocably and a new global epoch has commenced in which the non-whites, formerly regarded as inferior, and without a voice in the council chambers of the European power system, now stand as equals and active players on the historical platform of the world.[131]

As the security of South Africa depended on European power and that power had not only weakened but become an active ally in the emancipation of the black man, it followed that the white man in South Africa felt a great uncertainty about his future. At last the white South African realised that the colour quesion was inseparably interwoven into international politics and that the outside world would voice its opinion on any issue involving colour. The Afrikaners were no longer confronted with white imperialists outside their borders who intervened in the internal affairs of South Africa; it was now a case of the non-whites of Africa and of other continents opposing them at every step and predicting a sombre future for a white minority in South Africa that was outnumbered by a non-white majority within its borders – a majority that had no political influence.

It was now asked whether the whites would be able to sustain themselves – an island in the black sea of independent African states. It was no longer possible to argue that the non-whites were too primitive to rule themselves. South Africans realised that they would have to account for their actions before the bar of world opinion. In such circumstances an awareness of a state of crisis has manifested itself; the question of the future is a subject of continual conjecture and the authorities have formulated a policy designed to secure the "salvation" or "maintenance" of "white civilisation". This time of crisis has already had (and will continue to have) its effects on South African historiography.

A further change that has also influenced historiography is of an internal nature. It derives from the fact that since 1948 the Afrikaners have held the political reins. In the constitutional sphere South Africa was gradually detached from British symbolic attachments until a decision was taken on the 5th October, 1960 that it would become a Republic. The English-speaking part of the population reacted to this – just as there was once an Afrikaner reaction when the Afrikaner was under British rule. There was a reaction too among the non-whites of South Africa; their eyes were directed abroad whence came encouragement and support for their campaign against white domination.

The experience of contemporary events created an image that was often unconsciously projected into historical writing and which reflected the ideals, disappointments or changed values of the present time. In a certain sense we may refer to the commencing phase of a period of *revision* and *re-interpretation* of South African history.

*    *    *

The most significant trends in the historical writing of the *English-speaking section* are bound up with the Afrikaner government and Afrikaner nationalism, the intensified racial tension, and the failures of Liberalism and of the Empire in South Africa. The removal of British symbols and the exclusion of the English-speaking section from any major responsibility in the government have placed that section in a position in which they have become hypercritical, sceptical and distrustful spectators of national policies; their attitude is: "We have had no part in these things and we wash our hands of them". In the words of Mr. M. Gandar, they were reduced to the status of "an embittered and powerless minority", stripped of associations that were dear to them and compelled to live under an "alien" constitutional authority[132]; this gave rise to feelings of frustration and a sense of injustice and it reminds one of the Afrikaners' feelings after 1902. The English-speaking historians, in this mood of disappointment at the *present*, turned their attention to the future.[133] They had visions of impending catastrophe and looked back into the past to discover the turning points that had resulted in the current state of affairs.

A stream of political-historical writings – books and articles – reflects dissatisfaction with the present situation; these writings deal with our place in a changed world[134] and give the outside world a more or less negative picture of the Afrikaners and their policies – somewhat similar to the historical writing of the Imperialists on the eve of the Anglo-Boer War. Confronted with the Afrikaners' nationalism and racial policies, they seek to explain who the Afrikaner is and what one may expect of him. In her book *The Last Trek: A Study of the Boer People and the Afrikaner Nation*

(London) 1957, Sheila Patterson often hits the mark, but she is often wide of the target too. The following titles – I mention only a few of them – are reflective of the trend – *Background to Bitterness*,[135] *Twilight in South Africa*,[136] *The Anatomy of South African Misery*,[137] *Hope for South Africa*,[138] *South Africa's Eleventh Hour*.[139]

The need to grasp the present situation resulted in a re-interpretation of the past. Professor A. M. Keppel-Jones's article *"Where did we take the wrong turning?"*,[140] is a typical example. The enquiry is of a twofold nature: What led to the triumph of Afrikaner nationalism? and: why was the British liberal idea a failure in South Africa? These enquiries led to the discovery of "errors" in the past, faults that could chiefly be laid at the door of the Imperial government of the 19th century. Keppel-Jones considered that the "wrong turning" was the abandonment of the Orange River Sovereignty in 1854. This step finally split South Africa into Colonial South and Republican North and enabled the conservative frontier tradition of "no equality" and Transvaal nationalism to gain the upper hand.

In *Anatomy of South African Misery* and *The Jameson Raid,* Professor De Kiewiet and Dr. Jean van der Poel, respectively, condemn the Imperial government for its handling of the Jameson Raid; that episode resulted in the Anglo-Boer War and an artificial union followed instead of the natural growth of a federation in which latter it was unlikely that one group would have been able to dominate the other. A similar feeling of regret is apparent in Professor L. M. Thompson's excellent and objective book, *The Unification of South Africa*.[141]

The Festival of Union in 1960 too led to "stock-taking" on the past fifty years and the ideals and expectations of the fathers of Union were compared with the contemporary state of affairs.[142] In general there was much interest in the situation of the non-white majority and in the historical development of racial antipathies.

A third tendency noticeable in the English-speaking section's concern with history was a certain sensitivity to the Afrikaner's traditional presentation of history on the Boer-Briton on black-white basis. This sensitivity may be compared with that of the Afrikaners after 1902 in the matter of teaching of history at school. At that time the Afrikaners were sensitive and touchy at the way in which history was taught in schools from the British angle. To-day it is the English-speaking who are suspicious of Afrikaans textbooks and they assiduously search their pages to correct them or to "write them off".[143] After 1948 the teaching of history became a political issue. Afrikaans school history books came under the magnifying glass and the critics published their findings in the press.[143a]

It was also discovered – and with some measure of truth – that the Afrikaans historians had paid inadequate or no attention to the great role of the English-speaking in building up South Africa; that the past of the English-speaking community remained unknown and that matters were presented from a purely Afrikaans angle. In his book, *They were South Africans,*[144] John Bond asked that British pioneers be given recognition and he placed some of their achievements on permanent record. It was such considerations too that led to more of an interest being taken in the history of the British immigrants – note the attention of the politicians to this subject.[145] Whilst the Afrikaans-speaking generally tended to search for links with the past, the English-speaking showed a tendency to loosen the fetters of history, especially the over-stressed "struggle between Boer and Briton" which they saw as a dividing factor. There is a list of disputed subjects on which agreement will probably be difficult, for example, the roles of Dr. Philip and Maynier, the first annexation of the Transvaal, the causes of the Anglo-Boer War and especially the Concentration Camp issue. Some of these matters still give rise to heated debates in the readers' columns of certain newspapers. In the *Concentration Camps, Facts, Figures and Fables*[146] Colonel A. C. Martin presents the "true facts" from the British angle and "corrects" the findings, from the Afrikaans angle, in Dr. J. C. Otto's *Die Konsentrasiekampe.*[147]

\*     \*     \*

And now to turn to the *Afrikaners:* as a group they had lived in past times in physical and intellectual isolation – this self-sufficiency had protected them from the perilous threat of loss of identity. During the 19th and 20th centuries they were continually at loggerheads with the British just as the coloured peoples of the world (and those elsewhere in Africa) have come into conflict with Colonialism and Imperialism. The present-day demands of the non-white people have something in common with the Afrikaners' past.

The Afrikaner in the changed world of the 20th century, finds that his mental frame of mind in relation to the non-whites is still cast in the mould of the 19th century i.e. that the non-white, because of the difference in his colour and state of civilisation, cannot be allowed to exercise equal political rights with the white within the same state.

The Afrikaner had won the constitutional struggle against the Briton but at the very moment that he was about to reap the rewards of his victory in a new Republic, he stood confronted with the challenge of a non-white majority, which, in conjunction with the outside world, threatened to deprive him of his gains.

The question of the future is also foremost in the Afrikaner's mind: will the white minority be able to maintain itself in the southern point of Africa? And how can they achieve that? A national myth has already become established – that South Africa is an innocent nation and the victim of attack in an evil world; and that attempts to solve the racial problem by territorial divisions or separate development are "misunderstood". Whether he wishes to or not the Afrikaner is confronted with a changed world that undermines his historical certainties. Elsewhere in Africa non-white peoples control their own destinies and a responsible historian, Dr. G. D. Scholtz, has tried to bring home to Afrikaners the fact that there are no longer "inferior" races as the traditional Afrikaans view once held.[148]

This confrontation with a new world compels the Afrikaner to shed his introversion and at present he is undergoing an individual reorientation. His vision of the past will also change. Events within and without the country, bitter criticism from overseas, the coupling of the internal colour question to world politics, the rise of non-white nationalism in Africa – all these factors have already influenced historical writing, witness the books of South Africa's most productive historian, Dr. Scholtz, and they will continue to do so. Scholtz is the prophet of repentance whose mission it is to bring this changed world to the Afrikaner's notice. He wishes to help them shake off the shackles of intellectual isolation and equip themselves with knowledge so that "white civilisation can be saved from submergence".

In his *Oorsake van die Tweede Vryheidsoorlog* (1948–'50), Scholtz broadened the horizon – he sought the causes not in Africa only but in world politics. He was able to bring a greater objectivity to bear, although viewing it from the Afrikaner's standpoint, and he could dispel the Kruger legend and the supposed absolute innocence of the Transvalers. This book was followed by his *Hoe die Wêreldpolitiek gevoer word* (1952) and *Suid-Afrika en die Wêreldpolitiek 1652–1954;* he traced the applicability of internal affairs to international relationships in most original fashion. These writings served to emphasise that the time of isolation had passed and that the fate of the Republic of South Africa was linked inseparably with world politics.

In *Die Gevaar uit die Ooste* (1957) Scholtz pointed to the disposition and numerical preponderance of the Eastern lands and appealed to the Afrikaners to arouse themselves from their slumbers and "save" white civilisation by putting a real separation of the races into effect. He also published a massive work, *Die Stryd om die Wêreld* in which he treats the East-West clash and the dangers implicit in it for South Africa.[149] Scholtz sets himself out to pinpoint the Republic's place in the "one world" of to-day and pleads for a re-orientation in keeping with the times. Traditional historical writing has concerned itself with giving an account of the "sacrifices" that were required to achieve freedom and of the "struggle" for existence in the past; Scholtz, in his more global-orientated historical writings shows more concern with the "sacrifices" that will still have to be made to secure "the maintenance of white civilisation" in *future*.

This brings us to the influence of the non-white question on historiography. One is struck by the fact that the Afrikaans historian has not yet allowed himself to be harnessed to the *apartheid* car and has not acted as its apologist.

Although Dr. Scholtz's historical investigations have covered this field, he has confined himself in his books to discovering "faults" and "aberrations" in the past for which the "selfish motives" of our forefathers were responsible. His criticism of the past hinges on the use of "non-white labour" by our forebears; they should never have done this, he argues, and then there would have been no racial problem to-day nor would the future of the Afrikaners have been endangered. In his book *Het die Afrikaanse Volk 'n Toekoms?* he analysed "three historical errors"[150] on which he elaborated in subsequent pamphlets[151] and articles.[152] These were: the cessation of white immigration in 1707 that resulted in the Afrikaners being numerically a small people and the exclusive concentration of the Afrikaner on farming – a pursuit that led him into isolation. Furthermore he feels that too few took part in the Great Trek and that those who did should not have halted at the Limpopo; President Kruger erred in surrendering his claims to the land north of that river. Scholtz is also critical of the use of non-white labour by the Boer republicans and by the Natal sugar planters.

These are the arguments in which he finds an explanation for the presence of non-whites in the towns and on the farms or of the limited numbers of the Europeans; his historical labours do not result in a justification of "apartheid" for his critical analysis of South African history shows it to have been a three hundred year period of economic integration. His work is really a critical survey of the past from a Utopian point of view; it reflects the desire to see a well-ordered community in future in which everyone will be content. He divides history into two parts: that which has followed the paths of error hitherto and therefore has to be criticised and the "right" history that is to come.

In *Grensbakens tussen Blank en Swart in Suid-Afrika*, a thesis written in 1937 and first published in 1948, Dr. P. van Biljon gave a sketchy and incomplete account of relations between white and black in South Africa in the sphere of land ownership and division. The book was a plea that the white should remain in authority"; it compared the British policy of equalisation with the Afrikaner policy of "no equality" and considered that "territorial lines of separation" were the ideal solution to the "native problem". What he overlooked was the hard core of the problem, the established and westernised non-white population of the towns. The word "apartheid" was added to his book in 1948 only. Van Biljon's work may serve as a background to the present idea of "homelands" for the Bantu, but the advocates and apologists of "apartheid" on historical grounds have been drawn from the ranks of the sociologists[153] and theologians.[154]

*　　*　　*

It was only after the Second World War that the *non-white peoples* of the Republic of South Africa made their first contribution to historiography; we shall hear more of them in future. The historical writing of the Bantu was a product of the awakening of a political and national consciousness, related to the upsurge of nationalism in Asia and elsewhere in Africa, and the emancipation of non-white peoples who gave them moral support.[155]

The educated non-white too gave thought to his position and put queries that took him back into the past. In their newspapers and in their speeches it is clear that they saw themselves as "sons and daughters of Africa" – "Africans". But in their own country they felt themselves to be "aliens" in a position of inferiority. Although they formed the majority of the population, they were subject to "white supremacy"; they had no say in their lot and others ruled over them. They felt that they were an exploited, oppressed and cheap labour force, a voteless and voiceless majority,[156] placed under the daily burden of irksome discriminatory laws. They therefore had a sense of injustice and felt that they were wronged. They became aware of "Human Rights" and one of their speakers declared that "domination of one race by another . . . is a thing of the past".[157] They were alive to the "rising tide of nationalism"[158] and their "struggle for freedom".[159] In 1952 one of their leading spokesmen said: "I trust that the consciousness of the justice of our cause and a belief in the divine approval of our struggle will give us strength and courage to bear it (oppression) until victory is

151

won''. He praised "the sacrifices and courage" of the "sons and daughters of South Africa'' (Bantu) in their struggle to secure a voice in the government of the country. The whites are spoken of as the "enemies of our freedom"[160] and the native problem is reversed to become a "White Problem". The type of language used abounds in phrases such as "wrongs and oppression",[161] "national desires, aspirations and ambitions of the African People" – which may be equated with the slogan "Africa for the Africans".[162]

This language sounds very much like that of the Afrikaner of yore. It does not come as a surprise to find that during the Van Riebeeck celebrations a pamphlet appeared that was entitled *Three Centuries of Wrong*.[163] Its author, Dr. S. M. Molema, drew a historic parallel between the Transvaal Boers struggling against British domination and the position of the Bantu to-day. His conclusions amounted to this: the Afrikaners had become nationally-minded and had risen against tyranny and oppression; that too was the case with the Bantu. The Afrikaners were reminded that although they had forgotten their historical struggle as underdogs they should not forget that the subjected and oppressed of to-day might become the ruler and legislator of to-morrow.[164] When the Bantu interprets South African history he bases it on the principle of "struggle for freedom", just as the Afrikaner historians of earlier times did.

Two books based on a study of sources reflect this tendency – *The Role of the Missionaries in Conquest* by Nosipho Majeke[165] and *A History of South Africa in three volumes* by "Mnguni".[166] The approach to these books, the spirit that animates them and their content are similar and we may discuss them together.

The black man of Africa takes the centre of the stage and history is interpreted from his point of view. How did the situation arise in which the "Africans" find themselves in their present state? The inquiry is put into perspective and commences with the occupation of Africa by the whites during the period of European colonisation. History is then divided into halves; on one side are the subjected and oppressed Africans, struggling to be free: on the other side are the oppressors, the white conquerors and rulers. "Mnguni" declares: "The history of South Africa is a history of 300 years of struggle between oppression and oppressed" (p. 175), almost an echo of *A Century of Wrong*.

This historical writing is intended to make the non-white conscious of his historical and present position. It has to assist in his attainment of "freedom". These books have a characteristically pragmatic touch and are closely bound up with the political ideals of the Bantu. A further objective is that of unmasking the "distortions and falsifications", "untruths" and "legends" of the historical writing of the white man. In the pages of these books, therefore, one finds much censure and "correction".

The books were written in a spirit of bitterness; in their turn they create legends to which the Bantu can cling; they are virtually summaries of historical and present-day grievances arising from the "wrongs" inflicted on them, the first and oldest inhabitants of the country, by the "foreigners" who penetrated into the country and conquered and oppressed them.

In these books by Bantu authors no distinction is drawn between Boer and Britain, Conservative or Liberal – these all fall into the category of "white oppressors". The authors seem to be anti-everything – anti-British, anti-Boer and anti-missionary. Their version has an economic basis: as they see it there was first Boer feudalism with its slaves and retainers; then came the British urban capitalistic system – finally (a pinch of Marxist salt is added) the time will come when Bantu socialism will prevail.

What is the image that they create? "Mnguni" puts it like this: "The purpose of this history is to expose the process of conquest, dispossession, enslavement, segregation and disfranchisement of the oppressed non-Europeans of South Africa in order that the oppressed as a whole will understand better how to transform the status quo into a society worth living for and worth living in". Majeke's words are: "The story, if truly told, is one of continuous plunder of land and cattle by the European invaders, of the devastation and decimation of people, followed by their economic enslavement."

We cannot enter into details but I shall give a few examples to illustrate the Bantu style of historical presentation. The accounts they give and of the conquest of their *land* and of the imposition of *legislation* on them; the "Africans" are forced to go to cities and farms where they are subject to exploitation as a cheap labour force; Boer and Briton have "ganged up" against them as exploiters. Before the coming of the "invaders" their condition was idyllic; but afterwards these followed the systematic conquest of the country in "anti-Hottentot", "anti-Xhosa", "anti-Zulu" and "anti-Sotho" wars for which the whites had a culpable responsibility.

The authors have nothing good to say about any of the British governors or missionaries: Van der Kemp, Read, Philip Maynier and Stockenström are denounced as "spies" and traitors who were used as instruments of suppression. Nor do the Cape liberalists or the liberal historians find favour in their eyes. They see the Great Trek as "the flight of the Boers" and its results as "land-grabbing and the subjection of the Bantu".[167] Majeke feels that new labels will have to be found for the "so-called Great Trek" and other cherished conceptions of the whites. "Our future historians", he predicts, "wil strip the tinsel and velvet from those puppets who strut the stage of history from Van Riebeeck onwards".

In their view the "wars of conquest" far outshadow the Great Trek; the latter has as little significance for them as the Boer-British struggle in which they have no interest. Dingaan's "war" against Retief and "white invaders" is justified. Gaika was a "traitor"; Chaka, Dingaan, Mzilikatse and Moshesh were great heroes who offered resistance in the wars of conquest. The great "national suicide" of the Xhosas in 1857 was planned and inspired by the whites.

This image of which we have seen a few glimpses differs so radically from the traditional white interpretation that one might well speak of "Unwertung aller Werte". One might argue that the views are not representative of the Bantu but the books exist and their content reflects a spirit that is expressed in other writings and utterances. At its least it is the start of a development of which we shall have to take notice. One should not forget that the first history book in Afrikaans, *Die Geskiedenis van ons Land in die Taal van ons Volk,* was also written when a mood of reaction prevailed, that it was written purely from the Afrikaner's point of view and that it expressed anti-British sentiments.


8


To conclude I shall take a glance at the future of South African historical writing. Predictions concerning historical science are always risky. We know that some of the older approaches to it have been abandoned and that some of the new, that are still in their infancy, will be pursued, but one may ask whether any completely new lines of approach are likely to be evolved and whether as yet we can see any signs of their coming. Much depends on the actual course of history. If the sombre predictions of internal revolution and external pressure are realised, a main field of study will be "causes of the South African Revolution". And if the optimistic belief in the success of *apartheid* should become a happy reality then no doubt the praises will be sung of the Afrikaner's far-seeing vision and sacrifices. But let us leave it at that.

Our expectations should be based rather on present developments especially in the political field and in the region of race relations. We have already observed that the Afrikaner is undergoing a process of reorientation in which he will see future, present and past with a different vision; but this line of development can be checked if this is a return to the "laager" frame of mind i.e. a closing of the ranks that would now include the English-speaking and would form a greater "white laager" to bid defiance to emergent non-whites and outside pressure groups. This could lead to two possible approaches to the past, firstly, to a revision of the Boer-British relationship and secondly, to an investigation of the origins of the white/non-white community.

As to the first: the realisation of an historical ideal, the Republic of South Africa, may seem to the Afrikaners to be "amends" for the "injustice" that was done them in the past. The relaxation of political conflict over the constitution may result in the historical struggle ceasing to be of such force and interest. During the referendum campaign on the Republic issue, for example, Dr. H. F. Verwoerd declared that the two white language groups would "have to learn to look ahead instead of backward into the past"[168] and he repeatedly appealed to the whites "to forget past struggles".[169] He felt that a Republic was necessary to remove the sore points of history."[170] Professor S. du Toit's reflection on the result of the referendum was "1960 – year of the Republic of South Africa, a line drawn through the Treaty of Vereeniging. Merciful and crowning epilogue of the struggle since 1902".[171] Views such as these indicate that the Anglo-Boer War will be seen in a different light in the historical writing of the Afrikaner.[172]

Self-confidence and a feeling of greater certainty arising from so many years of rule since 1948 and from the realisation of the republican ideal, may lead the Afrikaners to reinterpret the historical conflict of Boer and Briton, especially during the 19th century. Emphasis will then no longer fall on grievances and injustices but on co-operation between the two white groups. The traditional image of Kruger and of the causes of the Anglo-Boer War (especially as regards the treatment of the Uitlanders) will probably be revised and interpreted afresh. The point of stress may gravitate from political history to constitutional history and to other branches of historical science such as economic, social and military history, to history of the humanities or to contemporary history.

In their political struggle (and in their historical writings) the Afrikaner historians have overlooked the intellectual development of the Afrikaner. We have, for example, no comprehensive work on the rise of the Afrikaner nor on the triumph of his nationalism, no book that answers the question of who the Afrikaner is and how he became his present self. Then there is contemporary history; this is a new development that as yet has received little attention here;[173] it is necessary to the grasp of our own time, especially since the attention of the world is now focussed on South Africa.

When the interest in past strife slackens it should be concentrated on an historical presentation in more universal terms; South Africa's place should be shown in relation to Africa and the colonial era; the withdrawal of certain European influences from colonial territories and the causes of European attitudes towards South Africa should be explained. Comparative studies would also be a fruitful field for arriving at a better understanding of our own history e.g. a comparative study of the American and South African frontiers and an account of the influence the frontier has had on our history;[174] or a comparison of Canadian and Afrikaner nationalisms that would put the Afrikaner's position into wider perspective; or comparative studies of various racial policies in Africa.

In conclusion: as attention will be diverted from the traditional Anglo-Boer strife, it will tend to concentrate on white/non-white relations and on race relations in general. What verdicts on the Afrikaner were passed (in former times and now) by foreigners, by the English-speaking or by the non-white? Or what was the white man's opinion of the non-white in the course of history? Such enquiries point to the need for a quickened interest in human relationships.

Since there will be reinterpretation one can be sure that historical debate will have a prominent place. Further studies of the theoretical basis of history will aid historians to arrive at sober reappraisals in future.

1. Published in Cape Town, 1869 and London, 1855, respectively.
2. For an assessment of these two books see my *Die Afrikaner en sy Geskiedenis* (Cape Town, 1959), pp. 74 and 79.
3. See, *inter alia*, his *History of South Africa under the Administration of the Dutch East India Company 1652-1795* (London 1897, 2 vols.).
4. *Vide* A. Wilmot and J. C. Chase: *History of the Colony of the Cape of Good Hope* (1869) in which they speak of "semi-barbarism" (p. 157) and John Noble: *South Africa Past and Present* (London 1877) in which the writer says (p. 15) that "their moral condition was scarcely higher than the Hottentots or slaves who were their household companions".
5. Chase in his *Natal Papers* (Grahamstown 1843) writes of the "errors of the unfortunate and much-to-be-pitied men" whilst in their joint history Wilmot and Chase refer to them as "unfortunate emigrants who were left at a perfect loss to know where they were or what they were" (p. 367).
6. See, for example, William Holden, *History of the Colony of Natal*

(London) 1855; he presents the Voortrekkers as a people inspired with "a violent antipathy against all British rule" (p. iv), refers to "disorder and crime" (p. 347), and to the "bad and fierce spirits" who were allowed "to pursue the course which their evil passions dictate, without restraint or control" (p. 350). In the joint work of Wilmot and Chase (p. 419) those taking part in the Boomplaats clash are "rebels" whilst the Transvaal is "a thorn in the flesh of the Cape Colony". John Noble, *South Africa Past and Present* (1877) writes of the "ignorant" Boers with their "natural antipathy to law and restraint" (p. 169) and their "acts of cruelty and wrong" towards the natives; they lived on the "margin of civilisation" – there was an "impotence of authority" and "dark blots upon the pages of the history of their country" (p. 173). On the other hand those (English) who established themselves in the Transvaal were "enterprizing settlers".

7. Examples are W. B. Boyce: *Notes on South African Affairs* (London 1839) and J. C. Chase: *The Cape of Good Hope and the Eastern Province of Algoa Bay* (London 1843).

8. See, for example, William Holden's *History of the Colony of Natal* (1855).

9. See the books of Boyce and Chase mentioned; also A. Wilmot and J. C. Chase: *History* p. 331, Noble: *South Africa*, pp. 57–58.

10. *Vide* J. C. Chase: *Some reasons for opposing the author of the South African Researches, the Rev. John Philip* (Cape Town 1836): D. Moodie: *The Record* (Cape Town) 1838 which refutes Philip's allegations; Wilmot and Chase, *op. cit.*, p. 332; Noble, *op. cit.*, pp. 57–58, etc.

11. See Wilmot and Chase, *op. cit.*, pp. 250 and 261.

12. See my *Teorie en Metodiek vir Geskiedenisonderrig* (Johannesburg 1960) pp. 92–87.

13. For details of Theal's life and work see I. D. Bosman, *George McCall Theal as die Geskiedskrywer van Suid-Afrika* (Amsterdam 1932).

14. Theal was the author of *History of South Africa*, 1505–1884 (10 vols.); *History of the Boers of South Africa* (London 1887) and many other publications. See the book mentioned in the preceding footnote for full particulars.

15. For details of these source publications consult A. J. Boëseken: *Theal as Baanbreker* in *S.A. Archival Journal*, 1959, No. 1, p. 33–42.

16. For particulars of Cory's life and work see *Die Huisgenoot*, 10 May, 1935 and *South African Railway Magazine*, vol. 21 (2020), December, 1927.

17. His purpose was "a straightforward, unbaised account of the circumstances under which the Eastern Province, took its rise" (*The Rise of S.A.*, Vol. 1, foreword).

18. Rider Haggard wrote in his book of the Boer's "absence of regard for the truth" (p. 97) and saw him as "ugly", "squalid and filthy to an extraordinary degree" (p. 98), with an "abhorrence of all government", "always in rebellion" (p. 99) and filled with hatred of Briton and Bantu (pp. 96, 100). He emphasised the "wholesale butchery" of the Bantu. John Nixon makes similar charges (pp. 14, 62, 213, 250).

19. In *The Story of the Expansion* Wilmot justifies the conquest of the Zulus and Matabeles. He viewed the non-whites as "the natural enemies of Europeans in South Africa" (p. 55). He therefore defended the colonists against missionary attacks on them (pp. 88, 101, 103,

104). Wilmot's main interest lay in the "wonderful expansion of the realm of civilisation" which brought with it "a gradual conquest of the savages" and he glorified the "mastery of that part of the continent which extends from Cape Town to the Zambezi" (p. 16 *et seq.*).

20. Wilmot's view of the Boers was that they were people with an "unconquerable hatred" of the British government and that they oppressed the non-whites.

21. Wilmot writes of the Transvaal government as an "oligarchy" and "a clique of prejudiced men" (*Expansion*, p. xxii) who oppressed British subjects. His hopes found expression in the words: "A revolution is possible, and if this takes place, the British flag may again wave over the public offices in Pretoria."

22. See, Annemarie de Ru: *Het Beeld van de Zuidafrikaanse Geschiedenis in Nederland van 1899–1956* in *Hertzog-Annale* (S.A. Academy for Science and Art), yearbook VII, Dec. 1960, pp. 74–117.

23. See, for example, L. S. Amery: *The Times History of the War in South Africa* (7 vols., London 1900–1909).

24. *The Tragedy of South Africa* (London, 1901).

25. *Vide* H. A. Bryden: *A History of South Africa* (1904); the author described the Boer as "ungainly in his habit", "litigious", "quarrelsome", grossly ignorant, superstitious, and self-conceited, careless and unclean in his dress and person, domineering and at times brutal in his intercourse with his slaves, natives and inferiors" (pp. 35–37).

26. See, for example, W. B. Worsfold: *Lord Milner's Work in South Africa* (London 1906); E. B. Iwan-Müller: *Lord Milner and South Africa* (London 1902), etc.

27. Examples of this are Cecil Headlam: *The Milner Papers* (London 1931–3, 2 vols.); E. Crankshaw: *The Forsaken Idea: A Study of Lord Milner* (London 1952); E. Wrench: *Lord Milner* (London 1958); Edgar Holt: *The Boer War* (London 1958).

28. W. T. Stead's *Methods of Barbarism* (London 1901) and J. A. Hobson's, *The War in South Africa* (London 1900) are good examples.

29. For example, see the article in *The Quarterly Review,* vol. 192, July and October, 1900: *Dr. Theal on South African History*. The writer rightly said that Theal's work was the basis on which "the modern school of writers upon South African History may be said to have been founded" and that in it "certain English writers and our Continental critics generally are able to find a justification of their undisguised sympathy with the course of the Dutch settlers in South Africa".

30. Iwan-Müller's opinion in *Lord Milner and South Africa*.

31. *Britain's Title in South Africa* (London 1901). Cappon launched a vehement attack on the Boers, referring to them as "half-barbarous pioneers". He endeavoured to correct Theal.

32. Iwan-Müller, *op. cit.* p.i.

33. W. J. Leyds: *De Eerste Annexatie van de Transvaal* (1906), p. 4.

34. C. Headlam: *The Milner Papers*, Vol. II, p. 243, memo Milner – B. Williams, 27.12.1900.

35. Objections were expressed to Gill's *Students Geography* and Russell's *Natal* (*De Volkstem*, 23.1.1912, p. 11; also to the Rev. J. Whiteside's *A New School History of South Africa* and Darter's *Geschiedenis voor Zuid-Afrika* (a translation). See pamphlet of F. Postma: *Zuid-Afrikaansche Geschiedenis op onze Scholen*, Potchefstroom, 1908. For

further details refer F. A. van Jaarsveld, *Teorie en Metodiek vir Geskiedenisonderrig* (pp. 102–107).

36. The book was reviewed favourably in leading articles in *The Cape Times*, 2.8.1918.

37. See my *The Afrikaner's Image of his Past* in this volume.

38. *Vide* F. A. van Jaarsveld: *Die Afrikaner en sy Geskiedenis* (1959), pp. 96–98 for a discussion of this book.

39. See the magazine's issue of March, 1878, pp. 140–142.

40. *Vide* Van Jaarsveld, *Teorie en Metodiek vir Geskiedenisonderrig* (1960), pp. 99–102.

41. On the subject of Odé see article by Dr. F. J. du T. Spies in *Historia*, March 1959, pp. 44–50: *G. A. Odé – Sy Bydrae tot ons Kennis van die Groot Trek*.

42. See, for example, *De Express:* 22.8.1887; 2.7.1889; 15.9.1891 for a defence of Theal; *De Volkstem*, 23.1.1912, letter of B. G. Brecher and Postma's pamphlet mentioned in footnote 35.

43. *De Volksstem*, 17.12.188, leading article.

44. See, for example, *De Volksstem*, 15.1.1885, containing a letter to the editor from members of the Afrikaner Bond: "As far as the whole history of the Afrikaners is concerned: (it is made up of) strife and suffering, always and everywhere occasioned by uncalled for intervention and malevolent mischief-making on England's part". In 1889 Piet Joubert reminded his people that their forebears had been "oppressed and driven from their country to seek freedom and a new fatherland" (*De Volksstem*, 21.11.1889. In *De Volksstem's* leading article of 6.6.1894 we read that: "In modern history there is practically no precedent for the systematic persecution of a small nation by so great and powerful a people: nor is there perhaps any precedent for the tough resistance and the unquenchable thirst for national self-determination, shown by the people of the S.A. Republic in the face of brutal displays of force and pressure on the part of the British Empire".

45. *Een Eeuw van Onrecht* was the work of Jacob de Villiers Roos except for the introduction and conclusion that were written by General J. C. Smuts. (See W. J. de Kock: *Jacob de Villiers Roos*, Cape Town, 1958).

46. Cf. Annemarie de Ru, *op. cit.*, (*vide* footnote 22).

47. The respective authors were General C. R. de Wet (Amsterdam – 18th edition 1903); General J. C. Kemp (Cape Town – 3rd edition 1946); E. Steenkamp n.d.

48. Van Jaarsveld, *Teorie en Metodiek*, pp. 102–105.

49. *De Volkstem*, 6.6.1903.

50. *De Volkstem*, 17.12.1904: report of speech of General de Wet; see too *Ons Taal*, 15.6.1908, p. 3.

51. For examples, see *De Volkstem*, 2.9.1903; 22.7.1903; *Ons Taal*, 15.6.1908; F. Postma's pamphlet (footnote 35); *De Volkstem*, 4.7.1911, report of a lecture delivered by Professor A. Moorrees. The complaints were directed at "unrealiable" and "twisted" facts, an "anti-Afrikaans spirit"; "mendacious presentation", "untruths and inaccuracies" and were supported by quotations from the text-books.

52. See my study of Leyds's work in this volume.

53. Preller, *Piet Retief* (7th ed. 1911), pp. 272–274, 278; Preller, *Dagboek van Louis Trichardt* (1917), introduction.

54. Preller, *Piet Retief*, p. 280.

55. Preller, *ibid.*, p. 274.

56. A report in *De Volkstem*, 4.7.1911 of a lecture delivered to the S.A. Academy for Language, Literature and Art.

57. See his introduction to the Louis Trichardt diary.

58. In 1912 he published: *De Stichter van Hollands Zuid-Afrika, Jan van Riebeeck (Amsterdam)*.

59. Professor at Cape Town University.                                      B

60. Author of the dissertation: *Die Rolle der Burenrepubliken, in der Auswärtigen und Kolonialen Politik des deutschen Reiches in den Jahren 1883–1900* (Nürnberg 1927).

61. Doctoral thesis: *De Ausdehnung der Kolonie am Kap der Guten Hoffnung, 1700–1779* (Berlin 1928).

62. E.g. by the Van Riebeeck Society.

63. *Précis of the Archives of the Cape of Good Hope* (16 vols. 1896–1906); on Leibbrandt's work as an archivist see J. F. Preller: *The Leibbrandt Appointment* in *S.A. Archival Journal*, 1959 No. 1, pp. 28–32.

64. His publications included *Basutoland Records* (3 vols., 1883) and *Records of the Cape Colony*, 1793–1831 (36 vols., 1897–1905).

65. E.g. *Kaapsche Archiefstukken* (1926–1935); *Kaapse Plakkaatboek* (1944–1951) – both published under the editorship of K. M. Jeffreys. A further series, *South African Archival Records*, includes the Resolutions of the Council of Policy at the Cape and the minutes of the Volksraads of Natal, Transvaal and the Orange Free State.

66. Includes *Historiese Studies* and *Historia*.

67. For an evaluation of the *Archives Year Book* series see the article by Professor W. P. Coolhaas entitled *Het Argiefjaarboek vir Suid-Afrikaanse Geskiedenis en zijn Betekenis voor de historische Wetenschap* in the monthly publication *Zuid-Afrika*, Feb. 1959, p. 20.

68. See the catalogues of theses and dissertations accepted by South Africa universities compiled, respectively, by H. M. L. Robinson (Cape Town 1943) for the period 1918–1941 and by S. I. Malan (Potchefstroom 1959) for the period 1942–1958.

    A particularly useful series of articles that will facilitate the work of future research workers and headed *Suid-Afrikaanse Kroniek* has been published regularly in *Bijdragen voor de Geschiedenis der Nederlanden* since 1949.

69. See his *Die Britse Owerheid en die Groot Trek* (Cape Town 1948).

70. For a discussion of Professor Thom's work refer to the essay on *Biographies of Voortrekker Leaders* in this publication.

71. Leo Fouché: *Die Evolutie van die Trekboer* (Pretoria 1909).

72. Leo Fouché: *Het Dagboek van Adam Tas, 1705–1706* (London 1914).

73. *Die Trekboer in die Geskiedenis van die Kaap-Kolonie*, 1657–1842 (Cape Town, 1938): *Die Noordwaartse Beweging van die Boere voor die Groot Trek*, 1770–1842 (The Hague, 1937).

74. By Dr. C. Beyers in *Geskiedenis van Suid-Afrika* Vol. I ed. Van der Walt, Wiid and Geyer), 2nd ed. pp. 183–184.

75. A. E. du Toit: *The Cape Frontier, a Study of Native Policy with Special Reference to the Years 1847–1866* (Archives Year Book 1954, Part I); W. J. de Kock: *Ekstra-Territoriale Vraagstukke van die Kaapse Regering 1872–1885* (*Archives Year Book* 1948, Part I, etc.)

76. E.g. A. J. du Plessis: *Die Republiek Natalia* (*Archives Year Book* 1942, Part I).

77. A. N. Pelzer: *Geskiedenis van die Suid-Afrikaanse Republiek*, Vol. 1 *Wordingsjare* (Cape Town 1950). There is a wealth of published material on this subject – see lists of publications in *Archives Year Book* and footnote 68.
78. E.g. J. H. Malan: *Die Opkoms van 'n Republiek* (Bloemfontein, 1929).
79. For example, J. J. G. Grobbelaar: *Die Vrystaatse Republiek en die Basoetovraagstuk* (*Archives Year Book* 1939, Part II).
80. D. W. Krüger: *Die Weg na die See* (Archives Year Book 1938, Part I); F. A. van Jaarsveld, *Die Eenheidstrewe van die Republikeinse Afrikaners*, Part I (Johannesburg 1951).
81. Examples are P. R. Botha: *Die Staatkundige Ontwikkeling van die S.A. Republiek onder Kruger en Leyds*, 1844–1899 (Amsterdam 1926) and J. S. du Plessis: *Die Ontstaan en Ontwikkeling van die Amp van Staatspresident in die Z.A. Republiek* (*Archives Year Book* 1955 Part I).
82. S. P. Engelbrecht: *Geschiedenis van die Nederduits Hervormde Kerk in Zuid-Afrika* (1922); A. Moorrees: *Die Nederduitse Gereformeerde Kerk in Suid-Afrika 1652–1873* (Cape Town 1937); G. D. Scholtz: *Geskiedenis van die Ned. Herv. of Geref. Kerk van Transvaal* (Cape Town 1956–60, 2 vols.). The ecclesiastical historians are divided into various "schools", a matter that cannot be dealt with in this study.
83. A. H. Lugtenburg: *Geskiedenis van die Onderwys in die S.A. Republiek 1836–1900* (Pretoria, 1925); J. Ploeger: *Onderwys en Onderwysbeleid in die S.A.R. . . . 1881–1900* (*Archives Year Book*, 1952, Part I, etc.).
84. Including D. J. Kotze: *De Eerste Amerikaanse Sendeling onder die Matabele* (*Archives Year Book* 1950, I).
85. The following were published, among others, in the *Archives Year Book*: J. B. de Vaal: *Die Rol van João Albasini in die Geskiedenis van die Transvaal* (1953, I): J. A. Mouton: *Genl. Joubert in die Geskiedenis van Transvaal* (1957, I).
86. D. B. Bosman: *Oor die Ontstaan van Afrikaans* (Amsterdam 1923); G. S. en P. J. Nienaber: *Die Geskiedenis van die Afrikaanse Beweging* (Pretoria, 1941); G. Dekker: *Afrikaanse Literatuurgeskiedenis* (Cape Town 1947, 4th ed.); Rob Antonissen: *Die Afrikaanse Letterkunde van die Aanvang tot Hede* (Pretoria 1956), etc.
87. For examples see D. J. Coetzee: *Spoorweg-ontwikkeling in die S.A. Republiek 1872–1899* (Cape Town 1940; H. B. Thom: *Die Geskiedenis van die Skaapboerdery in Suid-Afrika* (Amsterdam 1936).
88. J. H. Breytenbach: *Die Tweede Vryheidsoorlog*, Vol. II (Cape Town 1949).
89. G. D. Scholtz: *Die Oorsake van die Tweede Vryheidsoorlog* (Johannesburg, 1948–50, 2 vols.), J. S. Marais: *The Fall of Kruger's Republic* (London 1961).
90. J. H. Breytenbach: *Die Tweede Vryheidsoorlog*, Vol. I: *Voorspel tot die Stryd* (Cape Town 1948).
91. J. C. Otto: *Die Konsentrasiekampe* (Cape Town, 1954).
92. E.g. publication in the *Archives Year Book*: F. Vermooten: *Transvaal en die Totstandkoming van die Unie van Suid-Afrika* (1957, II) and B. Spoelstra: *Die Bewindsaanvaarding van die Botharegering oor Transvaal . . . 1907* (1953, II).
93. C. M. van der Heever: *Generaal J. B. M. Hertzog* (Johannesburg, 1944); N. J. van der Merwe: *M. T. Steyn* (Cape Town, 1921, 2 vols.).

94. See also Prof. Krüger's *Parties and Policies in South Africa* (Cape Town, 1960).
95. See footnote 67.
96. *Vide Dagboek van Louis Trichardt (1917)*, introduction.
97. *Archives Year Book* 1938, Part I, p. 34.
98. *Die Stellenbosche Oudstudent*, Vol. XII, April 1943, No. 1, pp. 9 and 18 (*Die Huidige Staat van Historiese Navorsing in Suid-Afrika*).
99. *De Volkstem*, 4.7.1911 (see footnote 51).
100. Cf. Van der Walt, Wiid and Geyer: *Geskiedenis van Suid-Afrika* and the Transvaal High School curriculum for Standerds IX and X.
101. See his *Die Sendeling Alexander Merensky* . . . in the *Archives Year Book* 1954, Part II, p. 99.
102. E.g. Van Biljon: *Grensbakens tussen Blank en Swart in Suid-Afrika*. (Cape Town, 1948).
103. E.g. A. E. du Toit, *op. cit.* (footnote 75).
104. *Vide* footnote 87.
105. Contributions such as Professor Abel Coetzee's *Die Opkoms van die Afrikaanse Kultuurgedagte aan die Rand 1886–1936* (Johannesburg, 1938) and Professor T. N. Hanekom's *Die Liberale Rigting in Suid-Afrika*, Vol. I (Stellenbosch, 1951) point the way.
106. A. N. Pelzer, *op. cit.;* see also M. M. Marais: *Armesorg aan die Kaap onder die Kompanjie, 1652–1795 (Archives Year Book* 1943).
107. About two-thirds of the publications in the *Archives Year Book* are in Afrikaans. Most of the published theses in English are of recent date; outstanding examples of the latter in the *Archives Year Book* are: J. F. Midgley: *The Orange River Sovereignty* (1949 II); A. M. Davey: *The Siege of Pretoria 1880–1881* (1956 I); N. G. Garson: *The Swaziland Question* (1957 II) and B. A. le Cordeur: *Robert Godlonton as Architect of Frontier Opinion 1850–1857* (1959 II).
108. The catalogues mentioned in footnote 68 include particulars of a large number of unpublished theses in English.
109. E. A. Walker: *The Place of History in University Education* (pamphlet 1918).
110. This book contains more "native policy" than "history"; Professor Brookes also wrote *The Colour Problems of South Africa* (Lovedale 1933).
111. *The Cape Colour Question*, pp. 10–11.
112. *Bantu, Boer and Briton* (1929, p. 5).
113. *The Cape Colour Question*, pp. 247–8.
114. *Vide* Julius Lewin: *Dr. John Philip* and *Liberalism* in *Race Relations Journal* Vol. XXVI, No. 2, April–June 1960.
114a. In 1961 prof. Marais published an excellent book on *The Fall of Kruger's Republic* (Oxford University Press). Cf. my review of it in *Historia*, March 1962, p. 65–67.
115. See his *Imperial Factor*, pp. 1 and 2.
116. G. B. Pyrah: *Imperial Policy and South Africa, 1902–1910* (Oxford, 1955); *The Cambridge History of the British Empire*, Vol. VIII *South Africa* (1936); R. M. Dawson: *The Development of Dominion Status* (London, 1937); H. E. Egerton: *A Short History of British Colonial Policy* (London, 1932 9th ed.); Paul Knaplund: *The British Empire*, (London, 1942), etc.
117. Reviewed in *The Cape Times*, 9.10.1941.
118. *The Cape Times*, 6.1.1928, leading article: *A Great Achievement*.
    Several historical surveys exist that are of an informative character

e.g. Leo Marquard: *The Story of South Africa* (London, 1955) and J. H. Hofmeyr: *South Africa* (London, 1931).

119. G. M. Theal: *Ethnography and Conditions of South Africa before A.D. 1505* (London, 1919); M. Martin: *Basutoland, its Legends and Customs* (London, 1903); G. W. Stow: *The Native Races of South Africa* (London, 1905); I. Schapera: *The Khoisan People of South Africa* (London, 1930).

120. J. M. Orpen: *History of the Basuto of South Africa* (Cape Town, 1857); D. F. Ellenberg and C. J. MacGregor: *History of the Basuto* (London, 1912); G. Tylden: *The Rise of the Basuto* (Cape Town, 1950); H. Ashton: *The Basuto* (1952).

121. A. T. Bryant: *Olden Times in Zululand* (London, 1929); J. Y. Gibson: *The Story of the Zulus* (London, 1911); E. A. Ritter: *Shaka Zulu The Rise of the Xulu Empire* (London, 1955).

122. *Vide* A. J. H. Goodwin (ed.): *A Commentary on the History and Present Position of South African Prehistory with full Bibliography* (1935).

123. A. J. H. Goodwin: *The Loom of Prehistory. A Commentary and a Select Bibliography of the Prehistory of Southern Africa* (Cape Town, 1946).

124. Published in *Annals of the South African Museum*, Vol. XXVII (1929); see also Vol. 8.

125. *Europe's Discovery of South Africa* (1935); *South Africa under King Manuel (1495–1521)* (1946); *South Africa under King Sebastian and the Cardinal 1557–1580* (1949); *Portuguese Rule and Spanish Crown in South Africa 1581–1640* (1950); *Portuguese and Dutch in South Africa 1641–1806* (1951) – all published in Cape Town.

126. *The Portuguese in South-East Africa 1600–1700* (Johannesburg, 1960).

127. See *Portugese Ontdekkers om die Kaap* (1957).

128. *Golden Republic* 1955) and *Storm over the Transvaal* (Cape Town, 1955).

129. *More Annals of Natal* (1936); *Later Annals of Natal* (1938) etc.

130. These include: P. M. Laurence: *The Life and Times of John X. Merriman* (London, 1930); I. D. Colvin: *The Life of Jameson* (London, 1922); S. G. Millin: *Rhodes* (London 1933) and *General Smuts* London, 1936, 2 vols.); E. A. Walker: *Lord de Villiers and his Times* (London, 1925), etc.

131. *Vide* W. Drascher: *Schuld der Weissen? Die Spätzeit des Kolonialismus* (Tübingen, 1960).

132. *The Rand Daily Mail*, 15.2.1961; *Die Transvaler*, 16.2.1961.

133. Including G. Allighan: *Verwoerd – The End* (1961); A. Keppel-Jones: *When Smuts Goes. A History of South Africa from 1952 to 2010* (Cape Town, 1947); Jan Toekoms: *When Malan Goes* (C.N.A., 1953).

134. E.g. E. Brookes: *South Africa in a changing World* (Oxford, 1953).

135. Written by H. Gibbs (London, 1954).

136. H. Gibbs (London, 1953).

137. C. W. de Kiewiet (London, 1956).

138. Alan Paton (London, 1958).

139. Jan Toekoms (C.N.A., 1958).

140. *Race Relations Journal*, Vol. XXVI, No. 1, Jan.–March 1959, pp. 18–30.

141. Oxford, 1960. See my review of this book in *Die Transvaler*, 27.5.1960.

142. L. M. Thompson: *Fifty Years of Union* in *Race Relations Journal,* Vol. XXXII, No. 2, April–June 1960, pp. 59–69.

143. See, for example, A. C. Martin: *History of our Schools, Mutual Respect or Antagonism* (Durban, 1953) and also my *The Afrikaner's Image of his Past* in this volume in which this dispute is referred to.

143a. Cf. my article in *Historia,* September 1962, p. 147–163: *Probleme by die Skrywe van Skoolgeskiedenisboeke.*

144. Cape Town, 1956.

145. E.g. H. E. Hockley: *The Story of the British Settlers* (Cape Town, 1948).

146. Cape Town, 1957.

147. Cape Town, 1954.

148. *Die Transvaler,* 16.3.1960, report of a lecture delivered at symposium in Cape Town.

149. The book was published in 1962, followed by a new book in the same year, *Die Republiek van Suid-Afrika en die Nuwe Wêreld* (Johannesburg).

150. Johannesburg, 1954, p. 70 *et seq.*

151. *Tydskrif vir Rasse-aangeleenthede,* July 1958, No. 4, pp. 143–168; *Die Ontstaan en Wese van die Suid-Afrikaanse Rasse-patroon; Het Rassenvraagstuk in Zuid-Afrika* (Brochure 1950: State Information Office).

152. *Die Transvaler,* 16–20 Feb. 1960: *Die Blanke Man in Afrika* (Series of five articles).

153. See Professor G. Cronjé: *'n Tuiste vir die Nageslag* (1945); *Afrika Sonder die Asiaat* (Johannesburg, 1946); *Regverdige Rasse-apartheid* (Stellenbosch, 1947); *Voogdyskap en Apartheid* (Pretoria, 1948); N. J. Rhoodie and H. J. Venter: *Die Apartheidsgedagte: 'n Sosio-historiese Uiteensetting van sy Ontstaan en Ontwikkeling* (Cape Town, 1960).

154. E.g. Professor A. B. du Preez: *Eiesoortige Ontwikkeling tot Volksdiens* (Cape Town, 1959).

155. *The Bantu World,* 18.10.1952, address delivered by Dr. W. F. Nkomo.

156. *The Bantu World,* 15.4.1952.

157. *The Bantu World,* 20.12.1952.

158. *The Bantu World,* 18.10.1952.

159. *The Bantu World,* 13.12.1952.

160. *The Bantu World,* 3.1.1953.

161. *The Bantu World,* 21.3.1953.

162. Quoted in *The Star,* 22.9.1959.

163. Melanchton publishers, 1952.

164. *The Bantu World,* 11.10.1952 and 18.10.1952: *A Historic Parallel and Warning.*

165. Johannesburg, 1952.

166. Cape Town, 1952.

167. Mnguni, *A History of South Africa,* p. 81.

168. Circular letter to the electorate, Pretoria, 20.9.1960.

169. *Die Transvaler,* 3.10.1960, address at Bloemfontein during the Union Festival.

170. *Die Transvaler,* 28.3.60, address at Meyerton.

171. Leading article in *Die Transvaler,* 31.12.1961.

172. See too the assessment of the situation in *Round Table,* Dec. 1960, p. 86.

173. An example is M. Roberts and A. E. G. Trollip: *The South African*

*Opposition 1939–1945, An Essay in Contemporary History* (London, 1947).

174. Professor E. A. Walker arrived at certain conclusions on the South African frontier that were independent of American influences; see his *The Frontier Tradition in South Africa* (Oxford, 1930). S. D. Neumark's *Economic Influences on the South African Frontier 1652–1836* appeared in 1957 but there have been no comparative studies. Subsequent to the preparation of this study W. B. Campbell's *The South African Frontier 1865–1885. A Study in Expansion* was published in the *Archives Year Book* (1959, I).

# ON OBJECTIVITY, SUBJECTIVITY, AND RELATIVITY IN THE WRITING OF HISTORY

## I

In the realisation of historical knowledge, just as in the case of Natural Science, there is interaction between the subject (investigator) and the object (a past reality or a natural phenomenon). Without the activity of the subject, no knowledge can come into being. The question is: what share has the subject in the creation of knowledge? If the *knowledge* is completely congruent with the *reality* it represents, i.e. independent of the subject, it is called objective. In this sense we refer to the *objectivity* of knowledge. If, on the other hand, the knowledge is not completely independent of the subject, i.e. if the investigator, as it were, leaves an imprint of himself on the knowledge, then it is subjective and in this sense we talk of *subjectivity* of knowledge.

In the case of the scientist who places his object in a laboratory test-tube and observes it there, the relativity of the subject can be completely eliminated by the experimental method. The object can be observed accurately and to the best advantage and general and essential knowledge is achieved that is in complete agreement with the reality of the natural phenomenon. The subject in this case is a medium, and is completely unconnected with the resulting knowledge. This type of scientific knowledge can therefore be completely objective.

Historical Science presents a different picture. In order to be able to discuss the possibility of objective knowledge, we should first examine the nature of the object and subject and then discuss their relationship with each other.

As to the *object,* we know that the past is not completely expressed in documents, and this makes a complete knowledge of historical events an impossibility. Secondly, our access to the past is indirect: the document is our key to the past. The past cannot be placed in a test-tube and repeat its course so that we can observe it directly. The realisation of historical knowledge depends upon the quantity and quality of the available documents. The intellectual life of the past is expressed in the document. The content of the document is coloured by the emotions, desires, partiality and prejudice of those who compiled it. It expresses certain values, objectives, ideals and conceptions of a nation, church or party. These are facets of mental activity that reflect the past.

As for the *subject*, this is always a person, i.e. a spiritual being having the same defects as the object of Historical Science. These weaknessess consist in the fact that he is limited by his own personality, aptitude, character and qualities. He may be inclined to falsify, to seek sensation, to lie or to be careless, so that we may say that he is bound by the limits of his own personality. In the second place the subject is restricted by his social environment, i.e. his community, nation, church or political party. He aspires to certain values, has certain ideals or a preference for the point of view of his own people. In this sense he is group-bound. In the third place the subject is fettered to the time in which he lives. Unconsciously he is imbued with the views of his time. He is born into a particular spiritual climate and way of thinking, which we call *a philosophy of life* or world-view. This influences his attitude towards the reality within which he moves or with which he comes into contact. In this sense he is time-bound.

Thus we see that object and subject are linked by a common medium – the human mind. The object is not purely material as in the case of Natural Science. In the realm of Historical Science we have, as it were, one mind penetrating another. The process of achieving knowledge is also totally different. In Natural Science the object is observed in a test-tube *outside* the subject: in Historical Science the subject enters *into* the object, i.e. loses itself in the object. Object and subject become one, yet they must at the same time be separate if knowledge is to be attained. Through this fusion the past is mentally resurrected: the past takes on form by virtue of the fact that the subject *re-lives* it; it is re-awakened, and comes to life once more in a "second now". It is "observed" by the subject who describes it and transforms it into ideas. The *image* of it that exists in the mind of the subject is conveyed to our minds. This image is not explained but *understood*. Natural Science explains its phenomena in terms of *laws*. Once the law has been formulated the phenomenon has been explained and the problem it posed has been solved. Historical Science understands its object by reliving it. This mental activity is called the *interpretation* or the explanation of the meaning of historical phenomena.

There is obviously a possibility since the relation between subject and object is a relation between mind and mind, that the mind of the subject may fuse so completely with that of the object as to make it almost impossible to distinguish them. The subject may be prompted by his personal inclination to make a deliberately partial selection of documents or to transmit his own prejudice, carelessness and misrepresentation to the object. The fact that he is group-bound may cause him to identify his own concepts of value, his ideals and aspirations with corresponding values of the past. The fact that he is time-bound may cause him to use his own philosophy of life as a criterion for the evaluation of past events, without being conscious that he is doing it. Thus the historian's person, group or time may pervade the object. Naturally the complete truth about the past cannot be reached. The sort of synthesis that is achieved is neither purely objective, i.e. in agreement with reality, nor purely subjective, i.e. in agreement with the subject. The resulting knowledge, therefore, stems from both subject and object.

Is truly objective historical knowledge possible? We would be very pessimistic indeed if we were to answer that it is not. On the other hand, we should not be over-optimistic. Despite our most earnest attempts at achieving objectivity, historical knowledge, because of the nature of both object and subject, cannot be absolutely objective. To be able to express an opinion on objectivity we must first explain the various degrees of subjectivity that exist.

In the first place we have *avoidable* subjectivity. When a historian approaches the past encumbered with a preconceived objective or party bias, he may be expected to select his documents to suit his point of view or his cause, in which case the resulting knowledge will be one-sided, false and subjective. He deliberately enslaves the past to his cause, i.e. he enlists it to promote his own interest or the interest of his group. His emotions come into play and his attitude is partisan. He finds in the past what he wishes to find there for the promotion of his own ideals. He represents the past as he thinks it should have been and not as it really was. His representation of historical reality cannot therefore be "true". We call this form of subjectivity avoidable, because it can be eliminated by strict self-discipline and the will to seek the truth.

Secondly we have *unavoidable* subjectivity or the subjectivity that is inherently characteristic of the human being and that cannot be eliminated completely. Whereas the subject or historian is able, to free himself from his personal and group ties by exercising strict self-discipline, it is virtually impossible for him to free himself from the influence of his time or from his adherence to a particular philosophy of life. A philosophy of life implies a particular point of view or position from which phenomena are observed and because of which they assume a certain colour and are interpreted in a certain way. Elements of a philosophy of life *unconsciously* pervade historical knowledge. This pervasion is not therefore always to the discredit of the historian. Relations or connected systems are involuntarily assessed in the light of the spiritual climate in which the subject finds himself at a specific moment. Because contemporaries move in the same medium, they remain unaware of it. Posterity is able to discover the defects as a result of the distance that separates it from the original work. In the light of a new philosophy of life or changed spiritual climate incongruities in the original work are easily perceptible. Distance lends perspective and makes one aware of the limitations of historical knowledge. The fact that the historical interest of the Afrikaner has centred on the Great Trek and Anglo-Boer War, illustrates what I mean.

In conclusion: No one can give an obsolutely objective account of historical reality. What then should be the historian's aim when he approaches the past, and what are the conditions with which he should comply to attain the highest degree of objectivity? In the first place he should show a sense of responsibility – towards the past as well as towards his own time. He should examine himself before he becomes involved with the past and should try to eliminate any element that might contribute towards the distortion and misrepresentation of past reality, i.e. he should be determined to reproduce the truth and no more or less than the truth. He should present the truth about the past as he finds it and not as he believes it ought to have been. He should be prepared at all times to subject his conclusions and judgments to the test of the indubitable facts of reality, i.e. he should aim at achieving critical insight into the past. That is his most important task. By showing respect both for the past and for his own time, he can minimise his personal and group limitations. The truth of the facts that he relates therefore depends largely upon his own integrity.

The historian should be made aware of the limitations imposed upon him by the fact that he is time-bound, and should try to see both his subject and himself in perspective. He should see the past, with which he has become familiar, from a new angle. Moreover, he should bear in mind that the values and criteria of the past differ from those of his own time. Contemporary criteria of values should not be applied therefore to the assessment or judgment of the values of the past. A false criterion gives rise to an unreliable image of the past. It is inevitable that the past should be approached from particular points of view. It is permissible for a historian to take a personal point of view provided that he is able to justify it scientifically in all circumstances. Man's mental faculties are limited and these limitations restrict his knowledge of historical reality. The nature of knowledge of the past is such that it can never be represented with absolute objectivity. Man can only strive for objectivity and truth, which although unattainable, can yet be approached.

2

We have seen that Natural Science establishes general and essential knowledge that everywhere and always, irrespective of place and time, serves as a valid explanation of natural phenomena. This knowledge is absolutely objective and disassociated from the subject that produces it. In Historical Science the knowledge of historical phenomena is dependent upon the subject, to a certain extent, who is bound to time and place. The knowledge that it tries to realise is unique and is non-recurrent. Whereas the knowledge of Natural Science is absolute, historical knowledge is *relative* and moreover dependent on perspective. This means, for example, that knowledge of a phenomenon that was valid a hundred years ago may not be valid today, or that the historical picture that is "true" for an Afrikaans-speaking South African, may not be true for an English-speaking South African. What is the basis of this relativity of historical knowledge?

The relativity is connected with the manner in which historical knowledge is acquired. If Historiography consisted in the compiling of dates or the drawing up of chronicles, absolutely objective knowledge would be possible. These, in fact, are *all* that *can* be presented objectively. History, however, embraces more than chronicles, facts and dates. To illustrate: It is an absolute and objective truth that war broke out between Britain and the Transvaal Republic on 11th October 1899; but the historian is not interested in this isolated fact. He wants to "understand" the war. The fact and the date tell him nothing. To understand the war, he must connect this isolated fact with the events that preceded and followed it. It is this that gives it meaning, and this is of primary importance to the historian. His object is to explain and interpret the war. To be able to do this, he must discover a significant sequence of events. This leads him to consider motives and causes, and thus to arrive at an image of the whole which is meaningful and intelligible. To interpret means to determine the connection. Without this there can be no reconstruction of the event. In evaluating an event, the historian forms an image of it. This image is a product of the mind.

The image is built up from description and interpretation, i.e. narration and evaluation. The basic facts remain unchanged but their interpretation is liable to change. The realisation of a historical image depends upon two things: the *available material* and the problem as posed. A historian writing immediately after the War about its causes, course and results, is limited in his interpretation by the amount of material available. Official documents are released by the archives only about fifty years after an event. It is obvious that if more material becomes available, a new presentation of the War will differ from the image of it that was formed immediately after its conclusion. The new presentation will be more complete, more exhaustive and more detailed. It will supersede the old image, which will no longer be valid.

With regard to the *problem posed* to the past, this tends to differ in the course of time. Fifty years after an event, people may have achieved a higher standard of development, and a shift of interest may have taken place. They may be faced with new social and political problems that condition their own questions on the past. Every period poses its own kinds of problems and the answer is also dependent upon the spiritual climate of the period. A historian writing immediately after the War may interpret it from a nationalistic point of view as an "injustice" inflicted with "fraud and cruelty" upon the Afrikaner, with the purpose of "exterminating and destroying" him. Another historian of the same period may see it as a necessary war that had to be waged in order to overcome "backwardness and suppression" with a view to establishing a united South Africa. After fifty years the same Afrikaans historian may see the war as a blessing in disguise and as a victory for nationalism. A second historian may possibly see it in the light of international politics and give a rational explanation of the causes. The War can also be approached from various other points of view, e.g. the economic, the national, the imperial, etc. each of which will give rise to an individual portrayal of events.

As time passes, the points of view from which the past is seen are apt to change, so that the perspective is altered. Being aware of the results of an event makes it possible to see the event against a wider background, across a longer period of time and in a larger frame. Judgments are therefore influenced by life itself, by existing ideas and by the prevailing philosophy of life. The image of the Reformation presented by modern historians differs completely from that presented by writers who lived during that period.

This means that even though the documents remain the same, they do not represent an immutable entity. They contain various aspects of reality and provide new answers to new questions. The object of History is therefore not a static reality, but one which changes as new documents are discovered or new problems develop.

Since the subject, too, changes in the course of time, it is obvious that historical knowledge can never be absolute and general. It changes as a result of changed points of view and situations. The historical picture is constantly being filled in, new touches are added and new perspectives develop. Every generation revises and rewrites History. As early as the 19th century Goethe and Ranke remarked that World History should be rewritten periodically and Croce asserted that all true History was the History of the present. By that he meant that historical knowledge provides an answer to the problems that arise as time goes on. This does not mean, however, that everyone is his own historian as some Americans have maintained. We have seen that there are certain norms to which Historical Science should conform. What is undoubtedly true, however, is Huizinga's conclusion that History is the form in which a culture considers its past.

Of its very nature, historical knowledge is preliminary and open to supplementation and correction. No historical picture is finally completed. This implies that a historian can also write the History of Historiography, i.e. can present a picture of how changing times have influenced the way in which the past has been viewed at various stages in the course of history. Today it is possible to write a History of the Historiography of the Great Trek. From all this we may infer that historical truth has many facets. The more aspects our research and interpretation elucidate in the course of time, the more nearly we approximate to the truth. Since the knowledge of the past is to a certain extent affected by one's philosophy of life, by personal points of view and by the fact that we are place-bound, it cannot be determined finally but is incomplete and represents, to use an expression of Prof. P. Geyl, "a never-ending discussion". Since this incompleteness is of a piece with human imperfection, the limitations of historical knowledge need not make us sceptics.

# THE PURPOSE AND SIGNIFICANCE OF
# THE TEACHING OF HISTORY

History the subject deals with men and of all school subjects it is perhaps the closest to life – its content is, after all, the being, the thoughts and the deeds of men who under certain conditions have lived in societies, and have struggled for survival and a place in the world.[1] This past life is made accessible to us in history books which are based on documents. But it is a heritage that has to be won. By re-living and living into the past in our imagination, and by understanding it with our intellect, we can reconstruct it in our mind's eye. We project ourselves into the past and interpret its reality to our pupils, who accompany us on our trip into the realm of what has been. Here, then, the "method" of initiation and transmission comes into play. The main purpose of "method" is to bring the pupils into contact with the "life" of the past, with its evolution and its patterns, and to get them to apprehend it clearly and to comprehend it critically. To what purpose?

It is only if we are clear about our objectives that we can speak of method. And objectives can be debated if the meaning or content of history has been grasped. Is it real, is it something remote or near, is it living or dead? Where does it exist, and how? Here we enter the field of theory, without an understanding of which history cannot be taught with confidence and sympathy. A subject cannot have meaning if its content is not understood. And if history has no meaning for the teacher, i.e. if he is not aware of its value or has no sense of history himself, how can it make sense to the pupils, to whom he has to transmit it?

It is not the purpose of this lecture to deal with questions on the nature of history. Yet, in discussing the meaning of history, I shall occasionally also touch upon its nature or content. To begin with, just this: he who thinks of "history", must remember that a duality is in fact involved: (1) a past reality, which actually was but no longer is, and can never be again, except in our imagina-

---

1. This lecture was written in 1956 (Cf. *Onderwysblad*, January and February 1956).

tion; and (2) the record of that reality, accessible to us in book or narrative, which can never be the reality itself, but only its reflection, or our own conception or representation of it. It is this "narrative" we make use of in school, but that is only one of four meanings of the term history which is of consequence for our teaching.

Under history as past actuality we can distinguish three other meanings: (1) past history *per se,* which can extend back thousands of years and by reason of its remoteness does not affect our lives so intimately; (2) a still-living history, i.e. such of the remote past as is not dead but survives in us (i.e. the Reformation or the Great Trek), and which stands much closer to us than the above-named; and (3) the recent past, i.e. history experienced by the generation now living or by us personally, and which may be regarded as the outcome of the two former. Our experience and participation in contemporary national or world history enables those of us who "transmit" history to draw analogies with the recent past and thence gain an insight into the remote past which can only benefit our pupils.

In discussing the meaning or significance of history as a school subject, we shall retain this threefold distinction: (1) man in past history *per se;* (2) contemporary man in relation to the still-living past; and (3) contemporary man facing the future.

I

We start with this first aspect. The infinite diversity of human existence in time and space can gratify our intellectual curiosity and we have the insatiable thirst for knowledge which distinguishes us from the lower forms of life. By virtue of the essential sameness of human nature through the ages, the bygone life of peoples such as the Egyptians, Greeks or Romans in the matter of customs, institutions, conflicts and the circumstances under which they occurred, struggles against adversity and calamities, their successes, failures, achievements, etc., can be understood. Knowledge of other peoples and civilizations, however remote they may be in time, affords insight into our own human existence, as well as an understanding of the eternally human. It enables us to appreciate and to assess our own circumstances better and more intelligently, and affords a basis of comparison, without which the things with which we are familiar cannot be clearly and objectively apprehended. In this way the mental horizon is widened and the faculty of observation sharpened.

174

Then there is also the intellectual pleasure to be derived from reading about the comings and goings, the foibles and follies, the trials and the errors of mankind, of its victories and defeats, its twists and turns. Because these things are locked in the distant past, only the imagination can open the door to them. You learn to "forget" the present for the time being, and to "transport" yourself into the unknown; and so the imagination is exercised, which in turn leads to the development of a historical sense – by which I mean viewing persons and phenomena in history in the setting of their aged and the unique circumstances of their existence or occurrence, i.e. viewing the past from within and with due consideration for its moral criteria, ideals and conceptions. It includes the urge to understand the past, instead of judging it off-hand, according to the criteria of the present, the vantage-point of the observer. A historical sense implies also a critical reflection upon and lively curiosity about the things of the past, instead of a mere memorizing of "dry" facts. It implies appreciation and understanding of life in history. Understanding in turn implies toleration towards those who thought differently in the past from the group to which the observer belongs; and toleration towards people in the past fosters a spirit of understanding and toleration towards opponents in the present. But that does not necessarily imply an acceptance of their views, just as it does not necessarily include an exoneration of the deeds of men in the past, for they have to be studied critically as well as sympathetically.

History teaches us not to sit in judgment on persons or causes before the facts and circumstances are fully known and understood. That does not exclude passing judgment on their failures or a moral actions on the ground of what they themselves could have known, nor does it mean that we relieve them of all responsibility. What does, of course, make it easier for us to judge is the fact that we are acquainted with the outcome of a particular event or train of events, whereas the person involved in it was perhaps, because of his lack of foresight, unable to take the right step in what, to him, was an unfamiliar situation. The historian must guard against the danger of being wise after the event.

This leads up to the ethical or educational significance which history can have. History brings us into contact with great personalities, men such as Socrates or Bismarck or Luther. In our everyday lives there is nothing more ennobling or inspiring, or more important in moulding character and personality, than the association with "noble" or "virtuous" men. The desire to emulate great men is a strong incentive. But such men are not to be found every day; only in history, which is our common possession, do we encounter people whose decisions affected the destinies of a nation or of mankind. It is they who acquire the stature of heroes. Their lives are usually distinguished by strength of character, perspicacity, prompt and decisive action, and keenness of judgment. By its very nature history cannot speak to us save through the mediation of persons who are "alien" to us. Since every person has an urge to shape and to develop his personality, the contact with the great men of the past can have a formative influence on his character, setting an example worthy of emulation, which can enrich and strengthen his personality and free him from his own environment. No-one can remain unmoved when brought face to face with the truly great, or can fail to experience pleasure or to show admiration.

Finally, we wish to know, not only what has been, but also how it came to be: how things originated, how each stage arose from the one before it and issued in the next, and how the chain of cause and effect is linked together. This applies to the history of mankind as a whole and as one whole. For example, how it has come to be that there is to-day one world and one great family of man, only the history of mankind as a whole can reveal. We can look back over a period of 6,000 years and trace the course of civilization, its progress and continuity and evolution. It is this history of civilization, extending over thousands of years, which forms the "backdrop" for the present, and which fills us with humility when we reflect on our place in it. There are so many instances of struggle, perhaps similar to ours, for the attainment of liberties to which we do not give a second thought today.

In and by means of history we learn to apprehend the realities of human existence. Though the origin and the ultimate purpose of history are hidden from us, yet written history can reveal the direction in which events are moving. Although the ultimate meaning of the great human pageant through time is known only to God, there remains for us the enigma and the privilege of seeking understanding. And even if the results of our quest for understanding lie strewn like wrecks on the highway of the centuries, they still contain broken rays of light which reflect in the direction of the truth. Acquaintance with the human drama in its slow upward surge leads us in the end to the mystery of human existence, to the more-than-human, the Transcendent, so that we can speak with Chesterton of "the divine story, which is also a human story".

The second aspect deals with the meaning of the past in its relation to the present in which we live. (i) We consider first "general" history. The fundamental difference between man and other living creatures is that man alone is able to escape from himself and to view himself and his environment from a distance, i.e. escape from its immediacy and become in his imagination part of a wider "environment" or "climate" which transcends his own and admits him to a wider world in time and space. If he can thus escape from himself, he begins to reflect on the origin of things – even the most simple, such as why there are 60 minutes to the hour – and only then does he begin to realize his dependence on the world of history. Then he sees that everything that has come to be, has roots in the distant past, and tenuous links stretching back into the mists of time.

General history can have the further significance that it throws light on the problems confronting man in the world. There is no present situation of which the roots cannot be found in history; this makes the complicated present more comprehensible. The elucidation of a problem affords background and perspective. It is the conscious apprehension of his present which distinguishes civilized from uncivilized men. A clear apprehension of the present is impossible without a thorough knowledge of the past. It orientates man in the world and explains his place in it. It yields perspective, distance and discernment. You learn to realize that the varying fortunes of your own country in the past or the present are not the result of domestic issues only, but are always determined too by extraneous forces and developments.

Then you come to see your own people's and your nation's existence in its proper perspective, belonging to a community of nations and a particular cultural sphere. And a knowledge of history becomes a means of safeguarding a nation from spiritual isolation. Complacency and "pride" in national "greatness" or achievements fall away, and the realization emerges that only by creating spiritual values can a nation give evidence of its spiritual richness and a progressive stage of development.

Familiarity with the history of other peoples prevents the spiritual life of a particular nation from flowing along narrow channels, and makes the knowing individual receptive to influences which, in synthesis with the indigenous, can refresh and invigorate the latter. Freed from the exclusive preoccupation with his own existence, he can view it with other eyes, and by comparing it with that of others, he becomes aware of its real worth and nature. History makes us "see". It also affords a basis of comparison which enriches our own spirit and enhances our appreciation of it, but which also makes it receptive to the achievements of others and fosters respect for what others have achieved in the world. In this way the urge is aroused to make some lasting contribution to the culture of the world. (ii) This brings us to consider "national" history which forms the background of our being in the present. While general history throws light on our place and our task in the world, national history reveals the variegated diversity of the society of which the state is composed. In it we discover the origins of racial groups, of parties and of churches. It throws light on their mutual relationships and reveals their inevitableness. It promotes realism and the acceptance of diversity. It moderates blind passions when the motives and aims underlying the actions of a particular group are understood, and there is sympathetic appreciation of what has come to be by the process of historical evolution. It need not lead to a weakening of one's own resolution or endeavour if the real passions of others or the true motives for the actions of opponents are studied dispassionately and appreciated. In and by means of history we understand social, religious, cultural, political or economic problems so much more readily. The "native problem" is a case in point, or the "republican issue", both of which have their roots in the remote past. Familiarity with the history of our own country leads us to an appreciation of the contribution of all the various groups to its development, so that each will be accorded its due and its right of co-existence.

The life of a nation reveals a certain pattern or regularity which expresses itself in its development. Though man is by birth a member of a particular nation, history can bring home a deeper insight into its true character, and help to initiate the youth into the national way of life. A knowledge of its development will also protect a person from alien ideologies and prevent him from acting at variance with the national norms. History also instils a sense of responsibility towards other cultural groups living in the same country under the same state. Thus where "cultural group" and "state" are not co-extensive, a knowledge of history can aid the powers-that-be to be considerate in their treatment of other groups and thereby promote peace and harmony. History initiates the young into the historicity of the national life, and makes them aware of the unity in diversity within the national community and of a community of nations in the world.

National history can also have the effect of attaching the youth of the nation to its traditions. In his familiarity with the past the pupil becomes acquainted with the lives of great predecessors who stood for, toiled and suffered for certain ideals. Thus inspiration can be derived for his own life, and loyalty to the national character be stimulated, a loyalty which includes appreciation for the good in other nations and the enrichment of the national life by its adoption. Knowledge of the past can be the spur to action, and at the same time evoke a feeling of thankfulness. National history also reveals heroes worthy of emulation, who can be venerated and respected, but not necessarily idolized. No-one can remain unmoved by the vicissitudes of his own nation. Anyone with love of his fatherland, cannot but be moved with feelings of pride, hope, loyalty or anxiety. Veneration, humility, love and gratitude towards past generations come naturally to a right-minded person. That is why initiation into the national past can lead to the cultivation of an "enlightened patriotism".

The mere fact of being born in the tradition is not enough to ensure an understanding of the national evolution. History alone affords the perspective for a just appreciation of the present and of the actions of past generations. A nation is not built in a day. Nor is its past dead. It carries its past within it, and has only to be made aware of it. Only then can it "see". Though every nation has an instinctive preference for its own country and people, a sound initiation in its history is the best safeguard against chauvinism. Only when the history of the world is known and the national past brought into relation with it, can intolerance and passionate nationalistic sentiments be avoided. What is good in the history of one's native country must be recognized and appreciated, but the good in the history of others must also be recognized and appreciated. Thus will we be safeguarded from arrogance and spiritual isolation. For then the recognition will emerge that one's own heritage is not the be-all of the world. Respect for others and respect for one's own – that is the key to wisdom.

### 3

This brings us to the third aspect of the meaning of history, namely in respect of man facing the future. This refers to "political" education and preparation for the assumption of responsibility in civic affairs. Because we are moving towards the future, the young should be trained for the task awaiting them. Nation and state are concepts which are involved here, and neither can be divorced from the teaching of history. The state is sustained by the nation, and is so organized that the whole nation is drawn into it. Every citizen has a place in the life of the nation and in the state, and he must be made aware of his duties and his functions. Nation signifies a supra-personal community, and towards the nation there is also a responsibility transcending personal interests. He who wishes to assume responsibility in a civic sense, to undertake responsibility for the solution of problems, must know the potentialities latent in the nation and understood the historical genesis of present-day problems. For that reason scions of ruling dynasties had to study history long before the sons of the bourgeoisie, who were excluded from political power, could share in this privilege. It was only when the extension of the franchise transferred political responsibility to the latter, that history became a compulsory school subject. The fact that most great statesmen were also well versed in history, attests to its importance as a preparation for the assumption of political responsibility. The functioning of our democratic system, public bodies and institutions, only becomes intelligible through and in history.

Finally, history can also be politically instructive. How would a politician ascend the rostrum without a knowledge of history? The problems of the present, such as the "native problem", have evolved historically and can only be understood historically. Possibilities inherent in a situation can be recognized and probabilities assessed. "Recipes" for the solution of practical problems will, however, never be supplied by history, for the circumstances in which things occur always differ. History is unique and cannot repeat itself, yet there are regularities which justify certain conclusions. Human conduct is unpredictable, and "laws" are foreign to history, so that the future can never be foretold. But though rules cannot be discovered, tendencies can be inferred by analogy to typical situations which can suggest directives for the future. A knowledge of the current situation set against the historical background can reveal the lines along which development may take place, so that there can always be conjecture (never certainty) about future development.

Because the forces of the past are still operative in the present, history can be of service to life. History is not dead, but survives in us. To understand the nature of the state in the present, and to bring the nation to know itself, the aid of history must be enlisted. Only then can the state be developed further. Knowledge of the past will always be imperfect without a knowledge of the present, and to understand the present a knowledge of the past is indispensable.

History can be practised and taken seriously only by a nation that is conscious of itself. When does a nation come to discover itself and its history? Only when it has come to demand an explanation of itself and its place in the world. Only by seeing itself and the things around it in the proper perspective, by discovering itself in relation to the world and the world in relation to itself, i.e. by attempting to orientate itself in a world which is its own, and in the circumstances in which its own peculiar situation unfolds, does it come to take an interest in history. The attainment of a certain stage of development awakens the desire to appropriate history to itself and to include it in its image of itself. And that is so because the past is the way man has come: history is man himself. By becoming aware of itself, of its individuality of personality, a nation or civilization also becomes aware of its history, which is an integral dimension of its selfconsciousness and its humanity. In history it sees itself, learns to know itself, learns who and what it is, and where it can go. If a nation asks who it is, it sees history in itself, and if it looks at history, discovers that it is but itself.

# DANGERS LATENT IN THE TEACHING OF HISTORY

I

It may seem strange that one can speak of the value and signifi-cance of history as a subject, and in the same breath of dangers latent in its teaching.[1] How can a school subject be both useful and dangerous? And where does the danger lie? Perhaps it is suggested by the proposition I made in the previous lecture: that of all school subjects history is closest to life: It deals with men and with the thoughts and deeds of men in society. It deals with the past and the present of a group or groups; thus with ideals, en-deavours, and realization of values. These are not achieved without a struggle. And that struggle is both historical and living in the persistence of the forces which gave rise to it in the past and which are not "dead". Thus the past is part of the present, particularly the still-living past, of which the memory survives in the minds of individuals and statesmen active in the present. When old enmities linger and are perpetuated in a later political system and when old and current political or national ideals seem to correspond, the dividing line between past and present is barely visible. What one group within the heterogeneous community regards as "sancro-sanct" in its past and as a struggle of "heroes" for survival and self-realization, the "other side", having had and still having others roots, ideals and loyalties, may regard as needless, as folly and narrow-mindedness. Here, then, is a possible difference of opinion, which is linked with different interpretations of the past. And interpretation derives from points of view which are bound up with the whole outlook and frame of mind of the groups within the same homeland. This difference in viewpoint is to be found in the living communities as well as in their interpretation of past history.

One need only compare a history of South Africa or of the Voor-trekkers by an Afrikaans-speaking author from an Afrikaans point of view, with a similar work by an English-speaking author from

1. This lecture was written in 1956 (*Onderwysblad*, April 1956).

the English standpoint – and perhaps a third by a Bantu from the Bantu point of view. What are these points of view, and is there a common truth somewhere "between" them? Here the idea of "truth" enters, with the "lie" or "legend" as its antipode. And the teachers who have to teach the same syllabus under the same department in the same "fatherland"? Will every teacher, to whichever group he may belong, transmit the same point of view to the pupils, the same "truth" in the same way, irrespective of language and race? What does the one language group expect of the other? If the Afrikaans community teaches history from the "Afrikaans" point of view, will the English-speaking community not say that it is "one-sided"? And vice versa? Here the problem of bias or prejudice arises.

What may be "true" for the one group, may be "untrue" for the other. Why are both sections of the white population – to judge by the newspapers – "afraid" that "wrong" and emotionally charged history will be taught to the pupils of the other section, and with what justification? Assuming that history can be completely objectively and "neutrally" rendered, what kind of history will it be? A mere recital of dates and battles and decisions; dead, spiritless and lifeless. Then it ceases to be history. And then history will no longer serve any purpose. For history is nothing if it does not become spirit and life. Otherwise it is devoid of inspiration. Suppose that history is deliberately misused for purposes of propaganda by one section of the white population, i.e. with the object of distorting the truth and discrediting "the other section", so that race hatred and racial discord results, will the "other side" not have reason to complain? But if the sympathetic teaching of "national" history without any ulterior motives, but with the object of inculcating a critical insight as objectively as possible, should lead spontaneously to feelings of patriotism, affectionate appreciation and understanding of the vicissitudes of a group in the past, its ideals for the future and its sacrifices for the living generation, has the "other side" then any cause to persist in charges such as the above? Does the history of a common fatherland belong more to one section than to the other? Here again the nature of our society is in question.

Suppose there is an English-speaking class in which the parents of 70 percent of the pupils have lived in the country since 1902; does the national history before that date "belong" to them emotionally to the same degree as to the children of the Afrikaans-speaking community, whose forebears may have lived here for the past 200 or 300 years? In theory it may, but can and will there be the same interest in, say, the history of the Great Trek? Do such children although South Africans, not also have other loyalties and a different background which derives from Europe? Here we again touch on difficult problems which throw light on the nature of the subject. For one pupil history is "inborn"; for another it must be acquired intellectually. And if such a pupil is not enabled to acquire it by compulsory study, how can he, too, become a citizen of the country without the background which will afford insight into the existence, ideals and aspirations of those who also live in the same country?

## 2

Thus far I have only touched upon problems. What of the dangers inherent in history? This raises the question: how is it taught? What history books are used? For the knowledge which is orally transmitted can only come from books. Here the nature of the society also comes into question, for in a unilingual society, i.e. where state and nation are co-extensive, – except perhaps in its social composition – the teaching of history is much simpler. It is not as complicated as for example in the case of South Africa with its racial diversity, which resembles Europe on a smaller scale. In Europe national history, if taught with a "nationalistic" bias, can have the effect of inflaming national antagonisms – and in fact the teaching of this kind of history has contributed in no small measure to perennial discord and dissension.

This poses at once the problem of the responsibility, on the one hand of the historian who supplies the information, and on the other of the teacher who has to transmit it in a simplified form to his pupils. In the first place, the history teacher must have at least a working knowledge of the process by which the past is discovered and made known; for otherwise he will not be able to judge whether a book is "subjective" or "objective". On the other hand it is possible that the historian, intent upon maintaining complete objectivity or neutrality, may offer a mere chronicle instead of true history. In such a case it is dead and without life and not true history – merely "technical" and having no meaning or bearing on life.

Fearing that the teaching or history-as-life may lead to the stimulation of certain sentiments in the pupils who listen to it, there may be those teachers who will fall into the same error as the chronicler, viz, to transmit to the pupils the dry bones of a skeleton, without spirit or life – series of unlinked dates and events. But this kind of teaching can also be the result of a teacher not having read widely in his subject or of his having no conception of its theory or nature. He is dependent on a text-book which the pupils must summarize and memorize. This may be one of the reasons why pupils consider history to be "dull" and why it fails to have any meaning for them. Merely to memorize chronicles does not afford a knowledge of the past. It is history which is divorced from life and which is itself devoid of life. To teach history in this manner is an offence against the subject as well as against the content of the past. To give our pupils an insight into history is our chief aim, and that requires "life".

## 3

History in the form of a chronicle serves little purpose, yet there are, on the other hand, dangers latent in history which aims at understanding the past. Yet that is the very object of our teaching. But if it is not done conscientiously and with discretion, it can be equally dangerous. The path of the history teacher is beset with many pitfalls. By history which aims at understanding, I mean history which tries to understand people and events from the point of view of their own circumstances, ideals and standards. It is the anti-thesis of the ideas of theologians or artists, who strive after eternal values or laws of beauty on which they then base their judgments.

In history the method which aims at understanding can easily result in making all standards – including moral standards – relative. In such a case everything depends on the event, which means that "understanding" implies little more than "vindicating" or justifying those who took the lead in these events, because everything has been "understood", and to know all is to forgive all.

He, who for instance, wishes to "understand" the murder of Retief by Dingaan must identify himself to such an extent with Dingaan's views, feelings and actions that, as it were, he shares his decision to murder Retief and his men. Now, it may be held that the historian has no right to sit in judgment in such a case, but should leave it to God and the Day of Judgment. We may agree that history has nothing to do with absolute ethical judgments, but what of the claims of common humanity? What of human judgment according to the dictates of one's conscience? That, surely, cannot be omitted from our apprehension of the past, but it depends on how our judgment is arrived at and whether it is clouded by passion – which implies that there is the curb of personal responsibility which the teacher must impose on himself. Understanding history in the sense of sympathetically comprehending and entering into the life of the past, does not imply relieving historical personages of their responsibility or justifying their actions on the score of circumstances, or, in the case of amorality, withholding judgment on the ground of what they themselves could not have known. If that happens, it can lead to moral relativism, but that need not be the case when we strive after understanding.

Such an attitude of indifference too can weaken our own resolution, for if everything in the past has been "understood" in this sense, it does not "affect" us. If ideals have to be upheld and furthered, such an attitude towards the past cannot but have an enervating effect on our conduct in the present. Here the old adage of "forgive and forget" comes in, which has been countered with "forgive but do not forget". We must appreciate the motives of the "other side" in order to understand, but that does not imply exonerating or justifying or abandoning our own standpunt and standards. Only when all the circumstances are fully known, can judgment be passed. The narrative must always be guided if it is to be history. To seek insight into the past need not imply understanding all and forgiving all, nor need it make our criteria and standards relative or paralyse our conduct, for the element of criticism always provides a corrective.

To understand the past means to aim at a critical insight into the past – with the emphasis on critical. This entails testing one's own judgment by the truth and the reality of the sources. For this reason this method demands so much of the devoted history teacher; he must always keep abreast of the latest publications in the field of history, and try to give his pupils a global picture of what he is discussing. Otherwise he cannot do justice to the demand for critical insight. Both history taught in the form of mere chronicle, and history taught with indifference in the sense of "to know all is to forgive all", can be dangerous, though elements of both are to be found in the teaching of history.


4


It must further be borne in mind that we always move and act within the field of human relations, that our society consists of diverse racial groups or communities, and that in the past we also meet with similar human relationships – albeit historical – this means that the past is directly linked to the present. If, in the one case, judgment can be made to depend exclusively on the criteria of the past, thus leading to an attitude of "to know all is to forgive all", it can in the other, if made solely dependent on the present in which we live, lead to an even greater error, namely that of projecting the present into the past, and reading into the past what it never contained. In other words, history here becomes more than history: it becomes propaganda for a party or church or group, intent upon maintaining its drive for power in the present. This is a violation of the spirit of history, leading to current human relations being embittered by the erection of artificial barriers within the national body, or to the stimulation of feelings of hate and division, which disrupts the unity of society and engender strife. History then becomes a manufactory of explosives which can have far-reaching and disastrous effects.

It is this kind of teaching which reduces history to an over-simplified design: all details are omitted, and what should be a variegated picture becomes a simple drawing in black and white: on the one hand are the heroes, the saints, the virtuous and the great – on the other, the villains, the knaves, the sinners. The villains are always lying in wait for the righteous, and the former must be cut down in size by bitter emotional judgments, while the heroes have to be defended, exonerated, elevated and purified. The past becomes the scene of conflict and bloodshed, denunciation, justification and vindication. Here the danger arises of legends being produced, which belie the complex reality and truth of the past. History may never be manipulated for political ends, for then it arouses militant, aggressive feelings among the listeners, and breeds intolerance. Both the past and the present will then suffer: the past, because its complex reality is over-simplified; the present, because the vision is so narrowed that perception and judgment are equally distorted. Only in its universal aspect, within the framework of the whole, can history be authentic and true, and can it discharge its function of leading to self-knowledge, of illuminating present-day situations, creating mutual understanding, and making the world a better place to live in.

5

It is this type of history, too, which produces a hazard of another kind, viz. that the past is invested with such a haze of romantic glorification that past generations appear as stainless heroes, and there is little left for the present generation to do – the better part, is, after all, dead and buried. This attitude can result in history acquiring the force of a kind of religion, which subordinates everything to it. He who wishes to create a future, must build on the past; but the mind can be so obsessed with the past, that it cannot return to the realities of the present, on which the future must be built. All this can have an enervating effect on our own endeavours, which seem to pale into insignificance beside the great achievements of the past.

On the other hand, the danger also exists that blind glorification of everything done by or belonging to one's forefathers may lead to self-glorification and self-complacency – indeed, even to self-pity, which directs the gaze on the past rather than on the future. This also weakens resolution. History should never be presented emotionally – though emotion does enter into it unconsciously – for a purely emotional apprehension of the past cannot lead to the broadening of the mind and the spirit which it should produce. In the understanding of the past man brings his intellect, emotion and will into play. The intellect must always be engaged: there must be logical insight as well as intuitive understanding, otherwise its value will be reduced. History teaching must consist of piety for the past only or of criticism of the past only; these must be combined, for piety without criticism is as dangerous as criticism without piety.

It is our task to raise the pupil above the narrow range of his own vision and to bring him into contact with the wider world. Only within such a framework can he discover his own task and mission. But all this merely serves to make us aware of the immense responsibility resting on the shoulders of the history teacher and the exacting demands made of his knowledge.

### I

We live in an era in which history is being made – but also in a time when much *thought* is being given to history. Little need be said on the subject of history-making. One only has to think of the historical implications of global changes taking shape before our very eyes. There is the retrogression of the West and the rise of the East that implies the whittling away of four centuries of European dominance over peoples outside their continent. In our era, for the first time – say from 1945 onwards – one may speak of a *genuine* world history. Prior to that there was only a "Europacentric" world history. In the contemporary period the world has really become *one*. Distances have shrunk to vanishing point and peoples and countries have come into closer touch with one another. It is obvious that in a world of this kind less emphasis will henceforth fall on national sovereignty than on aspects of international relationships. In this changed and changing world in which the West is dwarfed by gaint powers such as America and Russia that lie outside the European periphery and one in which the colour question plays so important a role, our country has to take stock of its position afresh, to find its bearings and to take its stance in relation to the outside world. What happens in Formosa or Israel or China may affect our position closely. As to our colour question – even the Norwegians or the Mongolians or the Japanese may be interested in it. Within half an hour of any event, it becomes the common property of *one* world.

In this world of change historians tend to set aside to some degree those *part*-interpretations that generally treat of *national* history and to turn their attention increasingly to the *whole*, giving prominence to comparative surveys of *world history*. The time in which we live has not only been a stimulus to this type of historical

---

* This lecture was originally delivered at a conference of history teachers in Johannesburg on the 19th May, 1956 and was first published in *Historia*, No. 1, 1957.

writing; it has also underlined the necessity for the synthesis in clearer and more urgent terms than ever before. Technological developments, the shrinkage of distance and massive weapons of destruction have made mutual understanding absolutely vital to humanity's continued existence. To further this idea of mutual understanding a historian like Arnold Toynbee[2] has ranged over the whole of humanity through all its former civilisations and has brought it together in one synthesis – like a family whose members can and should live together in one world. In Switzerland, Germany, Holland, America – everywhere in the Western countries, one finds this tendency. This was not always the case. The 19th century was pre-eminently the century of national historical writing with a nationalistic impulse; such writing had to swell the nation's grandeur and glory; had to dwell on wrongs suffered at the hands of neighbouring states and to expose the treachery, cruelty and dishonesty of "foes". This form of presentation was continued into the 20th century. At school – whether in America, Germany, France, Italy or Russia – the belief was implanted that there was only one nation that was worthy of recognition.[3] It is not surprising that responsible men of learning have concluded that the way in which national histories were taught in schools has to be held partially accountable for the discord in Europe and the spirit that gave rise to the great wars of the 19th and 20th centuries.[4]

It was the awareness of *one* world and of the need for universally acceptable historical presentations and fear of the deplorable consequences of war that made the West European countries and America realise that stress should fall on the idea of co-operation among the countries within the European framework of civilisation and not on their national difference; it was realised that international relations should take pride of place in a world whose watchword was unity and that this would create a better understanding of one another.[5] The results of this new sense of awareness can be traced in America, Holland and Germany. Old textbooks were revised and national history treated in such a way that it only found a place within the totality of general history. Naturally national history was not ignored, since no country could dispense with it, but it was reduced to more modest dimensions and perspectives so that it was seen as a part of the larger whole. And the dependence of the history of the fatherland on general history was given prominence. There was a chance in the spirit too. Undertones of bitterness receded and reciprocal understanding found a place. At this point I refer to German and French school history books.

Under the Nazi regime the Germans misused the history of their country for propaganda purposes. After the war the old textbooks were discarded and had to be replaced by new ones. One has only to page through the new books to realise what a great change has come about. Here too the emphasis falls on general history; the history of the fatherland is interwoven in such a way that the child cannot fail to appreciate that his country is not *the* only country, but that it was and is dependent on neighbouring countries and on the forces of world history. Moreover, these books have been written from a universal-historical point of view. But it does not end there: In 1950, the *Arbeitsgemeinschaft Deutscher Lehrerverbände*, in collaboration with the *Verband der Geschichtslehrer Deutschlands*, established contacts with similar bodies in France with a view to an investigation of certain points of difference in approach; what was then envisaged was that writers of textbooks should be asked to revise their books in line with the joint findings of this professional investigation. Similar moves were made in America and England. It is obvious that steps of this kind must serve to improve international relations since at school certain inclinations are impressed on the young. Incidentally, if these ideas were applied in South Africa, it would mean that Afrikaans history books would be subjected to a prior "vetting" by English-speaking South Africans and *vice versa*. In this case too where certain basic points of difference were involved, it would be necessary to adduce "scientifically" a set of facts that would be acceptable to everyone. Perhaps this idea merits our attention.

2

It is against this background of a changed and unified world that affects South Africa's position so acutely, that I should like to say something about the value of general history at school. The universal history tendency that I have already outlined and the changed attitude of the countries of the Atlantic community towards general and international history are my basic premises. My point of view is bound up with the most important requirement of our time – that the countries of the world should direct their attention "outward" rather than "inward". Let me add at once that by this it is not intended that one's "own" should be sacrificed in favour of the "alien', nor even that it should take a subordinate place. The necessary balance has to be kept. What I do mean is that countries of a world that has become *one*, countries that are associated so closely, should have their attention directed more forcibly than ever to events around them. In large measure the destiny and future of the parts have become dependent on the whole. The internal developments of a country cease to be the sole factors that determine its fortunes. By this we mean that the time of isolation has passed. What our new world has come to need, is knowledge of itself and its constituent parts. This is necessary with a view to the future and with a view to the past out of which this *oneness* of the world has arisen. It is necessary for the future since all indications are that oneness will grow, together with inter-dependence and the sharing of a common lot. Out of the past there arose a variety of civilisations and a knowledge of the broad lines of their development is needed for a better understanding of the present and perhaps to help us to distinguish vaguely the shape of things to come. This embodies the aims of general history and its content.

As to the aim or worth of general history, I see it as a means towards the education of *developed* or enlightened beings with a sense of civic and national responsibility. What distinguishes the uneducated man from the cultivated man? I should say a *conscious* living in the present, perceptiveness of its circumstances and an awareness of the conditions that gave birth to such circumstances. Also an insight into the possible turn of future events. It all boils down to the word *orientation* in the world, implying a sound judg-ment on connected circumstances and situations that may affect one's own country or cultural circle. It means *assessing* one's surroundings and having a *perspective* of situations and the course of events. It means *rendering* an account of one's own place in this changed world, of discovering one's own value and of establishing the part that one's own country should play.

It is only with the necessary *knowledge* that man can take his right place in the world, see the world in relation to his country and himself, and *vice versa,* and make the world really his oyster. A knowledge of the past is necessary, just as a knowledge of the present is necessary, for a comprehension of the past that will provide "background" and shed light on one's own place in the world. How can one grasp the problems of one's own time without laying bare the roots that lie in the past? A *conscious* experience of contemporary time means a "spotlighting" of that time and it is *general* history alone that can provide the beam of light. General history is also the pointer to future prospects since man can appre-ciate from it how he has arrived at his present state. Knowledge of general history gives man "eyes with which to see".

Where there is too strong an emphasis on national history, a feeling may be inculcated that one's own country is the be-all and end-all, the centre of the world and the most important state.

National history alone is insufficient to yield a full *conscious* experience of one's own time and insufficient to produce a well-balanced and civilised character. The perspective will be gauged incorrectly, the proportions will be out and one will live in isolation – as it were without cognition of the outside world. This would not be in accord with world developments of the past decade. The limited vision that would necessarily follow from an education of this type, would be inadequate in the reality of a world of *oneness*. It would mean retrogression instead of progress, intellectual poverty instead of intellectual enrichment. It is possible that on some unforeseen occasion it could give rise to fearful shock or an intellectual crisis. We should be receptive to the contingencies of *one* world and, by itself, national history is unable to induce that state of mind. Without a basis of comparison no intelligent formulation of opinion is possible. Neither is a historical sense and still less a comprehension of mortal man in relation to man the eternal.

As a source of instruction national history is insufficient to enable the pupil to find his bearings in a world that has become one and to appreciate his own relative importance and place. Still less to attach a true value to his "own". It is only within the frame of general history with its standards and bases of comparison of Western cultural values that he can discover and attach value to his "own". The scholar has to break away from an atmosphere of over-familiarity with his own country and weigh its achievements against those of other countries over the centuries; that will inspire him to acquire cultural and intellectual values. It is then that the discovery of one's "own" is made in contrast with the "alien", then that the deficiencies of one's "own" become apparent and then that attitudes of self-satisfaction are discarded. This awareness is the counter to life that runs in a narrow rut. The need for a synthesis of one's "own" with the wider sphere means that intellectual enrichment follows.

National history can only be of value when it reaches out beyond itself to the community of peoples and lands that go to form our circle of civilisation. Also when it extends to the countries that do not belong to this group e.g. those of the East. One's own history may be likened to the inner of a number of concentric circles; outside it is the large circle of the history of the neighbouring countries of its area; beyond that the circle of the Atlantic civilisation; and beyond that again a circle representative of the whole world in which both Russia and the East find a place. It is only within a pattern of this kind that national history can be valid and true. Only then that the pupil can be freed from intellectual isolation. And who is there who will deny that until recently the isolation of

South Africa was one of the most marked characteristics affecting our intellectual life? In support of my contention I need only point to the fact that until recently not a single South African university possessed a chair for the study of international relations.[6] The emphasis should fall on the manner in which our national history has been determined by influences from abroad, how the world around us has developed *oneness* and what place there is for us in this setting. The history of past civilisations should be studied – but only in outline. We should be able to distinguish the lines of development and we should then find our bearings and a true perspective. This could lead to a conscious experience of the present, or in other words, to cultivated beings who could easily be distinguished from the uncultivated.

Tested by these standards, the old syllabus still employed in our schools obviously fails to equate itself with reality. The fact that for many years most schools proceeded no further than 1871, and that some still do, leaves the pupil, as it were, poised in the air. How can he understand the present-day world without a knowledge of its antecedents after 1870? Moreover there is overmuch stress of detail, and that being the case, lines of development have become obscured. One is thankfully able to state that the proposed new syllabus has brought about a change. The pupil will be able to follow the history of the world beyond South Africa to the present time. And is there anything wrong with that? If it can be done in Europe, why not here too? Surely we are not intellectually backward to that extent?

I should be going against the dictates of my own conscience if I failed to offer constructive criticism as well. In our school syllabus one notes the absence of references to international relations between the two World Wars[7] and especially to the rise of the East to the prominent place it plays in the world of today. To my way of thinking the stress perhaps falls too heavily on our national history. Our times demand that we should pay more attention to general history since it is only within that context that national history gains sense and perspective. A very good knowledge of national history alone cannot make enlightened citizens of our young people – by itself it cannot assist them to life fully in the present with wide-open eyes. In South Africa, struggling to emerge from traditional isolation, a suitably stressed general history can mean much for her young people. Mean much, since it will enable them to take their place in this world of oneness and give an account of their acts of commission and omission in a fatherland that stands increasingly under the focus of international attention. One has only to think of the colour question that is no longer a domestic concern only but one that has become an international issue. We should take note of outside events since in them our existence is at stake.

1. *Vide* p. 189 of this book.
2. *A Study of History* (10 vols.), 1934–'55.
3. Boyd C. Shafer: *Nationalism, Myth and Reality*, 1955, pp. 184, 188.
4. H. Butterfield: *History and Human Relations*, 1951, p. 167. See also Sir Lewis Namier, *Avenues of History*.
5. Erich Weniger: *Neue Wege im Geschichtsunterricht*, 1949, p. 24.
6. In the meantime a professorship for the study of international relations has been created at the University of the Witwatersrand.
7. Fortunately a change has been effected in this respect. (Observation added in 1963.)

# ON THE TEACHING OF "NATIONAL" HISTORY IN SOUTH AFRICAN SCHOOLS

We begin by considering the fact that South Africa is a multiracial community, with several different language or cultural groups, each of which has its own background and traditions.[1] Nevertheless there is co-existence, in which both conflicting and concurring interests act together to unite the language groups within their common boundaries. However diverse their origins may be, they are all members of the same homeland.

For the past fifty years – and today more than ever before – politicians of all groups have been urging their common purpose: "to forge a nation", i.e. the ideal of "unity" or unification of the language groups. In this idea of nation building there is, however, an implicit awareness of the dualism in the white community, if we disregard for the moment the non-white section.

In saying that a language group has its own "tradition", we mean that it has, too, its own peculiar history, for the one is not easily dissociated from the other. A common citizenship within the same community also implies that there is a common tradition transcending the groups and linking them in unity. Besides the individual history of each group, there is then a general history of the "homeland", in which each group occupies its rightful place as an integral part of the global pattern.

All teaching of history is done from the present, the time in which we live; and those responsible for it belong to one or other of the language groups, with their own separate views of life and traditions.

Our primary thesis was that beside the history of particular groups there is also a general South African history, which embraces all the groups. This general history contains a hard core of facts common to all the groups. The history syllabus assumes that pupils will be made familiar with all these facts; but however "true" the facts may be, our interpretation of them will vary from group to group. Why? Because there is more than one

1. This essay was first published in *The Transvaal Educational News*, April 1959 under the title of "History Teaching and Responsibility".

196

tradition and because a teacher is bound by his group's *weltan-schauung*, i.e. philosophy of life or world-view. The facts of the past are related to the present, for present and past are connected in the same way as man and his history are linked in an existentialist association.

In the present we meet with differing points of view, conflicting ideas and individual group aims. Because we cannot dissociate ourselves from the present, we tend to notice differences, varying points of view and ideals, and to accentuate these, while neglecting those events which drew men together in awareness of each other. This is true of both language groups. Every member of a group looks for points of contact in his own tradition and in the past of his particular group, either because it is congenial to his taste or because he finds recognition there of his group or of himself. Our common South African history may therefore be interpreted according to individual points of view; and everyone is, of course, entitled to his own view of history, providing it is scientifically supported.

This, however, is the source and origin of the pitfalls in history teaching. Personal points of view, in rigid association with a *weltan-schauung* or world-view, may lead to such interpretation of group history that the overall picture of South African history, in which each group has its rightful place is distorted and thrown out of focus; the result is that pupils obtain only one interpretation, particularly of those issues which are the outcome of past conflicts. Consequently their impression of our history is one-sided.

This conception may be inculcated unconsciously, but there may also be deliberate indoctrination; and where this takes place history is perverted to propaganda in the service of a contemporary bias, which prescribes in advance what the nature of history teaching is to be. Since past dissension is correlated with present conflict with set purpose, this presentation of history assumes a political slant. Contemporary opponents are equated with "enemies" of the past, with the emphasis on injustice inflicted and suffered. The villains are all on one side, the heroes on the other. Such a presentation of history divides where it should unite, with the inevitable destruction of the very ideal proclaimed by politicians, namely "nation building", or "unity" between the two white groups. Group relations suffer, for the past is revealed as a course of dissension instead of unity.

A history lesson, infused with the party or group-bias of either language section, may indeed be a formidable weapon in the hands of an irresponsible teacher. To impair group relations is punishable by law today, yet we have no legislation to condemn or punish the irresponsible teacher of history who fosters the deterioration of group relations in his class-room.

It is of course an unquestioned fact that in the history of all nations there have been unpleasant incidents between groups, for which one section bore a greater share of guilt than the other. Must such incidents be ignored? No. That would be prejudicial to the very integrity of history. Integrity, too, is required of a teacher to impart such knowledge without extraneous motives. Essential facts are unalterable, but the use they are put to depends on us fallible mortals.

Let us take a particular example: The Imperial Government acted in a certain way in connection with the diamond fields and the annexation of the Transvaal. President Kruger took certain steps against the "Uitlanders". The former incident may now be treated as a source of "grievances" by a teacher from the Afrikaans language group, who may then throw it into vivid relief by relating the past to the present. A teacher from the English language group may point, in his turn, to Kruger's treatment of the "Uitlanders" as cause for resentment, adding realism to his argument by bringing it into the light of contemporary events. Neither of the two teachers gives thought to the fact that those problems have already solved themselves in the evolution of our history; that neither the imperial factor nor Kruger are with us any longer. The diamond fields as well as the "Uitlanders" have become part of South Africa, consequently the "grievances" associated with them have disappeared.

Only when a nation – in this case the South African nation – has become capable of laughing at the errors and follies of the past, can it lay claim to maturity. The "enemies" of the past are both extinct. We live in a different era, with common interests and problems, which we have to share. This positive attitude achieves far more than mourning over the graves of the past, or in reproaches and accusations concerning misdeeds for which our dead forebears were responsible. This does not mean, of course, that traditions are to be slighted.

Inasmuch as history is of all subjects the closest to life, there is always the possibility of its being misused. Then it fails in its high purpose of creating enlightened citizens. All this means that the teacher of history bears a tremendous responsibility. His first duty is to the past. He must omit nothing of truth, yet add nothing which may convert truth to falsehood. He must not oversimplify the complex facts of the past, which are to be grasped with sympathetic understanding of their significance in point of time. His emphasis must always be on positive, not negative values, for values peculiar to our time, if transposed to the past, violate the reality of history.

The teacher's second responsibility is to the present. Facts may not be misapplied according to personal opinion for the furthering of current political aims. Historical facts belong to an era dissimilar to that in which we live; they must not be abused to rouse feeling or passions against any group. The Zulus of today are guiltless of the evil perpetrated by their forebears on English- and Afrikaans-speaking Europeans. A history master with integrity will not use history as a means of propaganda but limit himself to the truth. He will aim at impartial insight into the past and elucidation of the circumstances by which events were shaped.

The history teacher has a third duty: to the future. If he wishes to do his share in promoting the ideals of our leading statesmen, "to forge a nation" or achieve "unity" between the language groups, he will stress their collaboration rather than their differences. Consequently his approach, instead of being merely negative, will be positive and rational rather than emotional. There is no one in the class-room to supervise the teacher's presentation of his subject. He has nothing but his conscience and integrity to guide him in giving his pupils a rational and universal outlook on affairs, to liberate them from their own limitations, to reveal their dependence on other countries, and finally, to determine their position in the history of the world and the international situation.

It goes without saying that to have this sense of responsibility the history teacher must be well-read. If he is ignorant of various and differing points of view and the large body of pertinent facts, he cannot perform his task. He must know his own era well too and he must think with honesty about the future. Certainly it is no easy task to be a teacher of history: it demands an awareness of responsibility.

PRINTED BY
NATIONAL COMMERCIAL PRINTERS
ELSIES RIVER